THRIVING IN SEX WORK

HEARTFELT ADVICE FOR STAYING SANE IN THE SEX INDUSTRY

LOLA DAVINA

THE EROTIC AS POWER PRESS
OAKLAND, CALIFORNIA

Published by:
The Erotic as Power Press LLC
248 3rd St. #646
Oakland, CA 94607

Cover design by Albert Ochosa | Sun Rising Media
Book design and layout by Rob Siders | 52 Novels
Copyedit by Felicia Gotthelf
Back cover author photo by Lisa Keating Photography

Note on front cover:
Images are stock photos posed by models, for illustrative purpose only.

Library of Congress Cataloging-in-Publication Data
Davina, Lola, 1968–
Thriving in sex work / by Lola Davina
p. cm.
Includes bibliographical references and index.
ISBN 978-0-9988920-6-1 1. Sex work 2. Self-care

I dedicate this book to every sex worker I've ever known,

the ones I haven't met yet,

and those lost along the way.

The principal horror of any system which defines the good in terms of profit rather than in terms of human need ... is that it robs our work of its erotic value ... Such a system reduces work to a travesty of necessities, a duty by which we earn bread or oblivion for ourselves and those we love. But this is tantamount to blinding a painter and then telling her to improve her work, and to enjoy the act of painting. It is not only next to impossible, it is also profoundly cruel ... The erotic is the nurturer or nursemaid of all our deepest knowledge.

—AUDRE LORDE FROM *USES OF THE EROTIC: THE EROTIC AS POWER*

The sexual drive, essential for our species' continuation, has been subverted into an agent of destruction by our own supposedly elevated moral principles. What should give the greatest pleasure has been turned into the source of the greatest pain.

—JONATHAN KHUNER

When I was growing up in Detroit, my mother told me lots of things that later turned out not to be true. She told me only tramps get their ears pierced. That those men in Washington knew what they were doing or else they wouldn't be there. That what makes you happy makes me happy. That enough was enough.

—LILY TOMLIN

CONTENTS

Preface, xi

My First Time, xii

Introduction, 1

Introduction, 2

Part One: Demons, 13

Fear: An Introduction, 14

Making Friends with Our Fears, 16

Practical Advice: Managing Acute Anxiety, 22

Practical Advice: Physical Safety, 25

Practical Advice: Learn Self-Defense (No Excuses!), 30

Heartfelt Advice: Surviving the Bad Call, 33

Practical Advice: The Law and Legal Trouble, 36

Practical Advice: Safer Sex, 45

Shame: An Introduction, 48

Shame, Low Self-Esteem, and Stigma, 50

Exercise: Spending Time with Shame, 55

An Open Letter to My Fellow Sex Workers: Shame, Fear, and the
Erotics of Discretion, 57

Coming Out and Being Outed, 60

Heartfelt Advice: How to Come Out, 62

Heartfelt Advice: If You've Been Outed, 67

Practical Advice: What to Do If You've Been Outed, 71

An Open Letter to My Fellow Sex Workers: Respect the Work, 74

Low Self-Esteem: An Introduction, 76

Feeling Ugly and Unworthy, 78

Aging, 81

Plastic Surgery, 85

Anger: An Introduction, 87

Anger, 88

Empathy Exercise, 94

Forgiveness Exercise, 96

Envy: An Introduction, 98
  Envy, 100
  Heartfelt Advice: Navigating Insecurity, Resentment, and Envy
    From Coworkers, 103
  Heartfelt Advice: Navigating Insecurity, Resentment, and Envy
    From Clients, 105

Part Two: Tools of the Trade, 107

The Biz: An Introduction, 108
  Building The Business You Want, 110
  Marketing, 121
  Motivation, 126
  Keeping Up with New Technology (Or Not ...), 131
Clients: An Introduction, 134
  What Do Clients Want?, 136
  Exercise: Your Ideal Client, 139
  Practical Advice: Cultivating the Clients You Want, 141
  Intimidation and Coercion, 146
  Review Sites, 149
  Heartfelt Advice: When a Client Makes You Feel Like Crap, 151
Money: An Introduction, 154
  Money Exercises, 156
  Practical Advice: Money Challenges, 160
  Voluntary Simplicity, 172

Part Three: Sex Work and Self-Care, 175

Sex Work and Self-Care: An Introduction, 176
  You Need a Buddy—Better Yet, a Bunch, 178
  Get Yourself a Good Therapist—No Excuses!, 181
  Have a Hero/Ine, 185
  Trigger States, 187
  Sadness, Depression, and Suicidal Thoughts, 194
  Practical Advice: Winter, 200
  Dissociation, 203
  Pleasure, 206

Part Four: Sex Work and Relationships, 209

Sex Work and Relationships: An Introduction, 210

Sex Work and Relationships, 212

Heartfelt Advice: How to Work with a Broken Heart, 218

Part Five: Life After the Life, 223

Life After the Life: An Introduction, 224

Heartfelt Advice: What to Expect Getting Out, 227

Don't Fear the Future, 230

When Falling In Love Means Getting Out of the Biz: Marriage
and Retirement, 234

When Falling In Love Means Getting Out of the Biz, 235

Heartfelt Advice: Work After Sex Work, 237

Practical Advice: Work After Sex Work, 240

Conclusion, 247

Conclusion, 248

Back to the Future, 251

Appendix, 253

Special Thanks &

Acknowledgements, 255

About Me, 256

Definitions, 258

Winter and Depression Survival Checklist, 263

Bibliography, 266

Resources Referred to in Text, 273

Additional Resources, 287

PREFACE

MY FIRST TIME

Hi, Sexy—

I'm so happy to see you here. If you're holding this book in your hands, I'm guessing you're a sex worker. So am I. Let me tell you about my first call as a working girl.

San Francisco, January 17, 1991. I'd been stripping at the Lusty Lady peepshow for about a year. Twenty-two years old, fresh out of college, I was a shapely, fair-skinned brunette cultivating a smart-and-sexy persona by wearing nerd glasses on stage. I was making great money, raising hell and riding high. I'd done girl-on-girl shows with other dancers and a few professional domination sessions with a friend, but up to that point, the job felt removed, like a sexy game. Now it was about to get real.

That night, I was going to the home of a major politician, a bit of a Big Damned Deal, sent by a fellow Lusty who had been working for a madam for the past few years. This client—I'll call him J—was her regular and always eager to see new girls.

My friend prepped me as best she could: J was brusque, not a conversationalist. In fact, the more he talked, the less he liked you. He'll be all over you the minute you walk in the door, she warned, and he was energetic in bed. But she assured me if I told him I didn't like something, he would stop. All of this had me nervous enough without the kicker—I was a birthday surprise from J's girlfriend, M, and she was going to be there, too.

I prepared like a bride on her wedding day—showering, shaving, inspecting every inch of my body for flaws. I was sure I'd show up and be rejected after one look. My mind spun out all kinds of crazy scenarios.

That evening, nothing went how I'd imagined. J opened the door, a shaggy lion of a man wearing a bathrobe. M, a foxy, petite Latina, stood in flawless black lingerie, stockings, and high heels. They whisked me off to the bedroom, lit with dozens of candles, in exactly two seconds flat. I guess they liked me just fine.

The scene was alien yet familiar. Although I was terrified, I also felt exhilarated and fascinated. Instinct kicked in, and while I had never had such spontaneous and strenuous sex with two strangers before, I knew when to act, when to react, and how to shift the energy when it all got to be too much. So did M, apparently, because after about fifteen minutes, without saying a word, she got up and left the room. When she didn't return, it became clear she had left altogether. Um ... **wow**.

Nothing in my instinct kit had prepared me for that possibility. J, however, didn't blink. He kept at his sexy fun for a few minutes more, finished, and then we lay there in the post-coital glow. I asked about M. He just shrugged—maybe she got bored. We chatted a few minutes more, then, in the most gallant fashion, he paid me and threw me out.

I stepped out into the foggy San Francisco night holding two crisp one hundred dollar bills, my body tingling. I was mortified because somehow I had offended M, and J would never want to see me again. But no matter. I'd crossed a line: I was a prostitute now. I knew I should feel bad, but for the life of me, I couldn't think why. Instead, I was on fire.

I had no way of knowing it then, but that night shaped the broad contours of the next fifteen years of my life. It turned out J liked me bunches, becoming my best client and remaining a friend to this day. I developed a loyal clientele. Earning stacks of bills would always be erotically charged, making me feel richer than my wildest dreams.

The Life gave me a life I loved: I earned the down payment for my first house as a call girl. I traveled to Machu Picchu, Angkor Wat, and Timbuktu on my ill-gotten gains. I earned my first master's degree on my own schedule and got my second master's without student loans. Along the way, I paid off more than one hundred *thousand dollars in debt, and when I hung up my phone for the last time, I had six figures in the bank set aside for my retirement. Just like that first night, I never lost the feeling that prostitution was my calling. Although stigma placed me squarely outside the protections of polite society, I knew I was born for the work and never felt ashamed. I learned things I couldn't have learned any other way. I wouldn't trade those years for anything. However, it never came easy.*

Striking out as an escort on my own, I encountered the terrors of screening strangers, risking my living situation, my legal status, my life. Friends in the industry helped keep me sane, but I never felt I measured up to their beauty or success. I dated both clients and civilians but wrestled with jealousy and sharing my hard-earned cash. I'd obsess that clients, cops, or the IRS would leave me penniless. Over time, I grew rageful, finding slights and hypocrisies everywhere. I struggled with loneliness and isolation. And always, always, always, my situation felt precarious. In an instant, something horrible could happen and I'd be an ex-hooker, washed up and unemployable ... or worse. It never ended well for people like me in the movies.

I retired more than a decade ago, and those years have given me perspective. I can see now that some of that pain was just a part of being alive, but a lot of it I brought upon myself. I don't want that same fate for you, Sexy Reader.

I wrote this book because my twenty-two-year-old stripper self used to react like a Roomba to the contradictory messages from life inside a peepshow booth, and because my thirty-three-year-old call girl self was racked by anxieties and hair-curling rage. I wrote this as a love letter to my sex worker friends and all their fears and heartaches, and as a tribute to those lost along the way. I wrote this for workers I've never met but only read about online — the whip-smart escort who loves her job but thinks she'll never get married. The pro dom sobbing at home alone after a client beat her up, who needs to keep working because she hasn't made rent. The day-spa masseur doing full service on the side, who now has to come clean to his boyfriend because a condom broke with a client. This is tough emotional stuff—sex work ain't for sissies.

If anyone can learn from my mistakes, feel less alone, or face the work with more clarity, then this book has achieved its purpose. Because sex is far too important to leave to amateurs. There always have been and always will be sex professionals, at least until the invention of the sexborg. We deserve to be safe, whole, healthy, and gratified while we do it. Let us find our way there together.

With my whole heart—
Lola D.

P.S. If you want to learn more about my work history, positionality, or cred, flip to my biography in the appendix on page 256 and study up!

INTRODUCTION

❋ INTRODUCTION

Supposedly sex work is "easy money," but as long as our society remains hung up about money and sex, it's going to be hard work. Most people might think of sex work as a physical grind, but usually it's not especially challenging. Besides, most job titles require our bodies do things they don't want to do, whether it's cutting hair, writing code, or mining coal. No, the toll sex work takes, the heavy lifting it requires, is **emotional**. Our job is managing stress, anxiety, anguish, loneliness, lust, and rage—other people's and our own. EMOTIONAL LABOR can be defined as the effort workers put into checking their emotional reactions within a professionally acceptable range. In sex work, that expands to account for a sex worker's responsibility for the positive emotional state of their clients, as well.

That makes for a whole lot of crazy, no way around it. Let's start with the fact that sex work can be intoxicating—after all, we're selling pleasure. Our job is to dress up naughty, strip down naked, and talk dirty. We experience the rush of turning people on. For many of us, the fast money and easy sensuality can make the normal world seem deadly dull.

At the same time, while we're in that exposed, unsettled state, we navigate weirdness, negativity, and potential violence. Our workplaces are unnatural, time bending, and boundary-warping. Dungeons, strip clubs, and brothels are soaked in drugs, alcohol, loud music, and bad behavior. We face hypocrisy, bigotry, and slut-shaming on a daily basis. We're casualties of our culture's warped ideas about beauty and pleasure and fantasy, and what they're "worth." Most of us don't get much support, living in secrecy and silence with few role models. It can be hard to find people to talk to who can fully relate. No question, sex work can be scary, disgusting, lonely, shaming, and thankless.

Well, that is just **not okay**. Sex workers deserve better. Here's what I want for you:

- ❀ *To love the work you're doing.* Most days, in most ways, I want fulfillment for your body, heart, mind, soul, and bank account.
- ❀ *To have a retirement plan.* You can only do this work voluntarily if you have the choice not to do it. And when/ if you do leave, I'd like you to transition gracefully into something that genuinely inspires you.

If either of those goals seems impossible, let's stop for a moment. Why do you think that? What's holding you back? What's poisoning your happiness? How is this work possible with more comfort and ease? This book will explore these questions from every angle, because sex work shouldn't just be survivable, but **thrivable**. (Not a word, but shouldn't it be?)

THRIVING IN SEX WORK

"Thriving" can be a loaded term, so let me be clear about how I'm using it. The goal of this book is to address well-being in all aspects of our lives, including feeling healthy, financially secure, at peace with ourselves, and connected to loved ones. When I talk about thriving in sex work, I mean:

1. You love yourself; you love your life.
2. You take care of your health and have interest in physical pleasure.
3. You have time and energy for outside interests.
4. You have love in your life.
5. You have a personal support network that gets you and your decision to be a sex worker.

6. You have a professional support network.
7. Your clients provide you with the money and gratification you deserve.
8. You understand, weigh, and make conscious decisions about the risks you take.
9. You have a financial plan.
10. You choose to do sex work.

These are lofty goals, and I don't want this list to feel like The Big Impossible. As they say, you can have everything you want in life; you just can't have it all at once. *You are not a failure* if you don't have everything all figured out right now. My hope is this book helps you get to where you want to go.

OVERVIEW OF THRIVING IN SEX WORK

Before we can discuss the life we want, first we have to get clear about the challenges we face. As I mentioned before, the job is profoundly emotional—at any given moment, sex work can trigger fear, shame, low self-esteem, anger, and envy in our coworkers, our clients, and ourselves. I call those negative emotions "DEMONS."

In Part One of this book, I discuss the dynamics of each of these demons beginning with fear, because no joy is possible without safety. It's important to make friends with fear, to harness it to work for us, rather than against us. I'll take you step-by-step through basic self-care of mind and body. Next we'll turn to shame and stigma, examining why sexuality can make us feel so bad about ourselves. We'll tackle low self-esteem, insecurities, and feelings of being old and ugly. Then we'll look at anger, which can feel delicious and energizing, but has the power to take over our lives. We'll finish with envy, an emotion so taboo that we hardly ever talk about it, but wanting what somebody else has drives all kinds of terrible behavior in the sex industry. Along the way, I'll share stories and provide exercises. If nothing else, know that you're not the only one to feel these things, and that there are ways to get to the other side.

In Part Two, I turn to what I call the "tools of the trade." Money, clients, and the industry itself can stir all kinds of emotions. I'll explore how money impacts us emotionally, how to manage time, and how to attract great clients. I'll offer advice on budgeting, keeping your money safe, and not letting technology drive you crazy, as well as dispel some of the most destructive myths of the industry.

In Part Three, I'll cover self-care and managing life's ups and downs. Our bodies are our livelihood, so we need strategies for those times when we get hungry, tired, lonely, bored, and depressed, as well as getting through the winter holidays and other slowdown periods. Part Four is dedicated to navigating the special challenges of romantic relationships, and I make a special plea to never forget that pleasure is our birthright.

Finally, in Part Five, I discuss life after the Life. What to expect, what to prepare for, how to cope with long-term consequences. How to transition gracefully into other enterprises, translating the skills we've acquired in sex work into the rest of our meaningful, rewarding lives.

STRATEGIES FOR THRIVING IN SEX WORK

Only when we see challenges clearly can we tackle them with skill. As sex workers, we need to pay special attention to our emotional health. A core premise of this book is that when we feel bad, first we have to get our heads right—only then do we take action. We get into trouble when we allow emotions to dominate our decision-making. I was angry and fearful so much of the time I worked—a client or coworker could leave me shaking with a throwaway comment. I look back and realize how destructive all that churning was. My younger self didn't know how to sit with negative emotions guided by curiosity and self-love. This book offers both practical and heartfelt advice on how to cope better.

I'm a firm believer in BOUNDARIES, or the limits one sets on one's behavior and others in order to maintain one's dignity and sense of self. These can be consciously stated, such as, "No sex without a condom," or, "No texts after midnight," or an unstated, internal limit that is only known once it's been breached. The sex industry profits from the myth that we're available for anything, but only by knowing and enforcing our rules can we keep ourselves healthy, protected, and sane.

I talk quite a bit about BURNOUT, and offer ways to keep the work vital and fresh. When we don't take care of ourselves, we shut down, making the work torture. While I don't have research to back this up, I believe burnout is one of the top reasons sex workers leave the industry.

Additionally, I believe in setting goals. For the record, I don't believe positive thinking is the solution to problems. Plenty of bad things happen that we have no control over, and the idea we can avoid them with happy thoughts is magical thinking. However, setting clear objectives through visualization, writing, talking, and making art is like GPS programing, telling our minds where we want to go. Imagining what we want our lives to look like is the first step to realizing those ambitions.

DEFINITIONS, PRONOUNS, AND GENDERED TERMS

This book is for sex professionals, so I presume most of the terms I use will be familiar to you. However, definitions matter. Terms defined in the appendix on page 258 are in BOLDED SMALL CAPITALS.

Just so we're all on the same page, I use the terms "sex worker," "adult performer," "erotic laborer," and "sexy professional" to mean a person of any gender performing sexual services or providing sexual products in exchange for money or other things of value. As a blanket term, "sex worker" includes STRIPPERS, BDSM PROFESSIONALS, PORN ACTORS and CAMMERS, SUGAR BABIES, and PROSTITUTES in the aggregate. I name specific occupations when referring to their particular dynamics. I use "SEX INDUSTRY," "sex trade," "adult industry," and "erotic labor," interchangeably. However, I use the terms "THE BIZ" and "THE LIFE" specifically: the mindset of living as a sex worker from direct participatory experience, rather than as an abstract concept or observed from a distance. They stand in contrast to the "STRAIGHT" or "NORMAL" world, meaning life outside the sex industry.

If you've ever done sex work or identified as a sex worker, I sincerely hope you find yourself in these pages. I tried to craft each line with every age, gender, orientation, race, class, and ability in mind. Although it would have been easy to refer to sex workers as female and clients as male, that erases the identity spectrum of sex workers and clients alike. Turns out when you address an advice book directly to the reader, there's a simple solution to the problem of gendered pronouns: eliminate them altogether and use "you(r)(s)" and "we/us/our" instead.

However, certain terms I use are traditionally gendered. "Slut" and "whore" for instance, casually thrown around in queer communities, historically have a special power when directed at CISGENDER females. Likewise, "BRAZEN HUSSY," or someone who is out as a sex worker or other sexual minority to engage in activism, doesn't always translate across genders or sexualities. I use these terms because they connote powerful archetypes that I hope can hold emotional truths for everyone.

Then there's the question of what to call people who pay for commodified sexuality. Terms like "tricks" or "johns" are often used as slurs, perpetuating the notion that in every sex work transaction, someone is despicable. So, my blanket term for anyone who pays for sexual services is "CLIENT." Strip clubs have "PATRONS." Porn stars and actors have "FANS." And while not all clients who use the services of BDSM professionals are submissive, I use the catchall term "SUB" for dungeon clientele. Why don't I use the term "customer"? Customers purchase goods; clients hire service providers. Sex workers offer their time, attention, and performances, not themselves.

As for pronouns for clients, the vast majority of clientele is cisgender male, no question, but plenty of TRANS* people and cisgender women patronize sex workers. Just as importantly, clients identify *in session* as gay and straight, trans*, cross-dressers, animals, aliens, even objects. Simply referring to them by their straight world presentation doesn't capture everything that goes on in pay-for-play exchanges. The trans* community offers many new, exciting pronouns, but I decided "they/their/them" are the most accessible to the average reader. I use them for clients, sex workers, lovers, coworkers, lawyers, police officers, and everyone else in this book. To all you grammarians out there gnashing your teeth, please recognize that our language is changing: thanks to gender radicals, we're learning that each of us, especially in our sex lives, contains multitudes.

TRIGGERS

This book is all about messy stuff like sex, money, and emotions, so somewhere along the way, something I say will likely strike a nerve and hurt, frighten, or anger you. Things to keep in mind:

- ❀ *Sex work varies wildly from person to person, and there is no "right" way to talk about or do sex work.* There is no universal understanding of the work or the industry. I've tried to make my observations as broad as possible, but there will be times when you don't see yourself reflected here.

- ❀ *I was a highly privileged sex worker.* My observations and advice will most likely be most relevant to those with similar advantages: working voluntarily, independently, indoors, with disposable income, internet access, and community.

- ❀ *I won't have all the answers.* What worked for me may not work for you. My analyses, opinions, and suggestions may seem completely off the mark, and that's valid.

Everything I offer is in the spirit of starting a conversation as a peer, not dictating as an expert. Take what's helpful, and by all means, set the rest aside.

Be warned—I'll repeat certain advice again and again: **Trust your instincts. Save your money. Happy clients equal a happy business. Self-care is essential. Don't beat yourself up.** I do this because some of you will hop around and won't read this cover-to-cover, and I don't want anyone to miss out. Just as important, there are some messages we can never hear enough.

SEX WORK AND CONSENT

This book is intended for adults engaged in SAFE, SANE, AND CON-SENSUAL (SSCA) sex work, with an emphasis on consensual. I don't presume to advise victims of sex trafficking, people pimped under fear of violence or deportation, or anyone working to feed a habit.

The concept of consensuality in sex work is contested; it certainly isn't black-and-white. Many of us grind along in jobs we hate because of limited employment options, and there is no way to argue SURVIVAL SEX is voluntary. But some see no possibility for consent in sex work ever. Anti-prostitution activists insist all sex work is exploitation by definition: because the work can be dangerous, stigmatized, degrading, and dehumanizing, it can never be compensated for like a straight job.

I believe blanket exploitation arguments are misguided. Sex work doesn't inherently harm, degrade, or otherwise diminish anyone. As I see it, sex is a normal human function. It's not intrinsically bad or dirty. Adults should have the right to be sexual however and with whomever they please. At the same time, no one should have sex with anyone they don't want to. Some people need or want to pay for sexuality; others are willing to provide it. As long as both client and sex worker act freely, whatever they negotiate is simply a labor exchange, not exploitation.

Sex work in all its forms, including prostitution, should be legal, meaning decriminalized. At the same time, I believe there ought to be fearsome laws fully enforced against anyone who profits off someone else's sexuality without their consent: nonconsensual sex work is commodified rape. I acknowledge there is tension in those two positions, but they aren't incompatible. Voluntary sex workers should enjoy the full protection of the law; traffickers deserve to rot in prison. I stand in solidarity with all sex workers, and hold a special place in my heart for those working against their will. I look to the day when we all can work free of intimidation and recrimination.

WHO IS A "SEX WORKER," WHAT IT MEANS, WHERE WE MEET

"Sex worker" and "sex work" were terms coined around 1979 by activist Carol Leigh, also known as the Scarlot Harlot, Unrepentant Whore. Defining prostitution and pornography as the labor of sex was a radical notion at the time. When I first entered the adult industry in 1990, it hadn't caught on yet. If anyone used "sex worker" at all, it meant "prostitute."

There was good reason for that. In that era, workers in the adult industry tended to be loyal only to their own. Strippers insisted on the term "exotic dancers," thank you very much. Porn actors affiliated with the film industry. Pro doms held themselves out as different because they kept their clothes on, but to much of the rest of the world, they were deviant freaks. And everyone shunned the prostitutes. Even if you worked in a strip joint or made pornos, by god, at least you weren't a whore.

Happily, in the past twenty-five years, there is greater solidarity throughout the industry. One measure of that trend is the term "sex worker" now does the political lifting that "queer" does in the LGBTQ community. It takes on stigma from across the spectrum. It's a label that says, *Think what you want about "People Like That." I'm one of them, too.* Of course, divisions and distrust still remain. Deep rifts run along race, gender, and class lines, as well as the ability to conform to beauty norms. We ignore and talk past one another. And prostitution remains taboo, especially working outside.

Additionally, there are many other sex industry-related job titles: adult video store employee, dildo maker, fetish designer, porn producer, phone sex operator, erotica writer, condom tester, and so on. These workers may face stigma and danger due to their job titles, but may not be readily included in discussions of sex work concerns. Whether or not you identify as a sex worker, if you work in the Biz and grapple with negative consequences, I hope my advice is helpful.

I'm always so proud to hear fellow sex workers come out, telling their stories; however, many of us don't have that freedom. Most writings on sex work are by white, diplomaed, able-bodied, conforming, cisgender female authors like myself. I promise to always try to be mindful of my privilege, aware that not everyone is in a position to follow my advice.

Having said that, if you picked up this book, you must have seen something of yourself in the title. Let me meet you there, in that place where we are not the same, but can share. May you find something you're looking for.

PART ONE: DEMONS

Turn your demons into art, your shadow into a friend, your fear into fuel, your failures into teachers, your weaknesses into reasons to keep fighting. Don't waste your pain. Recycle your heart.

—ANDRÉA BALT

FEAR: AN INTRODUCTION

Hi, Sexy—

Opening this book with the heavy stuff was scary—I was sorely tempted to start out with tips for conquering the winter blues and work our way up from there. However, security is foundational for any kind of happiness. In order to thrive in sex work, we need to start by addressing the threats we face.

As sex workers, we cross lines for a living, operating outside the bounds of polite behavior. We flaunt social norms, operate in legal grey areas, and smash taboos. Transgression can be liberating and exhilarating, but may result in very real negative physical, emotional, social, and legal consequences. Denying that fact leaves us even more exposed to danger—we cannot look away because we're too afraid.

What many of us don't realize, however, that when harnessed properly, fear can be useful. I'll use myself as an example. One of my worst nightmares is dying alone in a filthy room, starving because I'm too weak to care for myself, soaked in my own urine. This didn't come to me by accident. Brittle, sickly, helpless women raised me; they lived and died just like that. That terror is so powerful, it can make my heart beat faster and my muscles tense up, poisoning the safety I currently enjoy.

However, that fear has also been my very good friend. It's made me value friendship more than anything else in life. It's motivated me to make money and always have savings. My end-of-life anxieties have driven my work ethic, pushing me to be professional, cultivate good clients, and honor what I'm worth. Every day of my life, I've beaten that bitch back with a stick.

So, let's take some time and unpack our dread—it's never time wasted. We can use it to shape our lives into what we want them to be. Our strategy is simple: First we breathe. We listen to what fear has to tell us, fully feeling our anxieties, rather than pushing them away. Then, from our power, we act. Under threat, we protect ourselves. Anticipating future hazards, we mitigate risk. Cradling our most tender hearts, we honor our deepest desires.

As Gavin de Becker says, "True fear is a gift. Unwarranted fear is a curse." This chapter begins with heartfelt advice on getting to know our fears. I'll give practical advice for when anxiety threatens to become overwhelming. Then I'll offer suggestions on securing physical safety, along with self-care if something bad does happen. Staying on the right side of the law is so important—I'll offer a list of questions to discuss with a lawyer, and some ideas on how to find a good one. Finally, I'll outline safer sex strategies, because it's not always easy to keep our heads in the heat of the moment. Once we've made friends with fear, we'll be ready to address shame, anger, envy, and all the rest.

�֎ MAKING FRIENDS WITH OUR FEARS

Face fear, and thereby master it. Repress fear and be mastered by it.
—DR. MARTIN LUTHER KING, JR.

Sex work goes straight to the heart of the human condition. In his book *Think and Grow Rich,* Napoleon Hill lays out six universal fears: fear of poverty, criticism, illness, the loss of love, old age, and death. In sex work, these take on specific forms: getting arrested, getting found out, contracting an STD. A client turning violent, a criminal record, bad reviews. Aging out of the job. No romantic relationships or future career. Losing friends. And, of course, we all struggle with day-to-day insecurities and vulnerabilities. These grinding anxieties shape life in the Biz. Even though it can be a difficult conversation to have, let's talk through them together.

EXERCISE: GETTING TO KNOW OUR FEARS

In order to face our fears, first we must name them. These simple steps help clear out the emotional underbrush of anxiety, freeing us so we can find solutions. Find a blank piece of paper, and sit in a quiet place. Close your eyes, take a deep breath, and say, "I am afraid of…" out loud. What comes into your mind?

Write down the anxieties associated with your job. Be brutally honest. Include the gnawing worries along with the nightmare scenarios, from cellulite to stalkers. This isn't much fun—it's tempting to push those thoughts away, but unexamined fears have a way of snarling up in a big ball and taking over our minds. Once you've created your list, look it over, and take some time to get to know them. Give some thought to which ones would be the same if you worked as a bus driver or barista.

If you've got a therapist or friend you feel comfortable sharing with, by all means, get outside support for these next steps. Take a few deep breaths to calm yourself, then read this list out loud. Feel how these spoken words resonate in your body, your throat, your belly. Notice which fears are hard to wrap your voice around. Which ones make you feel small and powerless, or fierce and angry, ready to fight. Which ones make your pulse strong and eyesight sharp, and which make you feel soft and heavy and sleepy and dull.

Fear responds well to questioning. Try asking aloud, "*When* are you? Is something bad happening right now, or am I projecting the past onto the future? Am I reliving something I don't want to feel again?"

How does it feel to have your terrors hanging in the air out loud? Inside the chambers of our minds, they tend to rattle around, filling all space and time. It's easy to believe, on some level, that speaking them aloud will make them come true. Resting outside ourselves, some anxieties simply dry up and blow away. We realize how trivial they are, or that we've had the solution all along.

We can thank our fears for everything they've done for us. Let them know they can take a breath and relax a little—they don't have to do all the heavy lifting to keep us safe anymore. Consciously engaging fear lifts it out of our reptilian brains. Higher brain functions such as creativity and problem-solving can take over, identifying risks and preparing for the future.

NAMING OUR FEARS

Next step: now is the time to be your own best friend. Divide your fears into four groups: practical fears, imminent dangers, unlikely fears, and the "Worst Things in the World." Let's take a look at each of these in turn. Practical fears and imminent dangers are states of being and require action. Unlikely fears and our worst terrors are states of mind, and we need to address their underlying logic.

PRACTICAL FEARS

I can't run out of money like I did last month ... I wonder if my neighbors can hear my clients coming and going in the hall ... ? What if that nosy fan finds out I have a child or where I go to school ...?

Practical fears keep us on track, and self-protection is at their core. They make sure that we're discreet, and we keep our private lives private. That we lock our front doors, balance our checkbooks, and screen our calls. We need to reward that part of ourselves that's always on the lookout to keep us safe.

If you have a practical concern you aren't addressing, don't beat yourself up about it—you have your reasons. This is the moment to get curious. What's holding you back from taking care of business? Is there some solution you've been putting off? Is there someone you can ask for help? Active engagement helps release us from paralysis and procrastination.

IMMINENT DANGERS

I keep getting anonymous texts and hang-up calls ... That weirdo showed up again at the end of my shift. What if they follow me home ... ? Every time a client comes to my door, my neighbor is at the window watching ...

If you're in danger, you need to deal with it now—the question is how. There is no single right answer, but how we react instinctively tells us about our coping strategies. When you're threatened, how do you respond? Do you hope if you just ignore bad things, they'll go away? Do you make a scene or start a fight? Do you drop out of sight, quit your job, or move in the middle of the night? Do you call the police, or reach out to your friends, relatives, and FOUND FAMILY for support and protection?

Take some time to get in touch with why you respond like you do. Is it because you feel paralyzed? Itching for a fight? All alone? Assertive? Unable to speak? Are you desperate for other people to help you, or do you just want to withdraw and become invisible? However you feel is valid, but it's good to realize that your response isn't the only possible reaction, and others might respond differently. Inhale deeply and then exhale, taking a moment to acknowledge you're doing the very best you can to get through this.

This is how to deal with active danger: first we breathe, spending time with the fear, then we act. This is important: if you feel threatened, do not isolate. Predators count on this. In their twisted minds, we deserve what we get. What you deserve is help. Talk to your work buddies, your friends and family, or if you work for someone, tell management. Let other people know what's happening—do not try to solve this on your own. Tell your support system your plan for confronting danger before you do it. When we're scared, our minds spin out all kinds of crazy possibilities. Don't act without a reality check.

I know it can be hard to tell other people we're in trouble. We might feel like we should be able to handle things on our own, or we're afraid they'll blame us for bringing it on ourselves. But the fact is we all need help sometimes. If you're hesitant to tell someone, ask yourself: if your good friend were in your same situation, wouldn't you want to know?

Remember: You do not have to solve all of your problems yourself. You are not bothering the people who love you by telling them you're frightened for your safety. Talking about it is not what makes it real. Telling other people does not make the problem bigger than it already is. Talking about it does not make it your fault. Telling other people does not mean you'll have to stop working. Taking care of each other is what love is for. While you're at it, make sure to let your buddies know that you'll be there for them if they ever need help themselves.

UNLIKELY FEARS

What if my neighbor calls the cops, and I end up on the news ... ? What if my ex recognizes me from my ad and outs me all over Facebook ... ? What if a client secretly tapes our session and blackmails me ...?

As sex workers, we spend so much of our working day actually naked, or at least half-dressed, it's only natural that feeling exposed bleeds into other parts of our lives—it's easy to dream up all kinds of disasters. However, worrying doesn't change anything. We don't do ourselves any favors ruminating over things we can't control.

When you find yourself spinning out in the land of "what-ifs," stop for a minute and think about the odds. You're one sex worker out of many, many thousands in a multi-billion dollar industry. Do you see sex workers getting outed all over social media or cable news? If there's a video of you on some website somewhere, is anyone even going to notice? Focus on what you can do to keep yourself safe, and try to let some of the fear of the long shot nightmare scenario go. I outline concrete steps for managing intrusive worrying in the next section.

THE "WORST THING IN THE WORLD"

My mother is going to find out I work in a dungeon and disown me... I'm going to die homeless and alone... I can never have a partner because of my shameful secrets...

Every "Worst Thing In The World" boils down to the same core terrors: loss of love, loss of wholeness, loss of safety. They show us our true heart's desire. Unfortunately, terrible things happen all the time, and we are powerless to stop them. We do lose love. People get sick, they grow old, and they die. Someday, too, we will die. To live is to suffer, which can make it difficult to think clearly. Peace activist and Buddhist monk Thích Nhất Hạnh, in his book, *Fear: Essential Wisdom for Getting Through the Storm*, reminds us how powerful it is to remain present. He writes:

> Fear keeps us focused on the past or worried about the future. If we can acknowledge our fear, we can realize that right now we are okay. Right now, today, we are still alive, and our bodies are working marvelously. Our eyes can still see the beautiful sky. Our ears can still hear the voices of our loved ones.

When we feel that deep terror, we need to stop. First we breathe, reminding us that we are here, safe in this moment, grounded on this gorgeous earth. Then we act. If your fear is losing love because of sex work, the antidote is to build community. If you fear poverty when you're old, that's inspiration to learn how to earn, save, and invest. If shame makes you worry that you're destined to be lonely, your task is to seek out Brazen Hussy idols who live their lives out loud. Get started today.

Bad things happen to everyone, but living in terror is no kind of life at all. The "Worst Things In The World" are tremendous gifts. When we take time to listen, they point us to how we can live our lives to the fullest.

> *How much of our lives are wasted living in dread? Bravery is the gift we give ourselves by trusting the world, even with all the dangers and unknowns.*

❀ PRACTICAL ADVICE: MANAGING ACUTE ANXIETY

Anxiety episodes are no fun whatsoever: racing thoughts, elevated heartbeat, dizziness or lightheadedness, an inability to think clearly. We face a lot of uncertain situations in sex work, resulting in worry, stage fright, or just a general sense of dread. If you're in immediate danger, you must get yourself to safety right away. However, if you are safe in the moment but fear of the future is overwhelming you, here's my advice on how to feel calmer:

❀ *Realize what you are feeling.* The first step to confronting panic is to acknowledge it. Many of us would much rather ignore our anxieties, so we chatter, obsess, drink, overeat, or hypnotize ourselves online for hours. However, denial only exacerbates feelings of paralysis and powerlessness.

❀ *Voice what you are feeling.* Try saying aloud: "I feel super scared and wound up right now." Speaking the truth won't make whatever you fear more real. Instead, it will bring you into the present moment.

❀ *Breathe deeply.* Slowly inhale to a count of three, filling your belly first, then your chest. Gently hold your breath while counting to three, then slowly exhale to a count of three. Repeat as often as needed, until you feel your body soften. It's common to take shallow breaths when we're afraid, elevating the body's stress hormones. Breathing deep from the diaphragm activates the relaxation response of the parasympathetic nervous system, countering the adrenaline-fueled fight/flight/freeze response of the sympathetic nervous system.

❀ *Reconnect with your body, focus on the here and now.* Clenching an ice cube, snapping a rubber band on your wrist, or curling and uncurling your toes are ways to get you out of your head and back into your body. Even if you're in serious trouble, focusing on what's actually happening in the present moment will improve your ability to manage the situation.

❀ *Realize that your brain is playing tricks on you.* If you're in a panic mode but facing no immediate danger, your mind is outrunning reality. Say to yourself: "I am safe in this moment. I am healthy and whole. These feelings will pass." A friend of mine, when she's drowning in anxiety, puts on loud music, dances wildly, and sings, "This is silly, this is silly, this is silly," until she can get on top of how she's feeling. Acknowledging that our brains are in hyperdrive can help free us from any shame, guilt, judgment, or pressure we put on ourselves to "just get over it already."

❀ *Use positive self-talk.* Oftentimes during panic attacks, self-hatred tags along, fueling all those hideous whispers inside our heads telling us we're no good. I call those voices "hate radio." Talk to yourself with the same compassion you'd show to your lover or very best friend. Say, "This feels terrible right now, but I'm going to get through to the other side very soon. I don't let fear rule my life."

❀ *Visualize a calming situation.* Close your eyes and imagine yourself in a peaceful place out in nature, sitting in a park or by the beach or in the forest. As you inhale and exhale, imagine any thoughts or emotions that come into your mind are like leaves blowing on the wind—notice them, but let them go right on by. Just observe—don't judge or fixate on them in any way. This practice of acknowledging feelings without engaging them can be very powerful.

❀ *Question your thoughts.* When we get worked up, all kinds of horrible future scenarios can ricochet through our brains. Once your body and mind have calmed down for

a few minutes, and you are in a safe place, try challenging
your worries with these scripts:

- *My anxious reaction is out of proportion to the reality of
  the situation.*
- *I have friends and loved ones who can listen, soothe,
  and provide perspective.*
- *If the worst possible thing did happen, I am safe and
  strong and could handle it.*
- *I can alleviate anxiety today by preparing for a better
  future. Is there anything I need to be doing right now?*

❀ *Focus on meaningful activities.* When you're past the critical stage, a meaningful goal-directed activity like going
to the movies or the gym or making dinner can help
focus your attention elsewhere. It's fine to distract yourself—don't sit around obsessing about how you feel. Get
back to the business of life.

❀ *Listen to your body.* After an anxiety attack, it's common
to feel wrung out and exhausted; give your body the rest
it needs to recover. If you have excess adrenaline to burn
off, working out, taking a long walk, or sex can be relax-
ing and grounding, bringing body and mind back into
balance.

Worry pretends to be necessary, but serves no useful purpose.
—ECKHART TOLLE

✵ PRACTICAL ADVICE: PHYSICAL SAFETY

We can't have a conversation about safety in sex work without discussing the physical and legal risks involved. In these next few sections, I'll be tackling some difficult topics including violence, self-defense, getting arrested, and surviving a scary call. If you're not feeling ready for these topics right now, skip ahead to my discussion of safer sex on page 45.

DOMESTIC VIOLENCE AND WORKPLACE ABUSE

Because we operate at the margins of society, too many sex workers experience workplace violence at the hands of clients, management, pimps, traffickers, coworkers, or lovers. Many of us face getting outed, losing custody of our children, deportation, or arrest. Without exception, no one should be terrorized into doing sex work. Sexual coercion is a violation of human rights, integrity, and dignity. Furthermore, we deserve full control of the money we earn. I don't know who you are, I don't know your situation, but if you live with threats and violence, that is wrong. Nobody deserves to be treated like that. *Especially not you.*

We can talk ourselves into believing abuse is our fault. *I should've known better. I knew this would happen. I brought this on myself.* That is depression talking, anger turned inward. No one is responsible for your mistreatment except your abuser. Whatever you signed up for, whatever warning signs you ignored, and all the rest, none of that matters now—you need to get away from your abuser.

The National Domestic Violence Hotline (800-799-SAFE or 7233 | thehotline.org) is an excellent starting point for help. It's anonymous and confidential, which means no one will track your phone number or ask for any identifying information. Available to all genders and identities, they'll direct you to appropriate services and support in your area. I list additional sex worker-friendly crisis resources in the appendix on page 278.

WHO CAN I TELL?

When seeking help from the authorities, there are always worries: *No one will care. No one will believe me. My job will be used against me. I'll lose the only way I know how to make money. I'll be charged with a crime, and my abuser will walk free.* These fears keep many of us working in terror, undefended.

If you are in a bad situation, you deserve help. I am not a lawyer, and nothing I say here should be taken as legal advice, but I can offer basic guidelines for reporting abuse:

- ❀ *Crisis hotlines help victims—end of story.* They do not entrap sex workers and punish them. The person on the other end of the line is not going to turn you over to the police, the IRS, the DEA, ICE, or anyone else. Do not put off picking up the phone and calling for help **today** because of that fear.

- ❀ *When you call, ask whether your conversation is anonymous, confidential, private, and/or privileged.* Request an explanation so that you understand what your rights and protections are.

- ❀ *If you're engaged in illegal activities such as prostitution or selling drugs, ask for legal help.* Make it clear that you need to be able to speak without incriminating yourself.

- ❀ *Once you know you can speak freely, be honest.* Disclose everything, even illegal activities. You risk undermining yourself by holding parts of your story back only to be found out later, and your credibility is important.

- ❀ *Most social workers, crisis counselors, and legal advisors are decent people who see just about everything at their jobs.*

Of course, there will always be exceptions, but most likely you won't be the first sex worker they've met in their career. You probably won't be the first one they've laid eyes on since lunch! It can be hard to shake that instinctive fear of exposure, but most professionals won't bat an eye when they learn you do sex work.

SECURING A SAFE WORK ENVIRONMENT

One of the truly unjust aspects of sex work is that workplace violence is often tolerated. The industry is a magnet for criminal behavior, and we don't always enjoy full protection from law enforcement. However, sex work under threat is not inevitable.

You should be able to come and go from work without being followed or harassed. If management's security protocols are inadequate, make some noise. If that doesn't work, it's time to make a change. If a fan is stalking you, you can to go to the police and get a restraining order. If you work out of your home, and you don't have privacy, then you owe it to yourself to move. I know how horrible it feels to lose where you live because of safety concerns—I went through it myself—but you can't huddle in your apartment terrified your neighbors are monitoring your foot traffic. Thousands of sex workers all over the country operate in safe surroundings, and you deserve to as well.

VIOLENT CLIENTS

Is there any terror in sex work more vivid than the homicidal maniac? Popular culture works very hard to remind those of us who live on the margins that there is one force civilization cannot defend us from: the murderous, sex-crazed psychopath. Of course, most assault stops short of murder, but violence and rape are common in the populations who make up the bulk of sex workers: gay men, trans* folk, and women.

Unfortunately, there is no way to keep ourselves absolutely safe, but we can protect ourselves. My advice:

❀ *Trust your instincts.* Your gut is your first line of defense. If someone feels wrong to you, terminate the situation. As social animals, we know deep down from even the subtlest clues when something is off, but we're socialized not to be judgy, to smooth things over, to act nice. In sex work, **you do not wait for things to get weird.** When those little hairs go up on the back of your neck, you get yourself the hell out of there. I recommend a powerful book on this subject, *The Gift of Fear and Other Survival Signals that Protect Us from Violence*, by Gavin De Becker. As he writes, "The words 'I know it' are more valuable than 'I knew it.'"

❀ *Learn how to physically defend yourself.* (I discuss this more in the next section.)

❀ *Always have an escape plan.* When you do outcall, shoot porn in an unfamiliar place, or start at a new club, look for the exits and alarms.

❀ *Demonstrate good boundaries.* Act proud and assertive, like someone who doesn't tolerate nonsense.

❀ *Have a support team.* Let folks know where you're going, and check in with them after a shift, shoot, or scene.

❀ *Tell your clients about your support system.* Don't be afraid to inform them that you have people who know where you are and what you do.

❀ *Always, always, always* **have enough money to walk away** *if something doesn't feel right.* This means having twenty bucks stashed in your shoe or your bra so you can get home. This means having money set aside so you don't have to say "yes" to something you don't want to do.

❀ *Have a plan in case you get robbed.* How do you get home? How do you get in your front door? Is your cellphone, with all those hot selfies and client information, locked? Hopefully this never happens, but know what your next steps are if it ever does.

THE POLICE

Seeking out the police or other authorities when you need help is one thing; it's quite another when they come after you. The best offense is a good defense. When you're talking about cops who literally hold your life in their hands, you need excellent defense. Do not wait; do your homework today. Connect with a lawyer or a sex-work friendly legal defense organization. (More on that in a minute.) Always have their card on hand, right next to the condoms and lube, and memorize their name and contact information.

The police are less likely to mess with someone who calmly and clearly articulates their rights. I can't say this enough times: ***Know your actual rights***. Don't spout nonsense you picked up from action movies. This isn't always easy—I've got major authority issues myself, I confess. I get so mad I can't see straight when taking orders from bullies, so I know what a struggle it can be to stay cool.

However, always pick your battles wisely. The time to take a stand isn't when you're in custody. Keep your mouth shut, follow their orders, don't make a bad situation worse for yourself. I don't want to take anything away from folks who've been beaten, raped, and robbed by dirty cops—that is a brutal reality. However, I lived with an ex-cop for ten years and had several as clients. What they tell me is most of them don't want to arrest us. They can't admit it on the job—law enforcement can't pick and choose the laws they like—but many of them view shaking us down as a total waste of time. In the heat of the moment, try to remember they are just doing their job. Comply with their orders while firmly asserting your right to a lawyer. For more information, I provide a list of resources on how to interact with law enforcement in the appendix on page 278.

❋ PRACTICAL ADVICE: LEARN SELF-DEFENSE (NO EXCUSES!)

True story: Way back in the day when I was an itty-bitty call girl just starting out in my studio apartment in the San Francisco Tendernob, I kept a roll of pennies under the bed. Somehow in my mind, this constituted a self-protection plan. My thinking went, if a client got out of hand I'd reach under there and … And then what? Sock them in the face? As if punching someone with homemade brass knuckles would magically whisk them out of my apartment, leaving me intact. My psycho client insurance wasn't worth those fifty cents.

My other big self-defense strategy was daydreaming about coolly slapping wayward clients around. The *Kill Bill* movies hadn't come out yet in the early '90s, but the Bride was pretty much how I saw myself—ninja warrior in a banana-yellow vinyl bodysuit, minus the samurai sword. One tiny problem with this plan—total ignorance of any martial arts whatsoever. I'd seen movie stars performing all kinds of ass-kicking maneuvers, so somehow I figured if I ever found myself in trouble, once the adrenaline kicked in, all those techniques would flow through me, my assailant would crumple like a wet Kleenex, and I'd be safe.

There's no way to sugarcoat this truth: You need to plan for danger if you do sex work. If someone starts behaving erratically or in a threatening manner, you need a plan for getting away in one piece. Furthermore, you must commit in your mind to carrying that plan all the way through. If that means making a lot of noise and as a result, people find out about you, so be it. Don't be like my misguided younger self—***hope is not a plan.***

I strongly recommend learning self-defense. Check online—many martial arts studios, nonprofits, universities, community colleges, and police departments offer free or low-cost courses, teaching both defensive and evasive techniques, as well as how to spot aggressive behaviors and scheming maneuvers. Most of us don't have the opportunity in regular life to imprint our muscle memory by acting as if we're in imminent danger, shrieking at the top of our lungs as though our lives depended on it. For many of us, this may be the first time we ever punch, kick, gouge, or strike another human with full force, pushing through any inbred tendency to freeze when terrified. This is how we train ourselves to act.

Additionally, our body language, eye contact, and alertness can signal to potential attackers how easy it might be to overwhelm us—most rapes and robberies are crimes of opportunity. I'm in no way placing blame on anyone who has suffered an assault—the only person responsible for violent behavior is the assailant. With that said, it's good practice to project confidence and awareness, presenting as someone who doesn't tolerate bad behavior.

I also kept several self-defense tools on hand when I worked. I had an air horn stashed in my apartment, because 99% of bullies and thieves are cowards themselves—a big, loud unexpected noise isn't part of their robber fantasies. I carried pepper spray in my purse for outcall. It temporarily disorients an assailant, which is ideal if your plan is to run away. But if someone is in your work place just being obnoxious, pepper spray escalates rather than deescalates the situation, so it's not the best tool in all situations.

When I worked in my thirties, I kept a licensed loaded pistol in my apartment. I mentioned my ex was a former cop; she taught me how to handle a handgun properly. However, she trained me to draw it only when my intent was to shoot to kill. Don't make the mistake of believing a deadly weapon scares assailants off—a gun is not a magic wand that makes bad guys do what you want. In real life, drawing a gun you have no intention of using is the best way to get it used against you. Same with a knife. Very few of us truly have what it takes to stab a person in a way that makes them less, not more, of a threat.

I had a clear plan for which defense I'd use depending on how threatened I felt. I learned the effect each weapon would have on an assailant, and had an escape plan. I committed to risking eviction or arrest if that's what was necessary to survive. I'd rather my neighbors learn I was a sex worker than become a violent crime statistic. And I gave myself permission to cut off anyone who didn't feel right or follow my rules without feeling guilty about it afterwards. Better safe than sorry.

One more suggestion—there are now many self-protection phone apps that send an alert to your support circle or dial 911. If your life depends on it, do not hesitate.

> *A self-defense course is one of the very best things you can do for yourself as a sex worker. There is nothing to lose and everything to gain from learning how to handle yourself in a threatening situation. Master any weapons you have on hand, and be clear about when to use them. Don't let your fears about getting outed keep you from defending yourself **by any means necessary.***

❀ HEARTFELT ADVICE: SURVIVING THE BAD CALL

The worst has happened—a call turned ugly. A client or coworker or cop became violent, threatening, or otherwise out of hand. You're safe now, but shaken and scared. What do you do next? It's important to say first that in our line of work, an encounter does not have to rise to the legal threshold of rape, assault, battery, or robbery to feel disturbing, painful, dehumanizing, or traumatizing. If it felt bad to you, that is all that matters.

If you are the victim of a crime, reporting to the police is your decision. Unfortunately, in many parts of the U.S., sex workers face bias in the legal system. There is a chance your claims will not be taken seriously. If you decide to go to the police, I strongly suggest you enlist an ally to support you through the process.

In the days that follow, it is crucial to take extra care of yourself for as long as you feel affected by the event. Here's my best advice:

- ❀ *Take a moment to acknowledge this is tough stuff.* Give yourself credit for doing the very best you know how to get through this. Treat yourself just as your guardian protector or very best friend would treat you: gently, kindly, with ferocious protectiveness and bottomless compassion.

- ❀ *If you experience suicidal thoughts, insomnia, anxiety, or other distress symptoms, seek professional crisis counseling right away.* The National Sexual Assault Hotline (800-656-4673 | rainn.org) is available 24 hours a day. It's free, anonymous, confidential, and available to all genders.

- ❀ *Don't be silent; don't act like nothing happened.* Stuffing this down inside is additional self-harm.

❀ *Ask for support from friends and family.* Now is not the time to isolate.

❀ *Tell your buddies, coworkers, and management what happened.* Let them be part of your protection system. Additionally, they have the right to be informed in order to protect themselves.

❀ *Do not blame yourself.* You are only responsible for you, not for anyone else. You don't deserve what happened. You didn't have it coming. This is not your fault. You are not stupid. This is not your karma. ***Period.***

❀ *It's natural to feel vulnerable.* I encourage you, however, not to treat this event as evidence that you can't trust other people or yourself.

❀ *It's normal to feel depressed or lose interest in ordinary activities for a while.* Please don't beat yourself up. When traumatized, we need to grieve what we've lost: the hope that we will always be safe, the wish that nothing bad will ever happen to us. That sadness must be fully felt, but it is survivable.

❀ *Anger is common as well.* It can be an excellent motivator to make yourself safer in the future.

❀ *Take extra good care of yourself.* Go for long walks. Write in a journal. Make art. Be sweet to your body, including washing, grooming, and eating right. Connect with the things that make you feel good. Nature, sunshine, little kids, exercise, and animals are all excellent medicine.

❀ *If flashbacks flood your mind, stop what you're doing and be present.* Breathe into you, not the memories.

❀ *Avoid addictive or self-destructive behaviors as best as you can.* What starts out as a shortcut to make the pain go away can contribute to a spiral of shame and self-loathing.

❀ *Be proactive.* Self-defense courses and getting politically involved are powerful ways to take back control, as well as to find safe community. Support groups, both online and in real life, connect you to those who have had similar experiences, providing opportunities to learn from others how to cope.

❀ *It's natural to think about quitting sex work.* However, give yourself time; don't make snap decisions.

And finally, allow for the possibility that once you've processed what happened, this event will pass through you to settle where it belongs, in the past.

> *Few of us are actively taught self-care in response to trauma. As negative emotions come up, we must honor them, because they're telling us something important—our response cannot be to wish them away or to engage in yet more harm to ourselves. We must enlist all of our resources: friends, safety nets, self-love. Healing can only happen when we give ourselves time and space to acknowledge what happened and to grieve it. Only then can we absorb both the trauma and the truth of our resiliency into the story of ourselves.*

❊ PRACTICAL ADVICE: THE LAW AND LEGAL TROUBLE

The problem with living outside the law is you no longer have its protection.

—TRUMAN CAPOTE

The law ought to protect sex workers, and legal matters ought to be in the Tools section of this book. When sex work is illegal, it drives it underground, making it more dangerous while criminalizing the "victims" the laws are supposed to defend. The result is many of us, regardless of our job title, live with the fear of arrest and criminal prosecution.

Of course, plenty of sex work is legal, and you may think since you're not engaging in prostitution you're in the clear. But working for a legitimate strip club or massage parlor or porn company doesn't mean you won't find yourself in a bust someday because of someone else's actions, such as a nuisance complaint, drug dealing, human trafficking, or tax evasion. Unfortunately, our industry routinely attracts law enforcement. You cannot ignore your responsibilities, and ignorance of the law is no defense. It's especially true if you work for yourself. Only you know your precise circumstances—whether you have children, are on probation, are camming across state lines, are sending adult material through the mail, and so on.

Knowledge is power. What's considered free speech in one town can be prohibited in another. Laws written today may be overturned tomorrow. You can't fully assess risk if you don't know what risks you're actually taking. Wouldn't it be better to find out that what you're doing is legal than operating in ignorant fear?

I just have to shake my head remembering how clueless I was back in the day. I'd ask someone, usually a fellow working girl, what she thought the law was. She'd tell me something she heard from somewhere, but she wasn't quite sure it was true, because she'd heard the friend-of-a-friend-of-a-friend got busted for something like it just the other day. We'd all just stumble along in a haze of anxiety and half-truths.

Rather than that, my advice is to invest a few hundred dollars to sit down with a defense attorney to learn exactly what the laws are where you live. If that's financially out of reach, there are ways to get your questions answered through low-cost or free legal resources listed in the appendix on page 275.

As for me, I'm not a lawyer and don't play one on television. Absolutely nothing that follows here should be construed as legal advice. And I'm certainly not advising you to do anything illegal—heavens no! I'm instructing you to do the opposite: find out what the laws are so you can make good choices. However, be aware it's not only about what is on the books: laws aren't always equally enforced. Perhaps your newly elected district attorney plans to crack down on petty crime. Knowing the DA will press charges incentivizes the police department to make more nuisance arrests. Or perhaps your city leaders have decided adult industries boost tourism, so law enforcement priorities are directed elsewhere. Local legal aid nonprofits and criminal defense lawyers should know which way the wind is blowing in your area.

FINDING LEGAL COUNSEL

Where do you look to get the right help? I can't stress this enough: *do not* reach out to your lawyer clients. Don't ask to meet for coffee to get advice; don't offer a trade. First off, that is highly unethical on their part—not that you need to be protecting them from themselves, since they're the ones who are officers of the court, after all. But getting represented by someone who may have broken the law with you? You don't want any part of that if someone decides to investigate your client, trust me. And second, bad boundaries equal bad business. Keep clients as clients. Get yourself a lawyer who is sworn to protect you without any messy conflicts of interest.

Most legal aid nonprofits help people from every walk of life; I recommend asking right up front if they are comfortable advising sex workers. A former district attorney or public defender now in private practice will most likely have handled many sex work-related cases. Also, check out the Kink Aware Professionals directory, sponsored by the National Coalition for Sexual Freedom (ncsfreedom. org). NCSF stands up for the rights of all queers, kinks, and other sexually adventurous people. They provide a bulletin board listing lawyers comfortable with alternative sexual lifestyles. Additionally, check out the legal advice resources I list in the appendix on page 275.

Like all other professionals—doctors, tax consultants, and the rest—demand utter professionalism. Attorneys are obligated to be respectful regardless of their clients' circumstances. If your lawyer disses what you do, time for a new lawyer! Their job is to advise, not judge.

QUESTIONS TO ASK YOUR LEGAL COUNSEL

Once you find counsel, schedule an appointment to ask:

- ❀ Is what you're doing a misdemeanor or a felony in your municipality? What are the best ways to avoid breaking the law?
- ❀ Can using a fictitious name harm you? Should you ever use false identification?
- ❀ If stopped by the police, do you have to give your real name? What are the legal implications for using a false name?
- ❀ If arrested, should you talk to anyone other than your attorney? (Spoiler alert—the answer is always *no*.)
- ❀ What's the protocol if you are busted? What if you need to post bail? Discuss where the best place is to set aside funds if you ever need get-out-of-jail money.

❀ Should you deposit a retainer for bond and/or legal fees with your attorney? What are your rights to these funds if you do?

❀ How might getting arrested affect your living situation?

❀ If convicted, can you be evicted from where you live?

❀ Would you have to register as a sex offender?

❀ If you have children, what is the effect of an arrest/conviction/plea bargain on custody?

❀ If you're in the middle of a divorce, what is the effect of an arrest/conviction/plea bargain on marital dissolution proceedings?

❀ How can an arrest affect spousal and/or child support?

❀ Would you be obligated to tell anyone about your arrest: employers, judge in custody proceedings, future landlords?

❀ What are your state's laws concerning asset seizures? Can they take the cash in your home or place of work? Can they seize anything else—computer, cell phone, car, video equipment, or house? Can they confiscate your bank account, safe, or safety deposit box?

❀ What options are there to have an arrest or conviction expunged, meaning that it's removed from your legal record?

❀ What rights and/or legal exposure do you have regarding the internet? What cybercrime laws do you need to follow when advertising online?

❀ Can you protect your website's content from illegal use?

❀ What are the laws that govern working with other sex workers, including referrals or doubles?

❀ What should you do if a landlord or neighbor registers a noise complaint?

❀ If you are assaulted, robbed, or raped by a client, what are your rights? Can you report it to the police?

❀ If you are assaulted, robbed, or raped by a police officer, what are your rights? Who can you report it to?

UNDERSTANDING FELONIES

I advise you, in no uncertain terms, to stay the hell away from felonies. Felony convictions carry serious prison time, ruin your record, and can result in asset seizures, meaning the government can take your property and never give it back. If you're unfamiliar with any of these terms, talk to your legal counsel. *Do not skimp on learning what you need to know to keep yourself out of prison for years.*

❀ *Pimping and Pandering:* Laws intended to punish anyone who profits from or facilitates prostitution. Although well intended, these laws criminalize sex workers who coordinate with each other to share clients, schedule doubles, or even to protect themselves from dangerous clients.

❀ *Crossing State Lines:* Facilitating travel from one state to another to engage in prostitution. Another set of laws designed to save us from ourselves. (See #EliotSpitzer #EpicDownfall.)

❀ *Trafficking:* Moving or imprisoning people for the purpose of forcing them into prostitution or other work against their will. From what I read, massage parlors and strip clubs are prime targets for trafficking busts. Don't be naïve—just because you work someplace voluntarily, it doesn't mean you won't get swept up in a raid if management is involved in something shady.

❀ *Drugs:* While I've got nothing against drugs—I believe adults should do whatever they please with their bodies—I don't recommend exposing yourself to additional criminal charges. And obviously, selling felonious amounts of drugs or being around anyone who does is not a good idea.

❀ *Child Abuse/Child Trafficking:* Under no circumstances, without exception, ever involve yourself with sexual activity with a minor, and stay far away from anyone who does. If you know of such activity and do not report it, you can be charged with conspiracy and/or accessory.

❀ *Child Endangerment:* Just as it sounds: engaging in activities constituting physical or psychological abuse of a minor. Be aware that there are cases of people serving decades in prison for phone sex involving fantasies with children.

IN CASE OF ARREST

A lawyer friend once told me when it comes to the law, the single greatest advantage the rich have over the poor isn't having star lawyers defend you in court. It's pre-arrest counsel, or at the very least, counsel before being charged with a crime. (You ever notice how powerful people surrender to the police at a time and place of their choosing, rather than doing the perp walk in front of the neighbors? That's pre-arrest counsel privilege working big time.) Having a lawyer represent you at this phase of legal proceedings is the best defense to keep the police from throwing you in a cell to rot over the weekend while waiting for arraignment, threatening you with charges that force you to act against your own best interests, or otherwise taking advantage of you.

Unfortunately, most of us don't know we're going to get busted until the cuffs are on, so get your pre-arrest counsel *now*. Find out from your legal advisor the precise steps you need to take if you get arrested. Memorize that information, as well as your lawyer's name and phone number.

Additionally, the National Lawyers Guild (nlg.org) has a free online guide called *You Have the Right to Remain Silent: A Know Your Rights Guide for Law Enforcement Encounters.* Written for activists, it explains your rights in clear, easy-to-understand language: when you are detained or arrested; when you are out in public, in your home, car, or place of work; and whether or not the police need a warrant. Their message is clear: you have the right to remain silent, and you should. ***If you find yourself talking, stop.*** Think of it this way: the cops want you to incriminate yourself, to make their case for them. Don't give them the satisfaction—silence is your power move.

However, be aware that in some states, failure to give your legal name can be grounds for arrest, and giving a false name such as your working handle may also be a crime. Check with your legal advisor what your obligations are in your jurisdiction. I list additional resources in the appendix on page 278 for how to interact with law enforcement before, during, and after arrest.

If you do get arrested, do nothing until you have legal counsel present. *Say nothing other than asking for your lawyer.* Even if you have a law degree, nothing you say at this stage will improve on silence. Have a friend who knows your arrest protocol, including where to find your emergency bond funds, and what to do if your lawyer is not available right away. You can tell them you've been arrested and where you're being held, but that is all. Loose lips sink ships!

In general, if busted for sex work, you'll face a misdemeanor charge. It can get more complicated, however, if your arrest involves drugs, theft, minors, or assault, even if you are legitimately defending yourself from violence or robbery. In general, although not always, misdemeanors result in arrest and booking, followed by a plea agreement with a fine and/or probation and/or community service. In general, although I can't stress enough *not always*, if there are no other mitigating circumstances like a parole violation, there is usually no jail time. With a good lawyer, charges can be dropped and the arrest expunged from your record.

Finally, that one thing you hear again and again on cop shows turns out to be true: *You must tell your lawyer everything so that they can best represent you.* Everything you tell them is confidential and cannot be disclosed, unless you involve your counsel in a crime or fraud. Have them explain what that means so you understand the legal limits of your communications.

TRANS* RIGHTS WHILE UNDER ARREST

Our trans* colleagues are among the most vulnerable when in police custody. We all need be working towards a day when trans* people's bodies and identities are treated with dignity in our legal system.

Unfortunately, that day is a long way off. Most jurisdictions are under no obligation to place trans* people into jail populations that match their identities or make accommodations to keep them safe.

That doesn't mean you can't advocate for yourself while under arrest. Furthermore, your lawyer, whether or not they are court-appointed, has a fiduciary responsibility to advocate for your fair treatment in the legal system. Do not hesitate to self-identify your gender, request specialty protection while in custody, and demand your right to medication, if you are on hormones. To learn more, connect with the sex-work-positive trans* rights organizations I list in the appendix on page 278.

WHAT IF I CAN'T AFFORD A LAWYER?

If you can't afford a lawyer, you can ask for a public defender. However, you'll have to swear under penalty of perjury to your inability to pay and list your assets. If you lie and get caught, you will be charged with a felony of lying under oath. Which is another way of saying if you have the money, pay for your defense.

WHAT IF I WORK OUT OF MY HOME?

Different statutes apply whether you own or rent your home. If you own a condominium, covenants, conditions, and restrictions (CC&Rs) can be invoked if you're convicted of criminal activity, including operating an illegal business. When renting, there are nuisance statutes that can jeopardize your landlord's ownership. Know your rights ahead of time.

WHAT ABOUT MY KIDS?

If you're fighting to keep custody or have legal custody of children, please don't work without legal counsel. It used to be even unfounded accusations of engaging in sex work could seriously endanger parental rights. I'm old enough to remember when mothers could have their kids stripped from them if spotted with more than one "boyfriend."

However, as a general trend over the past twenty years or so as sex work has become more mainstream, in many jurisdictions, it's no longer automatic cause to void parental rights. It's not enough for a disgruntled ex to assert that working in a strip club or as a pro dom makes you an unfit parent, but naturally, it helps not to have any arrests or convictions. The court may well take into consideration whether your job affects your child's living environment. Common sense dictates it's best not to work where your kids sleep. And, of course, the court will want to know about mitigating circumstances: Are there drugs in the home, have the police ever been called, are other people working there with you? Answering "yes" to any of those risks felony exposure—yet another reason to stay away from those activities altogether.

THE IRS

When it comes to law enforcement, it turns out the IRS is a whole different beast. Again, while I'm in no position to dispense legal or tax advice, lawyers and CPAs tell me there is no structural linkage between local law enforcement and the IRS. Nobody in your hometown police department is going to pick up the phone to inform the taxman you just got nailed on solicitation charges with a fistful of ill-gotten cash—they just don't have the time. That said, all bets are off if you're convicted of a felony. The feds do talk to one another, and they will gleefully go after your assets—one of the many, many reasons not to ever mess with major crimes. (I'll talk more about the IRS in the Money section.)

> *Fearful ignorance is willful poverty. You may not have a lot of money in the bank, but **knowledge is wealth you can give yourself.** Connect with good legal counsel. Ask every question you can think of. Have a clear sense of the laws that govern the work you do, have a plan in place, and your lawyer's contact information memorized in case you get arrested.*

❀ PRACTICAL ADVICE: SAFER SEX

For those of us engaged in FULL SERVICE or CONTACT SEX, we face special challenges. It goes without saying, lovely Sexy, you need to take care of that sweet hot bod of yours when doing this work. You're not allowed to take unnecessary chances, because you're going to live to be old and fabulous!

I'm not going to run down all the details of the potential health risks here. You're an adult and know how to read, so I'm assuming that you know how to prevent pregnancy, if applicable. Also, that you know how to protect yourself from the really damaging viruses: herpes, hepatitis B, hepatitis C, HPV, and HIV. If you have any gaps in this important knowledge, check out the resources in the appendix on page 283. *Do it now, do it today.*

If you still have questions, talk to your health care provider. As of this writing, insurance companies in the U.S. can't deny coverage due to preexisting conditions or health histories, so for now, you can be as honest about what you do for a living as you choose to be. We all need to be aware of changing laws around health care privacy, however. If you have any concerns, ask what your rights are first before you reveal work-related information.

All that is well and good, but knowing about safer sex isn't the same thing as doing it. It's not always easy in the moment to make the best choices—we're turned on, we're scared, we want our clients to come back, but it's our job to do the right thing for ourselves, just the same.

When I worked, my rule was simple: no activities that exposed me to HIV, not for any amount of money. As it happens, that significantly lowered the possibility of contracting most of the other major icky bugs out there except for cold sores, the common cold, and the flu.

Now. Did condoms break on me? They sure did. Did at least one client slip the condom off deliberately and come inside me doing it doggie style? That did happen. Did I handle pre-cum or ejaculate while working with ragged cuticles, chapped lips, and other open cuts in my skin? Yes indeedy. There were times when I was unlucky or careless—working in a dungeon, I was once stuck by a contaminated needle. And don't let me give you the impression I was Saint Lola. There were times I had unprotected sex with clients because I wanted to. Then I'd gnaw on my fingernails through STD testing, sitting with uncertainty, guilt, and fear. So far be it from me to judge anyone.

However, we can limit our anxiety by establishing rules and sticking to them. Even though I wasn't always perfect in the standards I set for myself, I believe safer sex is **always** the way to go. My reason is that anyone negotiating to have unsafe sex with you is damn well trying to have it with everyone else, and that's a huge red flag. I used to say to my clients when they were trying to honey-talk me into bareback blowjobs, "Doesn't it worry you if I do that, Sweetie? It should. You should be glad I won't—I take good care of myself." In case you're still facing temptation, let's talk through it now:

- ❀ *More money.* When a client is waving bills, it's easy to think, "This person looks clean. What're the odds?" What I say is there is no amount of money on earth worth your health. Contracting an incurable virus means you'll be living with the expensive, painful, possibly life-shortening consequences forever.
- ❀ *The competition says "Yes."* Maybe so, but your client didn't book an appointment with any of them today, now did they?
- ❀ *They won't come back.* Well, maybe not. But a client trying to bargain away your boundaries isn't someone you want

to deal with anyway. The ones that do come back will re-spect when you say "no."

✻ *They'll write a bad review.* If a client does write something nasty about you and your unbribable ways, then at the very least, future clients will expect to wear a condom.

Some clients pouted when I wouldn't budge, and I'm sure some didn't come back because I stood firm. Not one ever walked out on me, though. On the other hand, much of my married clientele de-manded it, and we all know what a large percentage of clients are married males. Less risk while reducing their guilt. Win-win.

PrEP AND HIV PREVENTION

I'm even more leery of dispensing medical advice than legal advice. However, you should know that here in the U.S. there is a new HIV prevention treatment called pre-exposure prophylaxis, PrEP for short, with promising trials among groups at high risk of contract-ing HIV, namely sexually active gay men. Now, I don't like the idea of any pill giving you the false impression that you no longer need to practice safer sex, because PrEP won't protect you from herpes, HPV, hepatitis C, and other STDs. There is simply no substitute for playing sexy safer and smart. I encourage you to find a healthcare provider you can speak frankly with to explore all available options.

> *Navigating boundaries in the heat of the moment while making decisions for the long term, these are challenges we all face as sexual beings. Plenty of sex workers make a living enforcing a strict safer sex/ condom policy, and you can too, as a commitment to your health, long life, and sanity.*

SHAME: AN INTRODUCTION

Hi, Sexy—

Fear is the most primal emotion in every animal, but as social creatures, does anything cut worse than shame? It's called the "swampland of the soul." The belief that as sex workers we are dirty or bad or wrong keeps us in hiding. It lowers our expectations. Worst of all is the twisted damage it does to our sense of selves. Living, on some level, in fear of retribution from god or the universe, believing we don't deserve anything good because we do bad things.

The impact can be insidious. A dominatrix friend once confided to me while waiting for the results from a biopsy on a lump in her breast, "I wonder if I got cancer from all those years of wearing corsets." That was shame talking: cancer does not give two shits about lacing up in tight leather. Another friend had several hundred thousand dollars tucked away in a safe deposit box and a realtor client who wanted to help buy her a house. But she was too afraid to meet the seller's agent: she was sure he'd know she was an escort just by looking at her. A stripper I worked with was all bad and bold on the pole, but she kept her job secret from her family and lovers. She drank to drown out the dissonance.

*I want to say to everyone living with this pain: Nobody deserves to be punished for doing sex work. No one on this earth, **not even you**. Living in shame is a horrible fate, punishment in and of itself. No need to wait for Judgment Day—you're already living it.*

*This suffering can run deep, I know. We can't just turn off our culture's negative messages like a light switch. But I also know that shame shrinks in sunlight and doesn't hold up well under questioning: **Just***

exactly what is wrong with paying for sexuality? Who is harmed by sex as a calling? Is enjoying sex work a crime? It's a whole lot harder to swallow society's garbage when we think things through for ourselves.

In this next section, I'll discuss how and why shame pops up in sex work. (Spoiler alert: a whole lot of it is our clients' crap.) I'll point out the links between shame and its stinky kid sister, stigma, as well as low self-esteem.

On the practical side, I've provided an exercise for those times when shame does creep in, letting it have its say before sending it on its way again. I'll give both pragmatic and heartfelt advice for stepping out into the light—on your own terms and in your own time—as well as what to do if you get outed against your will. And finally, I've made a plea to respect all sex workers, because shaming any one of us shames us all.

❋ SHAME, LOW SELF-ESTEEM, AND STIGMA

"Shame" is defined many ways, but I find Brené Brown's description of how it *feels* to be helpful: "The extremely painful belief or experience of being unlovable, unworthy of connection or belonging." In the case of sex workers, I'd add "unworthy of protection, dignity, or humanity" for good measure. It is a dreadful feeling, like a soul death. When I spiral down into the shame pit, I wish I'd never been born.

SHAME, STIGMA, AND LOW SELF-ESTEEM

"Shame" is an umbrella term, but more precise language is helpful. Shame, stigma, and low self-esteem are interrelated but distinct, and can get all snarled up and feed into each other. Let's break them down in order to get to know them better. "SHAME" is a deep-seated belief of being bad, dirty, or wrong. "LOW SELF-ESTEEM" is feeling incapable, incompetent, or not good enough. "STIGMA" is the anxiety or pressure to hide because of judgment from other people.

If sex work is making you feel bad about yourself, it helps to know why. I'll tackle shame and stigma first, and then talk about low self-esteem and its BFF envy in the next few chapters. You may not agree with all of my conclusions, but hopefully they'll get you started thinking about why you feel like you do.

THE CASE AGAINST SHAME

So, let's start with the obvious question: Is sex work shameful? My answer: *No*. There is nothing inherently shameful about sex work; there is nothing inherently disgraceful about sex workers. Sure, the industry has problems, and many, many folks in it struggle and suffer—no different than the rest of humanity. Now, it is true the adult industry is … unusual. Our days are spent in places most people only visit for a short time, in environments that are disorienting, playing by different rules than polite society. Most of us want privacy when we're turned on, and sexuality out in the open or on demand can be shocking.

What's your take? Do you think sex work is dirty or wrong? How is it different from "respectable" employment? Do you think that makes sex workers **unworthy of love**? Disqualified from care and celebration? That is a spectacularly cruel fate. For the life of me, I can't see why.

Let me break it down three ways. First: There is no shame in *being* a sexual person. Sex is what got us here; sex is how we are made. In order to survive, our species needs to dance and to shimmy and to hum and to flirt and to fuck. The sexy fuels health, beauty, music, joy, creativity, inspiration, and curiosity—who would want to live without those things? Every single person alive on this earth today is a product of the erotic. Even test-tube baby-daddies need dirty magazines.

Second: There is no shame in getting *paid* to be a sexual person. Making a living tapping into the divine is no crime. If it were, linguists would be criminals for profiting from a love of language, dancers for their love of movement. Benefiting materially from being deliciously human is what professional cooks, artists, singers, models, actors, and writers do. Sex workers are no different.

Third: There is no shame in sexual *availability*. Getting paid to do things we otherwise wouldn't is pretty much the definition of having a job—not much shame in that. Of course, there can be "yuck" factors in sex work, certain unpleasant bodily realities. Also true in dog walking and nursing and plumbing and lots of other worthwhile careers. Nothing to make us dirty or disposable. Here's what I know: some of the most loveable people on this planet are sex workers. Know what *you* believe.

FUCKING UP

You might well agree that sex work is honest work—that doesn't mean you can't still feel lousy on the job. That's because all of us, at times, cross a line and do something we shouldn't. We say "yes" when we should say "no." We forget to count the money. We get caught in a lie. Because the work is so personal, it's easy to sink into a shame spiral: *I messed up. I sold myself cheap. I let myself down.* This can trigger terrible doubt: *Am I bad? Am I stupid? Am I damaged goods?*

Again, the answer is *no*. Not once, not ever. Never forget: Sex work is hard! We operate under crazy pressures, juggling all kinds of extremes. It's not like there's a job manual—the right thing to do is rarely obvious. We try our best, sometimes we fail, but we learn from our mistakes. Most important, we are *fundamentally and indisputably loveable*. Don't believe me? Let me ask you this: If your best friend messed up like you did today, could you forgive them? I'm guessing yes. I'm betting no matter what, love is bigger than the crime. Let that be your guide.

Now, if you keep letting yourself down again and again on the job, that's not good. You deserve to be cherished and protected, inside and out. Find someone you trust, a **BUDDY** or therapist or sponsor, to talk to about how you can be kinder to yourself.

CLIENTS BRING THE CRAZY

Getting our heads right isn't enough to immunize us from on-the-job shame. That's because clients show up with all their baggage, expecting us to deal. They want to be turned on; they want to get off. They crave beauty, kink, variety, danger, and role-play. They're insecure about their bodies. They want to be irresistible. They feel weird about fantasies that threaten to veer out of control. They want us to read their thoughts, blow their minds, and deliver peak experiences. But sex isn't something you're supposed to pay for—shouldn't you get it for free by looking fine, smelling good, and all the rest? Clients internalize the message: *There is something wrong with me.* So, strip clubs are for losers, dungeons are for creeps, and seeing prostitutes is pathetic.

Not only that: as high as clients soar, that's how far they plummet, and can you get any higher than having sex just for yourself? Clients crash back to earth naked and exposed. The sex industry reeks of the same sticky regret as carnivals and casinos. All that dislocation and self-loathing has to go somewhere.

Like black holes in reverse, clients bend badness and blame away from themselves. I call it "**OUTSOURCING SHAME**." They demean and objectify us, leering and groping and calling us names. The humiliation of their non-normative desires can be especially excruciating, so they dole out particularly dehumanizing treatment to **BBW**, people of color, pro doms, and queers.

Clients also wrestle with guilt. Many clients are married or partnered or come from religious backgrounds, taking a little taste of something they don't want anyone to know about. Nobody wants to feel bad while paying to feel good, so they shunt their ick onto us, sluts for pay.

It is not nice to be on the receiving end of bad behavior, especially as a reward for doing our jobs so well. In the immediate aftermath of getting slimed by a client, you may well be furious; I cover anger in a later chapter. If you're feeling ashamed, deflated, or gross, I recommend the shame exercise in the next section. In the longer term, we can build up resistance to toxicity through self-acceptance, self-respect, and not tolerating bad behavior. We can model how shame-free sexual adventurers behave. We reward the clients who treat us well; those who spread grief, we let them walk right on by.

STIGMA

Unfortunately, no matter how well you handle yourself and the Biz, there's still the rest of the world to deal with. Like a slow-moving zombie, stigma feasts on our brains. We've all heard the phrase, "You can't please everyone; you can only please yourself." Well, that's all good and fine, but on some level, most of us care what other people think. Stigma keeps us from living out in the open for fear the straight world will judge us as: out of control. Lazy. Stupid. Uneducated. Flaky. Messy. Sex-crazed. Diseased. Addicted. Damaged. Worthless. The irony is as many people outside the sex industry fit those descriptions as in it! But, unfortunately, those negative stereotypes stick to us.

My advice is to spend some time pulling stigma and shame apart. As tightly as they're woven together, they're not the same. Ask yourself: *Is there anything wrong with sex work?* If your gut answer is "no," but you still feel insecure, you're most likely grappling with the fear of other people's disapproval. **Which is fine**. Those consequences can be very real—I'll talk about them at length in the upcoming section on coming out. You are allowed to protect yourself from other people's bigotry by being discreet; that has nothing to do with shame. Here's the thing—if we lived in a world that didn't judge what we do for a living, I think most of us would feel pretty fine about it. Because deep down, we already do.

❀ EXERCISE: SPENDING TIME WITH SHAME

As Brené Brown says in her TED talk, *Listening to Shame*, "You gotta dance with them that brung ya." As sex workers, the sexy is the fun half of our domain. Shame is the other half, and we can't act like it doesn't exist. When you find yourself feeling gross about your job, or something a client did, or yourself, here is your meditation.

Close your eyes, take a few deep breaths, and experience that feeling. Give its heaviness its due. Carrying shame is a burden; let yourself truly acknowledge it. Pay attention to where it lives in your body—is it your belly? Your scalp? Your shoulders? Your jaw? Your solar plexus? Your throat? Place your hand there and breathe into that tender place that's holding all that hurt.

Tell yourself out loud the story of what happened and how it felt. Explain your role and what other people said, saw, and did. Make sure to include specifically what you thought was going to happen and what your hopes for the situation were. Part of letting go of shame is mourning the gap between wishes and reality. Between how far we wanted to fly and how far we fell.

Say out loud: "Shame is present, but I am not shame." Or, if you prefer, "Pain is present, but I am not pain." ***Breathe into yourself, not the situation.*** Then put a time boundary on it. Tell shame it has two minutes to make its case, and then you're done. It has to be quiet while you get on with the rest of your day.

It's no fun to sit with disgrace. It stings and makes us restless. We want desperately to escape this horrible state. But stuffed down inside us, shame has a way of building up, pervading our thoughts, making us feel we aren't worthy of self-care. Or we deserve to be punished. Or the bad things other people think about us are true rather than trusting ourselves. When shame comes to visit, we need to sit with it for a few minutes, listening to its snaky lies, while reaffirming none of that belongs to us. On the contrary—we are splendid and lovable, inside and out, sharing our treasures with the world. There is nothing wrong with who we are or what we do.

> *Shame is the lie someone told you about yourself.*
> —ANAÏS NIN

❋ AN OPEN LETTER TO MY FELLOW SEX WORKERS: SHAME, FEAR, AND THE EROTICS OF DISCRETION

Visibility, vulnerability, and shame are so snarled up together in sex work, I want to say a few words before we dive into coming out and being outed. Let's start by acknowledging that some of us are called to do sex work, and some of us are called to do it out loud.

I have so much love and admiration for those Brazen Hussies who live with their lives wide open, willing to say to the world, *Whatever you think of me, I'm not hiding to make you comfortable.* In the same way coming out puts names and faces to the LGBTQ community, sex workers who publically share their personal stories humanize an industry warped by both fantasy and demonization.

My friend, Carol Queen, paragon of Brazen Hussydom, wrote in her essay, "Dear Mom: A Letter about Whoring," about her need to explain to her late mother why she went into prostitution. She connects the lessons she learned from her parents' sexless, shame-filled marriage to her unwillingness to live in the shadows. She links her life-long journey of erotic exploration directly to the unhappiness she witnessed between her frigid mother and frustrated father. The depths of their silences committed her to living openly, refusing to hide her adventures from her lovers, her readers, even from her mother's memory.

For sex work to lose its stigma, the general public needs to understand that sex work can be chosen freely. For that to happen, sex workers need to be out and proud. The bravery of Brazen Hussies makes the Biz safer for all of us. And yet, at the same time, I don't believe all of us were born to march in the streets.

In this next section on coming out, I'm going to make the case that not wanting to live out loud isn't necessarily about shame. It doesn't even have to be about self-protection, although certainly that's a motivating factor for many. For some, a secret life serves as an enormous engine of creativity, excitement, power, and self-understanding. Many of us identify as member of a midnight band of underground sex radicals, straddling both the straight world and the demimonde. (True for many clients, too, I'm guessing.) I guard that source of arousal and inspiration jealously as one who has made the erotic my calling.

Now. I'm well aware that what I'm saying has political ramifications. I fully understand the resentment of those who are out doing the grinding, thankless work of changing minds about sex work, bearing the brunt of public opinion, while those who remain closeted reap the benefits of their activism. I get that. I hope all of us can come out into the light someday soon. It would turn more than a few heads and change many minds, for sure.

But let's set politics and personal erotics aside for now. There is another implication of living out loud that can feel daunting. Once people know you're a sex worker, there can be pressure to be a sexpert, someone who knows all, has seen it all, and has their shit 100% together. It can feel that only by appearing to be perfect can we combat negative stereotypes. So it may feel unsafe to admit that we're struggling with the job, for the fear it makes us look like losers. If we have a bad call, or fall in love with a client, or feel overwhelmed, didn't we bring it on ourselves? Vulnerability can result in a reflexive need for privacy, not wanting to put up a hard, sassy shield many of us don't authentically feel and that can be exhausting to perform. Carol also wrote *Exhibitionism for the Shy: Show Off, Dress Up, and Talk Hot!* The title acknowledges not all of us are born to be brazen. Some of us learn over time—we can't just flip a switch and put on a show.

A recurring theme throughout this book is to be as brave as you can be, maybe even a little bit braver—you grow into yourself as you do. But don't give into the pressure to be any bolder than feels right.

Discretion is a perfectly valid reason to keep secrets, even if you aren't clear exactly why. ***It does not mean you are ashamed.***

In conversations on coming out as sex workers, just as we need to feel safe to be visible, we need to feel safe to be vulnerable. There has to be room to acknowledge our demons, our doubts, our damage. Most of us muddle through sex work making all kinds of mistakes along the way. It should be okay to say so.

The opposite of shame is not shamelessness. It is accepting ourselves just as we are, knowing we don't need to be perfect in order to be good enough. Coming out of the darkness into the light should feel like stepping into our authenticity, tender hearts and all. Not trading a shroud of invisibility for a shield of invincibility.

❈ COMING OUT AND BEING OUTED

There's little cultural support for sex workers to help us debunk the myths about our lives—our friends and families almost can't help but swallow them.

—CAROL QUEEN FROM "DEAR MOM: A LETTER ABOUT WHORING"

N was lovely and lean with a hot yoga body. Intelligent and classy, she had everything going for her as an escort, and she made excellent money. There was just one problem: she lived in constant fear that one day she would pick up her work phone and hear her father's voice on the line. Everyone knew this kept her up at night because she talked about it constantly—not just with other escorts, she'd even discuss it with her clients. But none of us could figure out why. Her parents lived in Southern California; she worked north of San Francisco in Marin County—how in the world would they ever find out? Over time, her anxieties took control. She grew paranoid, reluctant to take on new clients, update her ads, or even answer her phone. She limped out of the Biz, never fully facing her fears. The "Worst Thing In The World" took over her mind, and eventually, her livelihood.

N's fears were extreme. But I'm guessing if you took a poll, right after serial killers, the greatest fear in the Biz is getting found out. Being exposed. Losing status and respect. At the root of it is the deepest fear of all, losing love. You can't blame people outside the Biz for having negative impressions about sex work when the only information the straight world gets is sensationalism from Hollywood and crime statistics from the news. So, many of us keep secrets to keep love in our lives. Our LGBTQ friends can tell us how living in the closet can breed shame, self-loathing, mistrust, isolation, and low expectations.

All of that may be true, but I am here to say there is no need to punish yourself if you don't tell the whole world what you do. It doesn't mean you're hunkered down like a troll living under a shame bridge. If your gut tells you someone isn't safe to tell, honor that. Don't come out just to make a point about what a free spirit you are—no one grades us for transparency in this lifetime. However, I'm going to turn right back around and make a plea for being as open as you can with the people who do feel safe. Fortune favors the brave in love and sex work alike. Letting people get to know all of you is a gift. Value your safety and privacy first, but be open to disclosure.

> *When we act without thinking, good things in our lives seem like nothing more than luck, and bad things feel like punishment. When we make conscious decisions, good results are fully earned rewards, and when challenges come our way, they feel bounded and tolerable.*

❈ HEARTFELT ADVICE: HOW TO COME OUT

Do I prefer to grow up and relate to life directly, or do I choose to live and die in fear?

—PEMA CHÖDRÖN

Open-minded people in your life are easy—you've probably come out to them already. The less likely someone is to embrace sex work as a positive choice, the scarier coming out gets. Here is my suggestion: Have a plan—don't do it impulsively. Think about what your response will be if they have trouble hearing the news. I've adapted excellent advice on coming out from the Colorado State LGBTQQA website (glbtrc.colostate.edu/coming-out-to-your-parents).

- ❈ *Do you know why you're telling this person?* Be clear on why you're coming out. I'd go further and ask yourself, "Once this person knows I'm a sex worker, will our relationship be closer and stronger?" If you don't have an answer, maybe you don't need to tell them in the first place.
- ❈ *Have you picked your time wisely?* Come out with a sober head for clear reasons, not off the cuff. Spouting off about your exploits in the Biz after you've had a few drinks to get a laugh or shock the room is not a good idea. Nobody ever woke up the next morning with a hangover and said, "I wished I'd said *more* last night."
- ❈ *Can you talk about your job comfortably?* When coming out, don't undermine your authority by making jokes or trivializing what you do. If you can't talk about your work

life in a straightforward manner, how can your loved ones trust that you're taking yourself seriously? Nothing is more impactful than speaking from your power. If you're doing work you believe in, that will come through.

- ❀ *Do you have support?* Have a trusted friend on call to talk it over with afterwards.

- ❀ *Are there any possible negative ramifications* like getting thrown out of where you live? Have a back-up plan, just in case things don't go well, or you need a cooling-off period.

- ❀ *Do you trust this person not to tell anyone if you ask them not to?* Just as importantly, if they do tell, can anyone in their social circle harm you? Remember: You are under no obligation to come out to anyone. Your sex work life is your private business. Literally.

If you're scared, let them know. Vulnerability has a powerful effect on people who love us. Say to them, "I've wanted to tell you this for a while now, but I've been afraid you'll be mad. That you'll throw me out of your life, and never talk to me again! But I wanted to be honest and let you know what's going on with me."

It's possible that your loved ones may not take it all in at once. If that's the case, you'll have to be patient. After all, you've been a sex worker for a while now; the news may be sudden for them. Be prepared for them to cycle through a range of reactions:

- ❀ *Shock.* Maybe they had no idea. Maybe you're the first sex worker they've ever met, and their brains are wrestling with how to react. If they've suspected but said nothing, they've been pushing the possibility away in their minds. Now they have to face reality head on.

- ❀ *Denial.* For some people, rather than face uncomfortable truths, it's easier to act like nothing was said. It can be jarring to reveal something important about yourself and have a person glaze over or change the subject. Try to remain compassionate and know that this reaction means your news was difficult for them to hear, and they're unable to take it all in at once.

❀ *Grief.* It's quite possible that sex work isn't what your loved one had in mind for you. Initially, this may land as terrible news. Allow them to feel sadness for the death of whatever dream they might have had for you, no matter how irrational it may seem. Understand that in their minds, sex work could make life harder for you in the future.

❀ *Anger.* This is probably the scariest scenario—someone flying off the handle. Needless to say, if you're afraid this person might become violent, think twice and then think again about why you're telling them. If you're in a situation where you must come out, don't do it alone. Have a witness by your side. Be prepared to set limits on emotionally abusive language. You have the right to assert yourself and to be treated with respect even when someone is disappointed in you. If they get nasty, you can walk away. Know that anger is *always* a front for other emotions. If you can, look past that angry shield, and address what's behind it—fear, love, envy, grief.

❀ *Self-Blame.* Family, especially, may see your choices as a reflection on something they did—somewhere along the way you were damaged, or they made a mistake. It's important for you to state firmly, and repeat as often as necessary, that this was in no way their fault.

If these negative emotions come up, here's some advice on how to handle them:

❀ *Encourage them to express their emotions and ask questions.* Christian Nestell Bovee writes, "We fear things in proportion to our ignorance of them." Now that your news is on the table, the only way out is through. Most likely the only impressions they have of sex work are negative—of course, they're going to be afraid for you! Painting a realistic picture of your job will help them digest your news.

❀ *Be prepared for them to want to save or change you.* One of the hardest things to do is not get defensive when our lives are under attack. It's easy to feel judged or infantilized. If you can, recognize that your loved one sees you as a part of themselves, and their desire to rescue you is an attempt to be helpful. Hear them out, and then say, "I hear your concerns. Please know I've given this a lot of thought, and I take really good care of myself."

❀ *Take a breather.* You may need some time apart to let your news soak in. Don't presume that if your loved one has a hard time initially it means your relationship is over forever. Trust that most people are as terrified of losing love as you are. Remain open to the possibility that although they're wrestling with this new idea, they have a deep desire to get back to a loving place where you are still very much in their lives.

AND NOW FOR ... THE POSSIBILITY OF JUICY GOODNESS

That's all the scary stuff—now let's make some room in our imaginations for amazing things to happen.

Coming out to an old college roommate, I was so scared because I'd known her my entire adult life. If she rejected me, I wouldn't just lose her sunny, silly friendship; I was risking our entire shared history. I told her I had been working in the sex industry for several years, currently as an escort. She sat silent for a second, and then blurted out, "If you're about to be homeless, you can come live with me." What a tender, revealing response! Her worry wasn't that I was having sex with strangers, but that I needed money. Once we talked, her fears lifted. I became her go-to sexologist, someone she could share her questions and fantasies with. Revealing myself to her opened the door to a deeper connection.

If you do decide to come out, allow for these possibilities: that your loved one's desire to have you in their lives gives them the capacity to accept something that they initially react to with fear or disbelief. That people can surprise you by how much they trust your judgment. That when you take the time to answer questions, your loved one's fears become realistic and manageable. That you can give the gift of a more realistic, humanizing picture of sex work, the people who do it, and the people who pay for it. That by revealing your authentic self, you invite deeper connection into your life. And last but not least: ***that the people that love us are proud of us for being who we are.***

❋ HEARTFELT ADVICE: IF YOU'VE BEEN OUTED

Coming out can be hard, but at least there's some measure of control. When exposed against our will, it can feel terrible. Over the years, I've been outed in various ways, and I'll share one experience: B was an old college lover I kept in touch with, even though I'd made a conscious decision not to tell him about my working life. As my ex, there were plenty of things I didn't share with him, and it felt fine to have him in my life on those terms.

Our mutual friend, L, got tipsy at a dinner hosted by B's brother. (Neither B nor I were there.) L had just gotten into the Biz herself recently, and she was flying high on the newbie's rush. She announced to the room, "I started doing erotic massage, and I really love it. You know who else is doing it too? Lola!" I never found out who said what after that, but B never spoke to me again. I don't know which betrayal felt worse—learning I was a dinner party scandal, or that B thought so little of our friendship. I felt sideswiped, powerless, and humiliated.

Turns out, I was not alone in that reaction. Interviewing more than a dozen sex workers about getting outed, they reported feelings of betrayal, loss of control, and helplessness. Shame from becoming an object of ridicule or pity. Humiliation as the butt of jokes. Fear of violence or harassment. Fear of loss of status. Fear of loss of privacy. Fear of being marked as dirty or different or less-than. Anger knowing someone else was defining them. Exposure as the subject of gossip. Fear that life will never be the same, or that the future is ruined.

These are potent, poisonous emotions. Fears scatter like dropped marbles when we feel violated. But before we react, we need to stop. We can inflict further damage on ourselves when we act without thinking. As bad as it feels, being outed means the universe has given us a homework assignment only we can do: dealing with our shit. Our job is to sit with how this makes us feel, and just as importantly, understand *why* it makes us feel that way. Only then can we operate from a position of power.

- ❀ *Set aside as much time as you need to absorb this new information.* This can be excruciating—just sitting with all the feels, letting the initial storm of emotions pass before making any decisions. As unpleasant as this can be, the silver lining is you get the opportunity to know yourself better.

- ❀ *Notice how your body feels and where your mind goes.* Do you feel numb? Is that a familiar feeling? Is your mind racing ten thousand miles an hour? Is that an old pattern? Are you desperate to act? To check out? To run away? To beat yourself up? Who do you become when something like this happens?

- ❀ *Do not blame yourself.* It's so easy to slip into self-hating scripts: *If I'd only been more careful. If only I hadn't been so stupid. If only I hadn't trusted so-and-so.* Well, maybe so, but what's done is done. If there's a lesson to be learned, make a note and move on. Don't punish yourself for other people's bad behavior.

- ❀ *What old stories does this scenario feed into?* Many of us have negative stories about ourselves from childhood: *Everyone abandons me. I'm unlovable. People are out to get me. I'm different than everyone else. No one defends me. Nothing good ever works out. Everything I touch turns to shit. Everyone's talking about me, and I can't stop it. If I died today, no one would care.* Do any of these sound familiar? These are sad, old storylines we learned as children, baked into us when we were small and defenseless, capable of feeling everything but understanding very little. We tell ourselves that's who we are, now and forever. While those feelings are entirely real, we're adults now. Those are the stories of a child.

❀ *What would RuPaul do?* Is there someone in the world, some Brazen Hussy, who if standing in your shoes might just say: "That's right, people—I'm hot enough to get paid, and y'all are jealous." It doesn't matter if it's someone you know personally or a character in a comic book or your imaginary friend. Your state of mind, while authentically yours, isn't the only reaction in the world. Try being curious about other ways of seeing your situation.

OUTING AND SHAME

I never felt shame doing sex work; I always believed it was an honest living. So in those times when I was nonconsensually outed, it'd come as an enormous shock when a rush of shame washed over me. Getting outed can push that button big time.

Don't beat yourself up—we feel what we feel. Take the time, as uncomfortable as it is, to ask why you feel ashamed. Do you believe that there's something wrong with what you're doing? If so, *what exactly is that?* Are you judging yourself by society's standards? Or does something about your job go against the grain of how you'd like to see yourself? If you think other people assume sex workers are [fill-in-the-negative-stereotype], do you accept that about yourself as well? Be clear on what you believe.

EMOTIONAL MATH: GRIEF + FEAR = PANIC

Some of the wisest words I ever heard were from my friend, life coach Fresh White. I'd received some out-of-the-blue bad financial news—a retirement plan I thought was going to take care of me when I was old might not be there anymore. I was deeply shaken, rattled to the core. After a week of sleepless nights and helpless tears, I called him. He listened, and then said, "I hear how terrifying this feels for you, but the fact is, you're harnessing your fear to your grief. You don't need to do anything today other than sit with the death of this plan. You wanted that safety so badly. Really let yourself say goodbye."

Instantly, I felt my body soften—he was so right. I crave security in my old age, and I was devastated thinking it was gone. As soon as I understood panicking was standing in the way of feeling that sadness, I felt the fear lift. Although I had no idea how I was going to do it, I knew I had time to fix my situation. All I needed to do in that moment was grieve.

When somebody outs us, a dream of ourselves dies: We are safe in our secrets. We can control what other people think about us and how they treat us. Bad things will never happen. These powerful wishes have no bearing on real life, but we hold onto them so tightly because we want so desperately for them to be true. Give yourself time to mourn what is lost. Once you've taken the time to really sit with what you feel, breathing through it, it's time to act.

❋ PRACTICAL ADVICE: WHAT TO DO IF YOU'VE BEEN OUTED

So, you've been outed. Now what? This can't be a comprehensive PR crisis management manual because everyone's situation is different, but I can offer some broad guidelines. First things first—if you're in immediate danger, you must get to safety *now*. Once you're in a safe place:

- ❀ *Get a reality check.* Relatives, found family, coworkers, and therapists help you see things from a different perspective. Talking with an ally is invaluable. Don't isolate when you feel terrified and violated—get the support you deserve.

- ❀ *Don't overreact.* That feeds into the idea you have something to be ashamed of.

- ❀ *Do not act impulsively.* Act calmly and strategically, once you've had time to think everything through.

- ❀ *Often the best course of action is not to act at all.* However, if you do choose this course, choose it actively. Don't fall into the trap of hoping if you ignore the problem it will just go away.

- ❀ *Pick your battles carefully.* If you don't care about the "outer" or the "outee," and they can't do you any harm, there's no need to get caught up in their opinion of you. The closer you are to either the outer or the one who has just learned the news, the more proactive, honest, and open you need to be.

- ❀ *Do not lash out.* As tempting as it may be, you run the risk of escalating the situation. You force people to choose sides, which isn't good either. Even if it's excruciating, you're better off in the long run taking the high road.

⚜ *Sometimes you can nip a situation in the bud.* You can state plainly that what you do for a living is nobody else's business. Say you overhear your gossipy neighbor down the hall blabbing about you. Pull them aside and say, "I want you to know I'm committed to keeping this building a safe environment for everyone who lives here. Respecting one another's privacy is what good neighbors do."

Being outed may feel like an unmitigated catastrophe, but life is rarely black-and-white. There may be more than one way to see your situation. For instance, gossip can be a social glue and isn't always harmful. Human beings connect by talking about each other. I know it can feel like a violation, but often the intent is benign—it's just conversation. Also, a big reason why people talk about sex workers is because they're titillated or curious. A common reaction when meeting a sex worker is excitement, like spotting a celebrity. So many times when I've come out, folks are initially nervous, but soon enough they calm down and act like it's no big deal. Sex workers are becoming more commonplace, mainstream, and accepted all the time. You might even make a new sex worker friend or ally along the way.

Then there's the possibility that people who don't know you well may not care what you do. That they aren't inclined to put much stake in gossip in the first place, or think much about it if they do believe it. Most people react with momentary curiosity to scandal, and then move on to more important things in their lives.

Finally, consider the fact that people who feel good in their own lives don't talk trash. While it might not mend matters with your landlord, the neighbor down the hall who busted you is probably living in a very scary world inside their head to see you as a threat. If and when you can, hold some compassion for their need to feel safe.

Visibility/invisibility, safety/exposure, being understood/misunderstood, secrecy/honesty, acceptance/rejection—these are at the core of what it means to be human. As sex workers, who-knows-what about us directly impacts our well-being. It's our job to take responsibility for our own lives while realizing we are mostly powerless over what other people say, think, and do. We must balance our fears against external realities. When we truly accept ourselves for who we are, we can accept the consequences of our choices with equanimity.

❋ AN OPEN LETTER TO MY FELLOW SEX WORKERS: RESPECT THE WORK

While we're on the subject of shame and stigma, I have a favor to ask: Please be respectful of one another and our differences. Now, I'm not saying you have to love everyone who works in the Biz. Of course, I'm not condoning bad behavior, and it's okay not to like individual people.

What I *am* asking for is to stop the trash talking, and there's a lot of it. "At least I'm not like those dirty/slutty/fucked-up [fill-in-the-blanks.]" "I can't stand those kinky freaks." "Don't ever be one of those whores who suck/kiss/swallow."

It doesn't have to be overt, just insisting on a nicer job title: "I'm a lingerie model, not a masseuse." "Oh, I'm a top—I never sub." "I entertain at bachelor parties—that's not stripping." "So I've got a Sugar Daddy—that doesn't make me a hooker." "I've got a driver and a scheduler and make eight hundred an hour—I'm not some crack-headed ho working a corner." To which I say, *enough*.

If you believe certain kinds of sex work are wrong, why do you think that? Who deserves to be harassed? Who deserves to be left behind? Sex work, all of it, comes from the same place. How close you get to strangers or how many people see you naked or how much you charge, these are distinctions without a difference.

I say this sweetly, but I do mean it: You are no better and no worse than the other trans* folk and women and men who do the work. You're no better or worse than those who do drugs or those who don't. It doesn't matter if you hate the job or love every minute of it. Whether or not you use condoms. Whether you work indoors or outside. Whether you make bank or are just getting by. Whether you work for yourself or someone else. You are no better or worse than those who love their clients or those who hate everyone. It makes no difference if you only have sex with members of your own gender or some other gender, or you only have sex with yourself, or you never have any sex at all.

When we are proud of what we do, there's no need to tear others down—that is offloading shame. We are all in this together, Sexys, and everyone deserves respect.

> His Holiness the Dalai Lama teaches, "Our prime purpose in this life is to help others. And if you can't help them, at least don't hurt them." Her Holiness the Lady Gaga teaches: "Don't ever fucking bully anyone, and just so you know, karma has everyone's address and a motherfucking stamp."

LOW SELF-ESTEEM: AN INTRODUCTION

Hi, Sexy—

I see you there. Can we get real? I want to talk about feeling bad, and by that I mean, baaaaaad. Crushing insecurities. Feeling ugly. Old. Not sexy. Not deserving. For many of us, low self-esteem is a constant background hum. If some days it's quiet, other days it can buzz so loud we can't think. And it feels so shameful, it can be impossible to talk about with anyone. If you struggle with insecurities, you aren't alone; most of us live in private pain. The sex industry is performance, and many of us make art out of those wounds.

Self-loathing can cause all kinds of irrational and destructive behavior. There were days I'd be so devastated about my appearance, I'd stand in front of the mirror between calls sobbing. Then I'd wash my face, put on my makeup, and greet the next client coming in through the door. No matter how many clients told me with words and money I was desirable, I just couldn't believe it. Like a paper jam, my brain wouldn't let that in.

It wasn't just me, of course. I watched my friends go on crash diets to lose weight. One escort I did doubles with used a breast enlargement pump on her magnificent tiny titties before every session. (If the pump made them any bigger, you'd have to squint to see it. To me, they were just as tantalizing before as after.) Then there was this one pro dom I never met, but she had the strangest ads—I'd stalk her website in fascination. She'd post clumsily photoshopped pictures showing her with a freakish wasp waist, which she clearly did not have. I could never figure out whom she might possibly attract with that marketing scheme, but she kept at it for years. The one thing you could be sure of, though—she didn't trust anyone would come see her if they knew how she really looked.

We see other people's fragility, and think, "That's so silly." But when it comes to our own vulnerabilities, it can feel as though our flaws are all anyone can see.

I have something important to say, and please take it to heart: low self-esteem has no redeeming value. Hating yourself doesn't make you better at your job, or help you lose weight, or clear up your skin. It's absolutely 100% wasted energy.

I know that logic is all well and good, but to feel something, we have to believe it. Sometimes what we need to know is that we are loved. So, listen up, Sweet Sexy. I don't know what you look like, I have no idea what you think you should look like. All I can tell you is, your friends, lovers, clients, they aren't blind. When you look in the mirror and hate what you see? You're missing the beauty you bring to this world. Promise me you'll find ways to let these dreadful feelings go. You only get one life on this beautiful earth. Spending it needlessly hating yourself gains you nothing.

In this next section, I'll discuss low self-esteem. I'll spend extra time on aging, since losing sexual value as we age is one of our culture's most punishing prophecies. I'll talk about how to determine if plastic surgery is the right choice, if you're considering making a permanent change. But mostly I'll offer heartfelt advice for grappling with feeling not good enough. You deserve to know you are stunning and treasured. Because that's exactly what you are.

❀ FEELING UGLY AND UNWORTHY

It's all about how you have to look a certain way or else you're worthless. You know when you look in the mirror and you think, "Oh, I'm so fat, I'm so old, I'm so ugly." Don't you know that's not your authentic self? That is billions upon billions of dollars of advertising, magazines, movies, billboards, all geared to make you feel shitty about yourself so that you will take your hard-earned money and spend it at the mall on some turn-around cream that doesn't turn around shit … For us to have self-esteem is truly an act of revolution, and our revolution is long overdue.

—MARGARET CHO

If I had a dime for every minute I felt ugly in this lifetime, I'd never have to work at all. I used to spend entire sessions waiting for my client to realize how hideous I was and leave. Even repeat clients who knew damned well how I looked dressed, naked, and from every angle. Hating how I looked was like a sickness, an addiction. It wasn't just me—so many of my friends struggled, hating their thick thighs, thin hair, wrinkled skin. No matter how successful they were, the mirror was always the enemy.

My heart bleeds for my younger self and my friends, all that pain, sorrow, and fear: *I'm not good enough.* Low self-esteem creeps into our lives in so many ways, causing us to reject compliments. Be crushed by criticism or unkind remarks. Undercharge. Lower our boundaries. Lower our expectations. Feel like we don't deserve good things, or like we don't belong (what's known as "IMPOSTER SYNDROME").

We're all constantly bombarded with impossible images of how we ought to look, because that's what sells teeth whitener and hair straightener and wrinkle creams and big plastic boobs. But as sex workers, it cuts deeper: our looks are our livelihoods. We're constantly being judged and rejected. Clients insult us to our faces. It's so easy to believe we'd be so much better off if only we looked different.

I want to talk about what it's like to perform sexually when insecure, because so many of us carry these terrible feelings in silence, too ashamed to share them with anyone. I know this sounds basic, but let's start at the beginning. If you worry that you aren't hot enough for this line of work, take this simple test: Has someone paid you to turn them on in the last six months? Then you are officially hot enough to get paid. You can stop worrying about whether you belong in the Biz. I understand it may not feel that simple, but actually, it is.

The fundamental rule of sex work is this: All you need to be is attractive **enough**. You only have to pass what is a remarkably humane bar of general attractiveness. You're more than halfway there when you're clean and well groomed, appropriately dressed, professional in bearing, comfortable in your own skin, and energetic. There is no body type, no age limit, no ability to pass that makes you unfit. Folks look every conceivable way doing this work.

What matters more is whether you're a good conversationalist, listener, dancer, lover; it also helps to be a former Scout with merit badges in knot tying. Now, it is true that the more conventionally attractive you are, the bigger the holes can be in your skill set to still get by. But that skill set counts for an awful lot, and it's far more important for long-term success than physical appearance. Spend any amount of time in the Biz, and you'll notice people trading in on their looks don't think they have to do much else except show up. They may score lots of first-time work, but it's rare that they build a career. Strippers and porn actors who don't play nice get replaced by those who do. The review boards are filled with HOBBYISTS warning about hotties with bad attitudes.

Beyond that, I've known many clients who actively seek out less conventionally attractive sex workers. Why? They feel shy. They think sex industry beauty standards are artificial or harsh, or find average-looking sex workers easier to talk to. For them, genuine connection is more important.

In addition to that, attractiveness is a wide-open construct, with few set rules. Magdalene Meretrix in her book, *Turning Pro: A Guide to Sex Work for the Ambitious and the Intrigued,* cites a study that found 20% of men surveyed preferred women with large breasts; twenty percent preferred women with small breasts. The other 60% were just grateful women have breasts at all. Those figures can be extrapolated to skin color, height, weight, age, level of fitness, how much you look like Barbie, or Ken, or any other impossible standard you want to hold yourself up to.

What it boils down to is this: there will always be a client pool that thinks what you've got is smoking hot. You'll leave some clients cold. The rest are just glad you are looking them in the eye and smiling. Really letting this soak in, focusing on the clients that find us attractive and letting go of the ones that don't, is tremendously freeing. Know that someone out there right now would weep at the prospect of the warmth of your body, the sound of your voice, the kindness of your touch. Not just one person—thousands. Don't waste time wishing you're something you're not. You have so much to offer just as you are. One of the very best things about this job is getting to feel hot-handsome-sexy-gorgeous on a regular basis. Go ahead and taste that sweetness—it belongs to you. There's no extra credit in this lifetime for starving ourselves of self-love.

> *Your skin is your skin. Your legs are your legs. Your hair is your hair. Your smile is your smile. Your past is your past. You can waste your life hating these things, but you may as well learn to accept them. Both routes are difficult and full of pain, but with acceptance, you will be happy one day, while with hatred, you never will.*
>
> —VIRONIKA TUGALEVA

❋ AGING

Nothing, and I do mean nothing, carries the fear that aging does, especially for those of us who rely on our looks to make a living. Over and over, the message is pounded into us that once you reach a certain age, it's over. Women feel it keenly; it's brutal in the gay male community as well. On the HBO show, *Looking*, Dom says glumly, "At forty, Grindr sends you a death certificate." All the while, our clientele get to go on buying youth and beauty for themselves, no matter how decrepit they get—it's so unfair! Age is terrifying because it seems to steal everything we hold dear. Because we've never been anything but young before.

Yes! I know all that, and I'm going to go ahead and say this anyway: As long as you work for yourself, you don't have to age out of sex work. Now, not so true if you work for somebody else. But if you're willing to do your own advertising, production, screening, and marketing, you can work until you say you are done. I've never met a single sex worker who aged out—there is no LAST FUCKABLE DAY in the Biz. By this I mean I've never known anyone who celebrated some black-magic birthday and suddenly their phones stopped ringing. The sex workers I've known who were forced into retirement either burned out or didn't make the right changes. Neither of those fates is inevitable, and neither has anything to do with how many candles are on the cake.

I'm not saying that age doesn't matter, it's just not the only thing that matters. I had colleagues who became physically unable to do the work, yet their former clients were still calling years later, hoping to coax them back into the game. If you don't believe me, check out the documentary, *My Granny The Escort*. The oldest woman interviewed started at age 83, has been working full time for four years, and charges £250 a session. "I'm quite sexy," she says. Apparently, her clients agree with their hard-earned quid. *Meet the Fokkens* is a documentary featuring twin sisters who worked in the Amsterdam Red Light District for more than fifty years. Growing old in this business is possible.

It's worth taking some time to look at this fear of aging, and what it's made of. The magical, unexamined belief that one day we're going to wake up, look in the mirror, and poof! Everything we had going for us is gone. Now, it's true if you're named Rip Van Winkle, and you wake up one day to find you've fast-forwarded twenty years, that would be a shock. But Rip doesn't fall asleep and age two decades overnight—*he falls asleep for twenty years*. His story is a parable about not being awake, alive, and responsive to change.

What's actually going to happen to you here in this real life is you're going to wake up each day exactly one day older than the day before. There's no sense agonizing over this natural state of affairs. Life happens so gently, so slowly. If you have what it takes to entice paying clients today, chances are excellent you will tomorrow. Always remember: your clientele is aging right along with you. Also, no matter how old you are, you'll always be younger than many, many clients in the prime of their spending power who are moving more slowly themselves. As my dear friend so succinctly puts it, "Boomers need whores!"

As we age, we crave quieter comforts: connection, conversation, romance, shared experiences—these are qualities that we can grow into. As a trade-off for the rosy glow of youth, we can develop skill, patience, wisdom, and the ability to more deeply connect. As we lose our exuberance, we can cultivate curiosity. We can always be learning, deepening our resiliency, and refining a more generous sense of humor. Even as we wrinkle and sag, we can learn to love ourselves better.

So, yes, there are comforts that come with growing older. But behind the fear of aging lurks the "Worst Thing In The World," some true disaster, forcing us to retire involuntarily. This is why you always need to have a Plan B. Waiting around for something better to drop in your lap is not a plan.

They say time is a thief, which is true enough. Time robs us of things we did nothing to earn—everyone gets to be young once; to grow old is a privilege. Take some time to face that fear of the future and what it will be like to make your way in the world in an older body. When you lose something precious due to aging, stop and take the time to grieve, to fully feel the sadness of what is irredeemably lost.

All that said, don't let society's idiocy shrink your future. If you want to keep working, plan for it—start today. Have a vision of what you want your clientele to look like five, ten, fifteen years from now. If you're able to monetize your brand in ways other than providing direct services, by generating video content, writing erotic blogs, etc., then start building your empire. If you see older sex workers with careers you admire, reach out to them to see if they'll mentor you. If there are lateral moves in your profession, educate yourself and build up work experience.

Know that you're going to have to keep up your end of the bargain. The things that once came effortlessly—staying in shape, summoning extra reserves of energy, moving without pain—these things get harder, but they are by no means impossible. Trust that the comfort of your body, the allure of your personality, the wisdom of your experience is something that remains valuable even as you lose the easy appeal of youth.

Let's go over some frequently unasked anxieties about sex work and aging and talk this all the way through.

- ❀ *Is the upkeep harder?* Without question. You'll have to evolve—this is not necessarily a bad thing.
- ❀ *Will my clientele shrink?* Not if you put the effort into maintaining, growing, and improving it. Focus on quality over quantity.

⚜ *Will I have to lower my rates?* Some do as they age. However, I've known sex workers who increased their rates as the years went by, culling and grooming their clientele to see only the regulars they wanted, clients who *adore* them. I know sex workers in their forties, fifties, and sixties charging top dollar—they just keep getting better and better.

⚜ *Does the work get harder?* Consciously cultivating a clientele looking for connection and companionship rather than swinging from the chandeliers will minimize the strain on your body.

We're living in a time when the collective erotic imagination is exploding for older people. I see people looking good not because they appear younger than their age—they simply look terrific *for* their age. So many women, gay daddies, and queers are creating breathtaking, groundbreaking imaginings for older sexuality. It's a future worth cultivating—reward those who do it well. We have to be the ones we've been waiting for.

> *Whatever age you fear, may you live to see it. When you reach that point that felt so terrifying before, may you be just as glad to be alive as you are today, learning more about your oldest, most wonderful friend: your body.*

❈ PLASTIC SURGERY

I don't know a single sex worker who hasn't at least thought about getting work done. (By this, I mean anti-aging, weight-loss, and cosmetic procedures; of course, for our trans* brethren, gender-affirming surgery carries a whole other meaning.) Plastic surgery isn't the big deal it used to be; it used to be shameful. Today people schedule nose jobs and butt lifts with all the angst of booking a spa day. There's such pressure to be young, curvy, flawless. It's easy to believe that if we improve our appearance we'll attract better clients and make more money.

If you're considering surgery, you've probably heard this before: Check your surgeon's record for qualifications, credentials, and complaints. Before-and-after computer simulations can give you some sense of how much a procedure can affect your appearance. Know that clients might like the look of plastic boobs, but many aren't crazy about the feel. As in most things in life, you get what you pay for, so don't skimp.

Those are the practical considerations; here's my advice from the heart: If you're contemplating surgery, you need to be realistic in your expectations. Beware of the fantasy that a procedure will A) magically transform you into the way you want to look without B) anyone suspecting anything. The reality is that if people can notice a change, most likely they can tell you've had work. And in 90% of cases, you'll still look pretty much your old self afterwards. It doesn't mean you won't look "better," but you have to accept those two truths going in.

Plastic surgery poses a fundamental question: Is your dissatisfaction "fixable," or something no surgical intervention is ever going to satisfy? Is it your path in life to change the things you don't like, or to make peace with yourself just as you are? A dear friend who has struggled with her weight her whole life summed it up this way: "Should I spend ten thousand dollars to get lap band surgery, or spend it on therapy because this is the body I'm always going to have?" No one can answer those questions but you. You need to be brutally honest with yourself. Plastic surgery is expensive, time-consuming, and painful. If you choose wrong, you'll end up still stewing in that original dissatisfaction.

Be aware that although your friends and partners want you to feel good about yourself, it can be hard for them to get past their own insecurities and projections. Most loved ones accept us just as we are. Our desire to want to change ourselves can feel threatening. Discussing your feelings with a therapist might be a better place for arriving at your decision than your social circle.

Building a robust clientele depends on how you make them feel, enjoying yourself, and loving what you're doing. If your goal is to stay in sex work for a long time, plastic surgery might well be a tool in your toolbox. But far more important than any nip or tuck is arriving at peace with your body, the work, and yourself.

> Remember the Serenity Prayer: Grant me the serenity to accept the things I cannot change, the courage to change the things I can, **and the wisdom to know the difference.**

ANGER: AN INTRODUCTION

Hi, Sexy—

Oh, lordy, when I worked, would I get pissed. I remember one afternoon: I'd been stood up twice, so naturally, I was furious. Walking to meet my girlfriend, some guy on the street muttered something in my direction. I didn't hear what, but it didn't matter. He was bothering me, so I went off, screaming in his face. My girlfriend came up to us, but I didn't even see her, I was so lost in a red rage. She gave me a long, hard look, and said, "Girl, you have lost your shit." She got that right. I had no place to vent my work frustration, so I took it out on a total stranger.

Over the next few days and weeks, I started to notice all my petty little aggressions at work: rudeness, impatience, cracking mean jokes. It was right in front of my face, but I hadn't seen it before: I was mad all the time. I also noticed how safe and familiar that anger felt. The thought of not feeling it terrified me. How could I possibly be safe without it?

Anger is tricky—it cuts all kinds of ways. Unlike shame and unworthiness and all those other soggy emotions, rage is fiery, protecting us from a dangerous world. But acting hostile and mean guarantees others treat us badly in return. Over time, anger grinds us down, eroding our trust in life. There are plenty of reasons to wanna holler in the Biz, **but you cannot let anger ride you.** Bitterness is the express train to burnout.

In this section, I'll discuss the dynamics of rage, and how it can take over our lives. I'll offer heartfelt advice on letting it go, and practical advice on how to detach from triggers while still allowing juicy deliciousness in. And I've included two additional exercises in empathy and forgiveness, because only through compassion for one another can we break the cycle of endless grievance.

ANGER

> *The moment you start to resent a person, you become his slave. He controls your dreams, absorbs your digestion, robs you of your peace of mind and goodwill, and takes away the pleasure of your work ... He is with you when you are awake. He invades your privacy when you sleep ... He requires you to take medicine for indigestion, headaches, and loss of energy. He even steals your last moment of consciousness before you go to sleep. So if you want to be a slave, harbor your resentments!*
>
> —ANONYMOUS FROM *101 MEETING STARTERS: A GUIDE TO BETTER 12-STEP DISCUSSIONS*

How would I describe the emotional state of the sex industry? ***Mad as fuck***. Grievance wrapped in self-righteousness soaked in outrage. Distrust, aggression, and bad behavior. Management, coworkers, clients, activists—everyone is the enemy.

As sex workers, we have every right to be angry. Our culture and the industry are riddled with hypocrisies that threaten not only our livelihoods, but our lives. Clients are draped in their mantle of unexamined privilege. They carry toxic baggage about sex, money, and their bodies, expecting us to make them feel good while shaming and devaluing us. Cops are paid to protect the peace-loving citizenry, yet don't defend us, even as we harm no one, even when our bodies and rights are violated. Anti-trafficking activists agitate for laws that make our work more dangerous in the name of "saving" us from our choices. The sex industry profits off **LOOKISM**, perpetuating ageism, racism, classism, able-bodyism, transphobia, homophobia, misogyny, slut-shaming, fatphobia, and other forms of body hatred.

Politicians court votes by creating moral panics centered on disease, trafficking, online predators, and endangerment of minors, all the while sidestepping any responsibility to improve the working conditions of SSCA sex workers. Capitalism requires us to make money in order to survive, and yet … our legal system makes it a crime to charge money for activities that are legal when free!

That is a lot to carry. And since we're perpetually on display and exposed, our jobs can't get any more personal. It can make it awfully damned difficult to get through our day when we're furious and defended.

A VISIT FROM THE RAGE FAIRY, A VISIT FROM THE JOY FAIRY

Here's a thought experiment: Maybe the first thing you read about when you wake up in the morning is the horrible treatment of a fellow sex worker—maybe someone you love—maybe someone just like you. Maybe at work, a client or coworker is disrespectful or selfish or cruel. You feel yourself flooded with the hot lava of fury. These injustices reinforce what you already know: the world is a hostile place. All throughout the day, you want to punch something, to lash out at those who don't get it. At night you go to bed only to lie awake with a racing mind and a tight stomach. A stiffened jaw. Joints that ache.

Let me ask you this: What if a joy fairy floated down from above and made the following offer: *One wave of my magic wand and all your bitterness will be lifted forever.* Would you take that deal—would you choose to let it go? Tricky, isn't it? Because secretly, that rage feels like a shield against an unsafe world. It goes deeper than that. Nobody ever says it out loud, but it's as true as the day is long: outrage is sexy as shit. Deep down addictive. A little hit we can taste any time we want. Why? Because we know we are *right*. And of course, resentment is never lonely. Unlike misery, who famously loves company but is no fun to be around, anger is contagious. Whole industries are built on it. Blogs, news organizations, political movements: if you aren't mad, then you aren't paying attention.

I get all that—I spent years in that headspace. But I also know how it feels not to carry around that kind of anger, and I can tell you right now—it's way better. If fury rules your life, let me ask you this: What is the very best thing your anger buys you? Is it worth how terrible it makes you feel? Because here's the thing: if you carry rage and blame because someone hurt you or hates you or because the world is unfair, you are doing your enemy's work for them. As Anne Lamott writes in *Crooked Little Heart*, "Holding onto a resentment is like eating rat poison and waiting for the rat to die." Anger is a kneejerk response to pain that only harms ourselves.

That day I went ballistic in the street, my anger did serve a purpose: it defended me against the humiliation of being stood up. It drowned out the slithery little voices inside my head that said: *Those guys think I'm worthless. I'm their punching bag whore and helpless to stop it.* But deep down, I was letting their shitty behavior define how I felt about myself. That rage felt like armor; instead, it was a prison.

Maybe there's no such thing as a joy fairy, but we can reduce the inflammation in our lives. Every day we put off this important work means living one day less in our true inheritance. I offer two anger management methods: engagement and detachment. With practice, you can determine which method works best for you in which situation.

ENGAGING ANGER

In the case of an acute flash of fury, I recommend engagement. The practice is not to react, but to sit still. As Thích Nhất Hạnh counsels, "Our attitude is to take care of anger. We don't suppress or hate it or run away from it. We just breathe gently and cradle our anger in our arms with the utmost tenderness." What happens when we're brave enough to be quiet with that restless pacing rage is it soon melts away, leaving our soft, sad emotions undefended. We're reminded how helpless we've felt in the past. We re-experience being unseen, unloved, uncared for. It's not easy to absorb, but we have to find a way to hold it and not reject it. As James Baldwin writes in *The Fire Next Time*, "One of the reasons people cling to their hates so stubbornly is because they sense, once hate is gone, they will be forced to deal with pain." The depth of our rage mirrors the depth of our unhealed wounds.

Every baby brought into this world deserves the knowledge, grounded in their perfect tiny body, that they belong, they are wanted, they are safe and adored. This is the legacy of early life for a lucky few. For the rest of us, it takes work. Dignified righteousness in the face of injustice means trusting we have the right to be here just as we are, and knowing nobody else has the power to define us. Only we can do that for ourselves.

That day I was stood up, what I needed to do was sit with my mistreatment, to recognize how heartbroken I was. I needed to let that pain pass, to allow for the deep sweet voice of self-love to speak: *They disrespected me, and it hurt so bad, but I did not deserve it. From now on, I'm only going to focus on clients who treat me well.*

DETACHING FROM ANGER

Sometimes we don't have the luxury to stop and sit with the feels. Sometimes we need to set that shit aside and finish our shift. That's when it helps to have a reservoir of well-being to draw upon, which is where detachment comes in.

I practice detachment when I find myself fuming over bigotry, racism, whorephobia, misogyny, slut-shaming, and the rest. Detachment doesn't mean these things don't exist in my perfect world—oh, no—they are very real. It doesn't mean I don't care—quite the opposite, I care very much. But I affirm my right to be healthy and whole. It's not my job to carry in my body the sickness of systemic injustices I don't have the power to fix.

When that bitterness boils up, when I hear my voice get sharp and my pulse rise, I stop and acknowledge that anger has come to visit. However, it's not allowed to unpack its bags and settle in. I take a few deep breaths, hear what it has to say, but then it needs to move along. My response is: *That is fucked up, but I do not let it fuck me up. In this moment, I am safe and whole.* Likewise, my policy towards difficult people is disengagement. Avoid them as much as possible, and limit interaction. My mantra is: *I don't pick fights. I don't take the bait. I engage wisely, only when it counts. I save my energy for the people I love.*

Think of anger as a gluten intolerance—a reaction to a toxin. It might be unrealistic to completely avoid wheat for the rest of our lives, but we'd feel a whole lot better if we stopped munching on a bagel every morning. Practicing detachment means cutting chronic aggravation out of our emotional diet. Like most compulsions, we think we can't live without it, until one day we realize we feel a whole lot better with it gone.

Here are my suggestions for reducing toxicity when you start feeling riled up:

- ❀ Disconnect from screens and social media.
- ❀ Avoid commentators, tweeters, and bloggers who perform outrage as their business model.
- ❀ Turn off the news when it gets to be too much.
- ❀ Boycott movies and shows that feature violence and hate.
- ❀ Steer clear of people who stir up negativity or act out.
- ❀ Put limits on snark and sarcasm.

We don't cultivate well-being just by what we cut out of our lives. We also generate it with what we invite in. So we can:

- ❀ Assert our boundaries, calmly and firmly.
- ❀ Take pleasure when we feel powerful and skillful.
- ❀ Adopt an attitude of gratitude.
- ❀ Cultivate people who treat us kindly.
- ❀ Practice mindfulness, forgiveness, and compassion.

- ❀ Notice the times when we diffuse anger and redirect bad behavior, both our own and other people's.
- ❀ Learn from others who use anger wisely.
- ❀ Sit with our emotions and learn what they have to teach us.
- ❀ Confront with care the people we love, letting them know when something isn't working for us, negotiating ways to make things better together.
- ❀ Effect positive change in the world through art, activism, education, volunteering, and other juicy goodness.

Sexy Reader, please learn from my mistakes: Don't be mad all the time. The most important work in this life is making peace with ourselves. I'm not saying for a second that you shouldn't defend yourself, work for change, speak out, or confront injustice, but do so from a place of dignified righteousness, not rage. The world may treat sex workers as disposable, despicable, and shameful, but deep down, we know self-love makes us whole.

> *When your heart contracts in anger, the air itself feels threatening. But when you're expansive, no matter the weather, you're in an open, windy field with friends.*
>
> —RUMI

❀ EMPATHY EXERCISE

Be kind, for everyone you meet is fighting a battle you know nothing about.
—WENDY MASS

Outrage perpetuates itself, providing ammunition to its enemies. We need strategies to keep other people's bad behavior from tearing us up inside. But self-protection is only the first step. To break the sex industry's cycle of rage and bitterness requires developing a reservoir of compassion. If you're having a hard time letting go of hatred, try this empathy exercise.

Imagine standing in a supermarket checkout line after you've just endured the crappiest client possible—there's not enough money in the world to compensate. All you want to do is to go home, take a shower, and put this terrible day behind you. Out of the blue, that same horrible client cuts right in front of you, as if they didn't even see you. How does it feel to stand next to this person? Does hating them feel good, or does it feel terrible? Do you feel small, invisible, and powerless, or do you feel jacked up and huge? Do you feel heavy and dull and just want to curl up into a ball and go to sleep? Do you want to lecture them? Humiliate them? Punish them?

Now, imagine this: same line, different day. Today, you're in a great mood because you just made a huge pile of cash doing something naughty and fun. You're riding high when that same evil client cuts in front of you without even a glance. How do you react this time? Do you shoot daggers into the back of their head with your stare? Do you defend yourself politely, or do you throw up your hands in exasperation, making some sarcastic crack: "Please, don't mind me. Act like I'm not even here." Or do you start a fight: "In a rush to get home to your empty, boring sexless life, you clueless asshole?" Snarky self-righteousness can be tasty, but stop and ask yourself—is that how a person who genuinely is at peace with themselves behaves?

Now take a deep breath and imagine the person who takes your rightful place in line is your grandparent, lover, or best friend. Perhaps this person is old or injured, in pain just from the act of standing. Through the eyes of love, you can see their frailties, their insecurities, their shortcomings. You can see how they might be tempted to behave badly, just as you have behaved badly in the past. You can see how they could be capable of cruelty or cluelessness, just as you can be capable of cruelty or cluelessness.

No matter how we feel, terrific or terrible, when we're confronted with someone we love or when we see someone suffering more than ourselves, we have room to say, *I can be patient with this person.* With compassion, we don't take bad behavior personally, even when they trigger us. We can see their suffering: perhaps they are grieving. Perhaps they are ill. Perhaps they are sick with hatred someone else taught them.

When we are at peace, no matter what anyone else does or why they do it, we know no one has the power to strip our humanity from us. Regardless of the pain we are in, how much money is in our pockets or how much food is in our belly, we recognize that we are whole, complete, and just as we're meant to be.

> *If we learn to open our hearts, anyone, including the people who drive us crazy, can be our teacher.*
> —PEMA CHÖDRÖN

❀ FORGIVENESS EXERCISE

For the longest time, I resisted the idea of forgiveness. I thought the phrase "forgive and forget" meant acting like whatever bad thing never happened. Pretending people always do their best, when the truth is a lot of the time they're selfish or cruel—another term for this is obliterating history. I know now that forgiveness isn't ignoring or condoning bad behavior. Instead, it's facing the humanity of those who have harmed us, while acknowledging our own faults.

This is a ritual I developed to set myself free from the rage I had accumulated towards bad clients over the years. I went to the beach and wrote a list in the sand in huge letters of those who had shamed, belittled, hurt, and disrespected me. For each name, I held an image of that person's face in my mind. I spoke out loud, so I could hear my own voice say these words:

- ❀ "I ask for [the universe/god/my higher power/my best self] to release me from this bitterness and anger."
- ❀ "I acknowledge [the fear/anger/neediness] that caused them to behave as they did, as I know it in myself."
- ❀ "I forgive them for [their bad behavior] because I recognize that they acted from their limitations."

After I spoke the story of each client aloud, I crossed out their name. (If you don't live near the ocean, you can write their names in bright paint on a huge piece of butcher paper, then rip it up and burn it. Shred with gusto—really let yourself feel it.)

Next, I forgave myself—this is a very important step. Without self-forgiveness, there is no way to build up a reservoir of compassion for others. I wrote my name in the sand, drew a huge heart around it, and said aloud:

- ✿ "I ask for [the universe/god/my higher power/my best self] to release me from this bitterness and anger."
- ✿ "I see [the fear/anger/confusion] that caused me to behave as I did."
- ✿ "I recognize, accept, and forgive myself, because I acted from my limitations."

I asked to let go of the humiliation I carried from all the times I didn't stand up for myself. I asked to let go of the shame I felt from letting myself down. I was able to acknowledge the humanity of the people who had harmed me, while taking responsibility for my role in my mistreatment. Thankfully, my anger lifted, allowing spaciousness and ease to enter my mind.

> *Forgiveness does not change the past, but it does enlarge the future.*
> —PAUL BOESE

ENVY: AN INTRODUCTION

Hi, Sexy—

Ah, envy. That magnificent dark queen—I saved her for last. Underbelly of the American Dream, engine of advertising, envy is virtually unexamined in our culture. Much of its power is taboo. Many of us would rather choke on our own vomit than admit to feeling less-than someone else.

It's been more than twenty-five years, but when I think about envy during my time in the sex industry, Cashmere immediately springs to mind. She was a lithe, golden-eyed, caramel-skinned New Yorker with an Italian mom and Tunisian dad. She had studied ballet from the age of three until she blew her knee out during her senior year of high school. A year later, she relocated to San Francisco and was dancing at the Lusty Lady.

After all this time, I can still remember how her poise and elegance cut me. There was nothing I wanted more in life than to look like her. Getting paid to spend time with half-naked women was my dream job—I was so insecure, I felt lucky every day I wasn't fired. But Cashmere—she had it all.

Back then, all I could process, all I could comprehend, was my envy. It blinded me. It's so easy to see now that Cashmere wasn't enviable. I mean, sure, she was stunning—she was also completely and utterly miserable. The job was a demeaning grind for her, beneath her contempt. Her icy demeanor ensured that no one ever talked to her; the other dancers universally disliked her. I never saw her smile, not even on stage. Her face was always a mask of fatigue, irritation, and defeat. How cruel it must have been, trained for years in classical dance, to spend her days *grinding in peepshow windows. When I looked at her, all I could think was: "I will never have those hips." When she saw herself reflected in that room filled with mirrors, what she knew to be true was: "I will never be a ballerina."*

In this section, we'll examine the dynamics of envy and how they permeate the industry in both clients and coworkers. I'll offer heartfelt advice on recognizing the underlying emotional dynamics of ugly behavior that stems from resentment, envy, and insecurity. And I'll propose strategies for staying safe from corrosive people, first by honoring ourselves and then by holding compassion for others.

✳ ENVY

It is no surprise the sex industry is drenched in discontent: money and sexual magnetism are two of our society's most important markers of status. Someone else always seems to have it all. Even if we're told the hottest people have their own insecurities, we don't feel empathy—we think: *Good! Hope they go home tonight and choke on a Twinkie.* Envy flows from and feeds other demons. So often, we experience it as hate, hostility, or contempt, but the fact is, it bubbles up from self-hatred, a direct by-product of low self-esteem.

Envy is a knife pointed at our deepest vulnerabilities. Its power comes from the belief that our imperfections hold us back from happiness. It's easy to take it a step further, as I did with Cashmere, magically believing that because she was so beautiful and talented, she must be happy. Every minute of her waking day had to be better than mine, because she had what I so desperately wanted. That, quite simply, is projection, mistaking surface for substance. Is there any way to claim that the most joyful, grounded, fulfilled people are the most beautiful? The most intelligent? The richest? There is absolutely no connection between the things our society prizes most and self-acceptance.

Whenever we experience envy, it's a wake-up call. We spot a bright shiny thing—the self-hating response is: *I don't have that, I'll die without it.* The loving response is: *What is the underlying gift? Where do I find that in my own life?* Here's what I mean—I wasn't envious of Cashmere for beauty's sake. I wanted what beauty gets: earning power, self-worth, confidence. These were things I believed I lacked. Of course, what I wanted more than anything was love. To be so irresistible no one would ever leave me, so I'd never feel heartbreak ever again.

But notice I said "everything I *believed* I lacked," because, in truth, I lacked none of those things. I was good at my job and a great earner. Most days, in most ways, I felt fine, with plenty of love, security, wealth, and freedom. Pulling that even further apart, there's no way to ever know if looking like a supermodel would have made me a happier person. What is true is I was successful just as I was. And being spectacular wasn't enough to keep Cashmere from despair.

The moral of this story is, when we feel envy, we need to stop and spin out the story of "If Only":

- ✼ *If only I looked like Kim Kardashian—she's so beautiful.* True. She's also having Kanye's babies. Your life makes sense.

- ✼ *If only I had smooth skin, bright teeth, a flat tummy, huge breasts or cock, clients would pay three times my rate.* No matter what we look like, we can cultivate a loyal clientele, so our phones will never stop ringing. We can get good at money, so what we earn feels like enough. We can take charge of our business, so we don't ever have to feel less than anyone else.

- ✼ *If only I was ten years younger, I'd never have to worry about anything ever again.* No matter how powerful those feelings are, none of that is true. Whatever our age, we are exactly where we need to be.

Regardless of our flaws and shortcomings, we are objects of desire. We have family, friends, and lovers who adore us. We have gifts other people would kill for. So, even though it's an unwelcome guest, envy can remind us of our own abundance, then motivate us to get more: more love, more success, and more ease. When we understand our desires, we can use our unique gifts to get them. Growing into someone we admire is the basis of self-esteem. Other people's excellence can't cut us when we like who we've become.

ACCEPTANCE

When envy pops up its ugly head, sometimes we need to take inventory of what we already have, sometimes we need to strive for more. But sometimes, we need to stop and make peace with what is.

All the years I worked, I kept my hair long, past my shoulders, but no matter what I did, it was heavy and dull, with dead ends and flyaways. As a stripper, I'd get so envious of other dancers doing their sexy hair flips. What I'd advise my younger self now is to feel that sadness completely, then let it go—long hair will never be my look. However, nothing's cuter than a pixie cut. No hair flips in my future, but I don't have to mess with snarls and bad hair days either. I love the sanity that comes with short hair. More importantly, now whenever I feel that jab of jealousy, it's a reminder that I'm fine just as I am. I have love in my life. I'm desirable and desired, content with my choices.

Covetousness is such a small, mean emotion, turning us into trolls, despising ourselves and everyone else. Self-acceptance is envy's kryptonite. Giving thanks for what is, practicing feelings of enoughness, we grow expansive and joyful. Melody Beattie writes: "Gratitude unlocks the fullness of life. It turns what we have into enough, and more."

> *Overcoming envy is a lifelong project. Learning what's worth working towards and letting the rest go are powerful tools for appreciating our own lives more fully. We may still want things we can't have, but we can make the best of our native gifts, acknowledge love in our lives, and celebrate excellence in others.*

❋ HEARTFELT ADVICE: NAVIGATING INSECURITY, RESENTMENT, AND ENVY FROM COWORKERS

Inadequacy triggers all kinds of nasty behavior in the Biz. The fact is, every day we face scrutiny and rejection in ways that couldn't be more personal. Competition is often zero-sum: If you get picked for a lap dance and I don't, I get nothing. Unfortunately, some sex workers have to harden their hearts to do the job, taking their frustrations out on everyone around them. To thrive, we need strategies to identify and deflect the coworkers who are bullies, blamers, schemers, shamers, and enforcers. If a fellow sex worker is making life hard, try being curious why:

- ❋ *Insecurity fuels a lot of bad behavior in the Biz.* Consider the high-school valedictorian who makes it into Yale, but then hits a wall when they're suddenly average among their peers. Someone who gets by on their looks can feel threatened if they don't believe they are the most attractive person in the room.
- ❋ *Hot people beat off unwanted advances every day of their lives.* Often, the world doesn't feel safe for them.
- ❋ *Envy inspires hate.* People who inspire envy know that, so they reflexively push others away.
- ❋ *Many attractive people believe others only like them for their looks.* Much like the rich person who suspects their friends only love them for their money.
- ❋ *Some sex workers believe they are ugly.* Everywhere they turn in the adult industry is proof that they aren't good enough.

❀ *For many, working in the sex industry is shameful.* Rather than face it, they tear others down. Anyone who spends all their time listing other people's faults, most likely they feel small and powerless.

❀ *Strip club dressing rooms, porn shoots, and dungeons are sexually charged environments.* For many of us, they might feel playful, even liberating. But for someone whose sexual boundaries haven't always been respected, these spaces can feel chaotic and intimidating. When cornered, even the sweetest dog bites.

If you encounter excessive negativity, good self-care is essential. Steer clear of anyone who spreads damage. Don't try to change them—there is no need to lecture, punish, correct, or fix. They've chosen their path for reasons you know nothing about, leave them to it. Be respectful and courteous if you have to interact with them, modeling how someone with healthy self-esteem behaves. Cultivate coworkers who spread love, and if you can, hold compassion for those who spread suffering. There is no possible way they enjoy a quiet mind.

✳ HEARTFELT ADVICE: NAVIGATING INSECURITY, RESENTMENT, AND ENVY FROM CLIENTS

I had one client come right out and say it: "You're so lucky, getting to lie around having sex all day. I wish I could have your job." I could've laughed out loud. In a way, it was a compliment to my ability to project that fantasy. To him, I was living the dream.

So much unspoken, undigested envy circulates between sex workers and clients. Although we dress up and smile, although they bring us offerings, we resent the ever-living hell out of each other. To start with, clients are the ones with the money. Upstanding citizens with fancy jobs, shopping around to make their fantasies come true. We conform to their desires—they look us over like meat. They live in the light, yet don't lift a finger to make us safer. Their review sites detail our most intimate body parts to avoid getting "robbed," while we cobble together phone numbers to prevent getting raped or killed.

But envy cuts both ways—clients resent us as well. Clients crave connection, arousal, and release to avoid feelings of emptiness, loneliness, and poverty. They project onto us all the pleasure and fulfillment they lack. From their perspective, we sleep on stacks of cash, while they slog away at straight jobs. Our lives are one long erotic adventure, while they are no more than paying guests, welcome only as long as their money lasts. We radiate shamelessness, while they feel humiliation for their desires, their impotence, their need. How our beauty must cut them if they feel ugly inside. No wonder clients hate us so much: they desire us so badly. From where they sit, we have it all.

The result? Passive aggression, straight up aggression, and contempt. Haggling over fees. Demeaning comments and insults. Frustration out of all proportion. Obsession with our cleanliness, our "looseness," our emotional stability. Hang-ups calls and no-shows. Erotic envy is at the root of much of clients' bad behavior, and oftentimes dealing with it feels like it's not worth all the money in the world.

As sex professionals, it's our job to recognize their pain, to understand the true motivations at play. When clients act out, we can say: "Stop—no more." There's no need to flip the power dynamic—that solves nothing. Lashing out just feeds into their hostility and aggression. It's enough to calmly and firmly assert ourselves, to love who we are as sexual beings. We're fortunate to be desirable, and generous enough to offer ourselves for a fee. We can provide an honest, friendly service *as equals*. Clients who can meet us halfway will be delighted. Those knotted up in bitterness, we let pass. When we can identify their underlying pain, perhaps we can hold compassion without the need to react or take it personally.

> *Inside every one of us, there is a gap between our sexual ideal and who we believe ourselves to be. All kinds of toxicity can fester there. However, when we stand in our power, we are whole. We demonstrate what self-love looks like, and we offer that gift to the world.*

PART TWO:
TOOLS OF THE TRADE

Without work, all life goes rotten, but when work is soulless, life stifles and dies.

—ALFRED CAMUS

THE BIZ: AN INTRODUCTION

Hi, Sexy—

Saturday nights at the Lusty Lady, the Private Pleasures booth was my bitch. A precursor to camming, the booth hosted individual sex shows. Built to look like Amsterdam's Red Light District, it was made out of Lucite, with curtains for privacy. One side faced out onto the Lusty's common area, so anyone could walk by, tap on the window, and stare.

The booth was the jungle. So many lines of power were on display there—desire, aggression, resentment, greed, domination, menace—many Lustys would never go near it. It was more than a little nuts to be locked in a plastic box, enticing strangers to pay to watch them masturbate. I loved it, though, and was a good earner. Management scheduled me every Saturday to work the longest and most grueling shift on the Lusty calendar: 9 P.M. to 3 A.M. Six hours of facing drunken hordes spilling out of the surrounding North Beach nightclubs, cruising for a thrill.

Sides of myself I didn't even know I possessed would show up on those nights as packs of men strolled by my window, stopping to leer and jeer, ordering me to show them my ass. Naturally averse to confrontation of any kind in the real world, in the booth, I was a warrior. I'd morph into a wild child, comedienne, carnival barker, lounge crooner, bully. Armed with a microphone, armored in my lingerie, I was cruel in the knowledge I could have anyone bounced in a second, which I did some nights just to prove I could. Pickled in rage and glee, I'd pick out the rowdiest member in a pack and bait him until he pissed me off. Then I'd call security, waving and singing as he was escorted out.

We can't have a serious discussion about staying sane in the sex industry if we don't first acknowledge how crazy it can be: competitive, cutthroat, often scammy, constantly changing. Disorientation, overstimulation, and altered states aren't bugs—they're features. It can make it hard to feel centered and safe for sex workers and clients alike.

In this next section, I'll discuss doing this work with clarity. Visualizing what we want and working towards it. Honing our image. Making ourselves available. Showing up all the way. And if that doesn't work, knowing when it's time to make a change. I'll specifically address technology, since this brave new online world we encounter every day is rarely a safe place. Then I'll expose marketing myths that are easy to fall into. Much of what follows is directed to the self-employed; however, since we all develop working personas, calibrate how real we want to be, and manage emotional downturns, my hope is everyone can get something from my advice.

❋ BUILDING THE BUSINESS YOU WANT

The universe can only respond to the identity you truly believe you embody. Any lack of belief will show up in a lack of action. There is no escaping this truth.

—HOWARD FALCO

What does success in sex work look like? Amanda Brooks, author of *The Internet Escort Handbook* series, counsels, "When you discover your niche, you'll be happy because you get the clients you like. Your clients are happy because you meet their expectations. Your business stays healthy, you stay healthy. Life is good."

Her point can't be overstated: We suffer burnout and exhaustion trying to be something we're not; when we're just going through the motions, clients know they aren't getting good value. However, when we follow our passions, the right things tend to happen. We can tap into our natural reservoirs of energy, creativity, generosity, and good humor. We attract people looking for what we uniquely offer—this is what we want to work towards. That kind of alignment is only possible when we're honest with ourselves. When we understand our strengths, are clear-eyed about our weaknesses, and don't ignore what's not working.

If some aspect of the Biz is driving you nuts, stop and take a good, long look at it. Feeling crazy, doing crazy, going crazy—that's dreadful. Finding that place where the world makes sense and the work makes sense and you make sense, ***that is true power.***

IT'S NEVER AS GOOD AS THE FIRST TIME

Let's start with beginner's luck—it's a very real pitfall for those in the adult industry. What no one ever tells you is when you first put up an ad, no matter how amateurish, you'll get a ton of interest. When you're the fresh face at the club, even if you can't dance to save your life, patrons will be desperate to meet you. A whole class of client waits to pounce on every newbie. Naturally, we believe if we keep on doing what we did when we first started, we'll keep getting the same results. But our initial success is nothing personal—those clients soon move on to the next.

I've heard so many sex workers talk about wanting to get back to the rush of those first weeks and months, like the desire to fall in love again after a relationship has turned predictable. Managing that inevitable business downturn is a challenge. It can be easy to get discouraged when what came so easily before starts feeling like work.

It helps to acknowledge that what goes up must come down. Unless you move to a new city for that brand-new-sex-worker bounce, it's unlikely that initial business will come back. It's also helpful to make the distinction between the rush from *starting out* in the business and *having* lots of business. Don't make the mistake of hoping that popularity will make the adrenaline return—I hate to be the one to say it, but it won't. You're a different person now. That early tingle of transgression from sexual experimentation, from making your first fat stack from fucking or flogging or dancing will fade. It only returns if you step away for a while. Like sex itself, the Biz feels like a whole new world when you first discover it. After a while, though, it loses some of its giddy power.

Time will bring challenges to your marketing. Maybe when you started out you were lucky enough to have landed on a timeless ad campaign right away, and you'll always score enough work without ever having to make a change. But chances are you'll see a drop-off in activity, so you've got to keep innovating and improving. That's where good marketing skills come in. (I discuss this more in the next section.)

TIME MANAGEMENT

As your business matures, it's easy to fall into the trap of making yourself more and more available to generate business. After all, it makes a certain amount of sense that to make the most money, clients need to be able to reach you. If you never return emails or texts, it's like that famous *New Yorker* cartoon, "How's never? Does never work for you?" However, being too accessible projects a desperation that turns off good clients and attracts predators.

Scheduling is just as much a feature of your professionalism as your appearance and your fee structure. Your goal is to have a calendar filled with repeat clients, and more potential dates going through your screening process every day. At the same time, you want a well-rounded life, so that you have the energy to greet your clientele with anticipation. None of that is possible sitting by the phone all day like a slug in your sweats.

I'll share how I did it, and let me just say, I didn't land on this system right away. It took me more than a year to get to the point where I had enough regular clients to be sustainable, so, I'm suggesting this as something to work towards.

First, I posted clear time windows in my ads and on my website. "I'm available to speak on the phone [or text or email] in person between the hours of 10 A.M. and 12 P.M. every business day. If you've reached this message, I'm either on the other line or unavailable. I return all messages within four hours during business hours or by 10 A.M. of the next business day." This did so many good things for me, making me look professional, busy, and exclusive. Then, I honored my callback rules, *no matter what*, because nothing is flakier than flaking. Keeping my word demonstrated professionalism and trustworthiness. That consistency generated client loyalty and, over time, allowed me to command higher fees. When I went on vacation or was otherwise unavailable, I posted it to let my clients know, demonstrating that I valued their time.

Just as important is not working when you're not working. I recommend turning off work gadgets on your off-hours. Let your well-crafted voicemail message and website copy spin their sexy magic. Don't check your email right before bed—it can keep until morning. Don't feel guilty, don't fantasize about that client you're crushed out on calling you for a quickie. When you're off, be all the way off.

The hardest part about adopting this policy is the fear of losing what I call "CONVENIENCE CLIENTS," or clients that want to drop by on short notice. It can be a challenge to let go of the prospect of fast, easy money, but you can't build a long-term business that way. They aren't loyal—disappoint them once or twice, they move on. They distort your priorities, too. Drop-in clients may seem like quick money, but that doesn't take into account all the unpaid hours spent making *yourself* convenient. When you can afford to, let them go to make room for something more sustainable. Cultivate clients who schedule in advance, so that the rest of your time is your own. Who know you have a life, who think about you days or weeks ahead of time. Who want to make a genuine connection, invest in your relationship, and support you well into the future.

STRATEGIES FOR A WORKING PERSONA

Our job is unusual. We cross boundaries, display our bodies, play with ourselves, and talk dirty. Few of us do this work simply as ourselves. Most of us change our names, and many of us slip into character. This doesn't mean necessarily we split off from our authentic selves—quite the opposite. We can explore parts of our psyches that wouldn't otherwise get out to play. This can be a deeply appealing feature of the job.

In my years in the Biz, I saw many personas up close. My working image was very close to who I actually am: a brainy nerd, a news and politics junkie, and sex positive activist. In my ads, I'd mention I read *The New York Times* every day and do the crossword puzzle in ink. At the same time, I offered peekaboo hints about my private life: kinky, bisexual, and SAPIOSEXUAL.

The advantage of presenting a work persona so close to my authentic self was I didn't have to lie much. My story was simple, making it easy to remember, with clear boundaries around the parts of my life that were off limits. For example, I'd happily tell my clients in juicy detail about my first time having sex with another woman, but never speak a word about my current girlfriend. For the most part, I presented as an integrated, unified whole. As long as I had interest in the job, it worked fine. However, when I hit burnout, there wasn't much of an imagination gap for me to draw upon to recharge my erotic and creative batteries.

One friend of mine had a completely different strategy, creating a separate dominatrix personality. (I have no hard data to back this up, but it seems to me pro doms have an easier time keeping their stories straight than the rest of us.) My friend is a natural performer, and when she became Mistress X, her walk, tone of voice, and speech patterns changed. Working in Mistress X's dungeon was to be in the presence of a ruthless queen, a completely different person than my sunny, goofy friend at Sunday brunch. She was wildly successful—clients adored her, and other pro doms respected her. As Mistress X, she had a confidence, a competence, a drive she confided she lacked in regular life. She thought Mistress X was gorgeous in a way she wasn't, decisive when she often felt unsure. Mistress X drove her creativity and success, no question.

Another friend of mine, her persona was a worldly courtesan whose clients underwrote her intellectual and artistic pursuits. She'd figure out her next challenge, whether it was to learn a new language, live abroad, or pursue an apprenticeship with a spiritual teacher, then put a call out to her clientele, sending her alter ego out into the world to achieve her life goals. The upside of her strategy was traveling to fantastic places, staying in world-class accommodations, and studying around the world. The price, however, was dealing with high net worth individuals with huge egos and endless demands. When it worked, it was spectacularly successful, but when she got burned out, she was forced to retreat.

Who are you when you work? Where does your mind go? Your working persona does a lot of heavy lifting, making clients happy as well as keeping you safe. Pay attention to which parts of your persona tap into your natural underground springs of adventure, playfulness, and discovery. Notice what parts feel liquid and lively, and where you feel stunted and dull. Are you freer than in regular life or more inhibited? Do you take more chances, or need a routine to feel safe? Do you mix things up to keep from getting bored? Do you rev up to get into character; does it take days to come down? Does your work persona feel grand and showy, or calm and grounded and wise and true? Do you like who you are when you work? Because you should.

Do you feel safer presenting as someone ordinary and approachable? That makes you the sweetheart next door. Do you want to do the sexy without much conversation or connection? Sounds like you're a porn star. Do you enjoy the rituals of dating and romance? You offer the Girl/Boy Friend Experience. If you like letting your imagination run loose and are always ready for adventure, that means you're the wild sexy one. Never letting anything get too serious means you're the silly fun one. When enforcing strict boundaries is what makes the work worthwhile, then you're the exclusive recluse who plays hard-to-get.

Try telling yourself the story of who you are when you work, as if describing this person to someone who has never met you before. Explain where you feel free and where you get stuck. Where you feel brave, and where you get scared. What you're great at, what overwhelms you. Your motivating goals and deepest fears. Your wildest dreams, and the one thing you would never, ever do. This can be a powerful practice, telling the story of your intentions to yourself.

AUTHENTICITY VS. REALNESS

Authenticity is related to, but not the same as, your working persona. Before I get to that concept, let's break down realness first. Anxieties surrounding "the real" pervade our industry. Many clients are obsessed with it: real pictures. Real names. Real tans. Real breasts.

Real turn-ons. Real hard-ons. Real fantasies. Real orgasms. It's easy to understand why—nobody wants to spend good money on a bogus service, and the Biz is riddled with liars. Bad actors make the work harder for the rest of us, scamming clients with false advertising and empty promises.

But there's something else going on. Lap dances and scenes and dates are artificial situations. No matter how aroused a client may be, some part of their brain can never let go of the fact that they have to pay. As sex workers on the other side of the exchange, we do all kinds of things we wouldn't do otherwise, like spending time naked with a stranger, to start with. So the job is always a performance, and nobody ever really forgets it.

Realness can never be for sale, only given freely. However, a good actor can make us feel deeply even when we know everything they do is make-believe. As sex workers, when our working personas access spontaneity, generosity of spirit, humor, and unvarnished opinions, we can tap into our authenticity. When I was working, I gave myself permission to react wholeheartedly, within my boundaries. Clients were drawn to that genuineness—it flattered and soothed them. It took the sting out of the artificiality of the exchange, and gave them room to be vulnerable as well. Offering authenticity while showing up all the way is a powerful combination that many clients respond to with gratitude and generosity.

SHOWING UP ALL THE WAY

Such simple advice, but sometimes hard to follow. The most successful sex workers aren't the best looking. They don't have the wickedest moves on the pole or in bed. They attract a devoted clientele by conveying that they are present and there to have a good time. They listen, make eye contact, laugh, and smile. Ask questions and have opinions. Remember what's been said to them. Good clients can tell if you're stressed or distracted or bored. You best believe, they know when you're faking it.

Of course, plenty of clients don't care about any of that—human interaction knocks them out of their focus. Their minds constrict into a narrow tunnel of arousal, and any attempt to connect on a deeper level is distracting. There's nothing wrong with those clients; some make steady regulars. But performing as a sexbot is no way to feed your mind long term.

TRANSITIONS

One friend, a stage performer and escort, used to tell me, "Smooth transitions are the mark of the true professional." She is so right. Whenever I'm a client at a strip club or dungeon, I notice transitions are where so much energy and intention is exchanged. What separates the amateur from the pro is managing the beats as a scene begins, progresses, and ends. Rather than obsessing over things that don't matter, like costumes or hair styles, better to focus on smoothing out these pulse points for casting a magical, sexy spell:

- ❈ *Show up/be ready for a call or shift on time and focused.* Avoid the inevitable annoyance when a call starts late, or that awkwardness while a client waits because you're not prepared. In their minds, you aren't taking them seriously, wasting time they've paid good money for. Before you've even started, you've undercut your value, and they'll want you to make it up to them.

- ❈ *Be sure your initial contact is warm and genuine.* Make eye contact and flash a big smile with a "hello there" and a hug.

- ❈ *Remember your client's name and use it.* People like to hear their names, especially when they aren't sure if someone really likes them.

- ❈ *Conduct payment in a firm but fun manner.* I've watched so many sex workers either count out bills mechanically like a bank teller, or rush like they're ashamed. The money exchange is an opportunity to flirt, to act surprised or excited, but above all, to connect by expressing gratitude.

- ❀ *Move from small talk to flirtation, seduction, then to the initial physical contact playfully, purposefully, and gracefully.* Momentum is important. When you seem aimless or stuck, it's distracting.

- ❀ *If something not-sexy happens—a fart, a fire alarm, a phone ring—acknowledge it with a shrug and a laugh.* Deal with it only if you must, but don't let it interrupt the flow.

- ❀ *If something isn't feeling fun, or they need to stop doing something **now**, redirect them before using the words "stop" and "no."* Give them another task they can be rewarded for. Most clients aren't trying to be annoying—they just want to be told how to please you.

- ❀ *After close contact, move away smoothly, not abruptly.* End the session or dance in a natural, fluid, and friendly manner. Thank them. Tell them you had a wonderful time, and ask them to come again. People like to be told you that like them. Lots of clients are shy—if you don't clearly state you want their business again, they'll assume you don't.

All that being said, it's important not to be a pushover. Do not undermine your authority. Not only does that send the message you have no boundaries—never, ever a good idea—it cheapens your service. Studies of customer service dynamics show that an overly friendly waitperson makes fewer tips than one who maintains a friendly yet noticeably professional distance. Sociologists speculate this is because appearing too eager to please signals lower status. Asserting equal status signals that the interaction is only complete when service is fully rewarded. The result is larger tips.

INVESTING IN YOURSELF AND YOUR BUSINESS

Ever found yourself sitting in a Chinese restaurant where they haven't updated the plastic molded chairs and fluorescent lights since the 1970s? You think to yourself: *Why don't they spend a little money on this place? New coat of paint, some mood lighting—they could double the price for the same plate of lo mein.*

You run across sex workers stuck like that. Dancers, escorts, and pro doms who landed on a look years ago and are still at it. In an industry driven by novelty, it's a shock to encounter them, but for a handful of people, it works well enough. Wearing the identical costume every day to go through the same routine feels safe. It attracts a certain kind of client, driving the rest of the world away. One thing you can bet about these folks is that they experienced early success. They made more money than they ever dreamed possible, and on some level they thought to themselves: *I'm not going to do anything to mess this up.* Any deviation might break the spell.

If you're one of those people who needs your Wednesday to look like your Tuesday and your Monday and all the other days that went before, then you've found what works for you. But for many of us, exploration is why we love the work. If you find yourself falling into a rut, ask yourself: Do you believe, consciously or unconsciously, you can only work a certain way?

Successful entrepreneurs plow a portion of their earnings back into their business. Growth requires balancing constancy with experimentation. How else can we dream, grow, expand? Our business is pleasure, so remember to have fun. Set aside funds to invest in:

- ❀ Clothes, shoes, toys, gear, and household supplies.
- ❀ Decorating your work environment. Make it a fun and inviting place for you and your clients to spend time in, as well as keeping it clean.
- ❀ Pornographic and erotic images, writings, and videos. It helps to have inspiration in order to provide it!
- ❀ Caring for your body. (Massage, nutrition, personal training, yoga)
- ❀ Education and travel. Keep your mind active and keep learning about the world—clients love to hear about what you're studying.
- ❀ Experimentation and diversification. Some sex workers offer multiple services under different names.

A pro dom friend of mine called her toy-shopping excursions "tending her kink garden." Your business, regardless of job title, is a creative, organic entity—make sure to give it plenty of love and attention.

❇ MARKETING

When self-employed, good marketing is critical. Since we're all soaking in advertising—we're exposed to several thousand ads a day on average—it seems like promoting ourselves should be one of those things we're automatically good at. Really, though, most of us aren't. When I worked, I did the barest minimum needed to keep my phones ringing. If you despise promoting yourself, can we just stop for one minute and acknowledge: it is emotional to sell our sexuality! We put ourselves out there asking the whole world to vote with their dollars: *Am I worth what I ask*?

If marketing feels hard, take some time to figure out why. Is it the technical stuff? Notice how you feel when you say the words, "search engine optimization," "web design," and "Google analytics" out loud. Do you feel sad, sluggish, heavy, distracted, bored? If so, marketing depresses you, and you're probably better off hiring someone so you can focus on what you do best.

Do you dislike the pressure of coming up with new material, or feel like you keep falling into the same stupid rut? Do you feel intimidated when you compare your ad to others? Have you tried things in the past you thought were going to cause your inbox to explode, but the response was underwhelming? It's not easy to put ourselves out there, trying new things, taking risks, never quite knowing if our efforts are helping or hurting. One time, I posted fresh photos I thought were red hot, and calls actually dropped off. I don't know if someone wrote a bad review, or it was a full moon, or what, but it burned my confidence for months afterwards.

You don't have to figure out everything yourself—you can ask for help and inspiration. Reach out to your buddies and coworkers—not everyone will want to talk marketing strategies with you, but someone will. If you can't find someone to do it for free, look online for a marketing consultant. And don't forget, you can talk to the folks who have already responded to your ads. Ask your favorite clients what drew them to you, and for any constructive advice they might have for attracting more of the same.

On the flip side, if marketing makes you feel excited, curious, ambitious, and creative, by all means, get good at it. These valuable life skills translate directly to the straight world, so invest in yourself and take some classes. You can make your talents available to others in the Biz for a fancy fee.

Two great books on marketing yourself as an independent sex worker are *The Internet Escort's Handbook Book 2: Advertising & Marketing* by Amanda Brooks, and *The Sugar Daddy Formula: A Sugar Baby's Ultimate Guide to Finding a Wealthy Sugar Daddy* by Taylor B. Jones. Regardless of your gender or job title, they provide knowledge you can really use about writing catchy copy, figuring out how high net worth individuals think, standing out from the crowd, and so much more.

While I'm no marketing expert, I did learn some lessons the hard way, which I'll share with you, in a little segment I like to call "Debunking Sex Work Marketing Myths."

MARKETING MYTH #1: CHARGE LESS AND MAKE MORE MONEY

It's been a few weeks, business has slowed, and the end of the month is looming. You get online, and all these gorgeous new people are advertising. The competition is looking hotter, fresher, and more intimidating by the minute. You think, *What does every other business on earth do when business is slow? They have a sale! I'll offer a special discount, get a ton of new business, and in a few weeks, raise my prices again.*

It's easy to think like this, but it doesn't work that way. If you're new in town, your rates are twice the competition, maybe you've overpriced yourself for the local market. However, if you've been at this for a while, charging what you've always charged with no other substantial change to your service, then the problem isn't your rate. Maybe your advertising is stale, maybe someone wrote a bad review, maybe the slowdown is seasonal.

Now, it is true if you lower your rates, you'll get new clients. Laws of supply and demand hold true in sex work as in any other business. But attempting to make more money through volume creates all kinds of problems. First off, it takes the same amount of time and effort to see a client no matter what they pay. Earning less money for the same work is demoralizing and a quick way to crash and burn. Also, bargain-hunting clients tend to want something for nothing. You want clients who are comfortable paying your fee, expect to pay for good service, and know that they're getting excellent value.

Another problem is that lowering your rate, even for a few days, sends a terrible signal to your regulars. You'll find even your tried-and-trues will try to negotiate you down because once you've lowered your rate, why should they ever pay your full fee again? Worse, reviewers pay close attention to rate fluctuations, and they spread the word. One time, I thought I'd be nice and took fifty dollars off my hourly rate for someone new because he said he was in medical school. Clearly that's what he wrote in his review, because years later I still had people calling saying they read I offer a student discount.

What happens when you try to raise your rates again? Clients balk. And your bargaining position is weakened because of your special rate last week. You'll find yourself having humiliating negotiations about what you're "worth" instead of what you charge.

Here's the bottom line: you can afford to raise your rates when you can afford to turn business away. When you have enough work lined up so that at the first sign of haggling, you can cheerfully hang up the phone. When you can say, "These days I only have a handful of slots available, and this is what I charge to connect with new friends." End of discussion. That's only possible from a position of strength.

Consider a rate restructure only after business has slowed for several months, and only after you've exhausted all other methods to boost traffic, by updating your photos and ad copy, advertising in new places, making yourself reliably available, and getting constructive criticism from a working buddy, a consultant, or clients.

Have savings set aside so you can ride out an extended slowdown, with enough time to make deliberate changes to your marketing strategy. Don't lower your rates in a moment of panic thinking it'll just be temporary. You'll be shocked at how long the negative consequences last.

MARKETING MYTH #2: I'M SELLING A FANTASY, SO I HAVE TO BE PERFECT

This belief is so persistent throughout the entire industry, and it brings so much pain. Most of us fall far short of the fantasy, and none of us is perfect.

So, just how does the sex industry keep generating billions of dollars every year by mere mortals doing the work? Turns out, what you're selling is *reality*. You provide a sexual experience only you can offer, so just be yourself. Let go of thinking that you have to be flawless. Not only do you waste energy feeling bad about yourself, you squander your very best asset: who you really are. By all means—get professional photos taken with good lighting, look as fabulous as you can. But present honestly. Don't hide what you think are your imperfections in your advertising.

This does two huge things for you: Clients know what they're getting, and when they get what they expect, they are satisfied. And it frees you from the fear your clients will reject you because of those imperfections. Because if they know ahead of time about your acne scars, your dimpled ass, or whatever you think is so weird about yourself, and they still want to see you anyway? Then it doesn't bother them. Maybe it's not as noticeable as you think, maybe you remind them of someone else, maybe they have a cellulite fetish—who knows? The important thing is you can let go of that insecurity, and the two of you can get down to whatever sexy trouble you can make for yourselves.

Imagine the reverse. If your images are airbrushed and cropped and photoshopped—what will clients think when they first lay eyes on you? You're a liar. Projecting a glamorized image of yourself may drive traffic, but it sets clients up for disappointment.

MARKETING MYTH #3: BE EVERYTHING TO EVERYBODY, BUT JUST LIKE EVERYONE ELSE

You spend any amount of time looking at adult ads, and after a while they all look the same. You get the sense that everyone is reading from the exact same script. But as Coco Chanel said, "In order to be irreplaceable, one must always be different."

It's hard to stand out when you're trying to be just like everybody else, only better. My advice is, be unique. Have a point of view. I realize too much "personality" can be off-putting—you do need to market yourself as accessible, not erratic. But as Erika Lyremark points out, author of *Think Like a Stripper: Business Lessons to Up Your Confidence, Attract More Clients & Rule Your Market*, "Originality is filled with energy that everyone is naturally attracted to." Successful brands are based on individuality, not copycat cowardice.

Clients cruising ads are on the prowl for something to catch their eye. Make sure your copy pops and your images capture something specific to you. Have faith that the right clients will find you, because you're sending out signals that you have something unique and wonderful to offer: yourself.

❋ MOTIVATION

One of the hardest things about sex work, whether you work for yourself or someone else, is remaining motivated during tough patches. Only you can determine whether a slow period means it's time to step on the gas or drop out, but it helps to be aware of the signs that you've gone astray. I talk a lot in this book about burning out, but there's another syndrome that is just as pernicious, and that's **FIZZLING OUT**.

FIZZLING OUT

Burnout is **HITTING THE WALL**: *I can't do this anymore!* It's a conscious state—you and everyone around you know when you've reached it. Fizzling out is indifference, complacency, an unwillingness to change. Like a frog in a pot brought to a slow but deadly boil, inertia can accumulate over months and years. Sometimes we are the last to realize how depressed, bored, or frustrated we've become.

What does fizzling out look like? Not doing the little things right. Giving your boss reasons to fire you or your clients to move on. Things like:

- Turning down good work for no good reason.
- Forgetting/skipping calls or shifts.
- Not honoring your posted hours of availability.
- Leaving the same ad up months after responses have dropped off.
- Not keeping up with a work blog or social media account.
- Not returning calls or emails.
- Sending sloppy, unspellchecked emails.

- ✿ Being curt, dismissive, or otherwise off-putting in communications.
- ✿ Multitasking while on the phone or during calls.
- ✿ Arriving late.
- ✿ Not allowing enough time between calls.
- ✿ Showing up unprepared or missing essential gear.
- ✿ Forgetting names or requests.
- ✿ Working while distracted.
- ✿ Working hung over, sleep-deprived, starved, high, drunk, sick, or otherwise not fully present.
- ✿ Oversharing with clients.
- ✿ Overstepping sexual boundaries you regret later.
- ✿ Not keeping your workplace tidy.
- ✿ Not investing in new outfits, toys, linens, gear.
- ✿ Letting your grooming slip—not brushing your teeth, shaving, or showering.
- ✿ Not keeping your costumes, laundry, or toys clean.
- ✿ Forgetting which outfits you've already worn for a client.
- ✿ Taking out your resentment towards one client on other clients.
- ✿ Doing nothing when your photos are robbed and posted on sleazy websites.
- ✿ Not keeping track of cash.

Now, look—I'm not saying you have to be perfect every single minute of every day. Heaven knows, there were times I could barely stay awake through a call, I was so sleep-deprived. I saw clients with five minutes to prepare and the stubbly legs to go along with it. Once you're in a cycle of neglect, though, your business won't get better doing more of the same. Ask yourself if you want to keep doing this job—there's no shame in wanting to quit! You owe it to yourself to choose the work every day that you do it. Don't take your commitment for granted.

Here's an example. A formerly successful incall escort in my social circle noticed that her business had dropped off, so she asked me to help with her ads. Visiting her apartment, I noticed she never dusted. I dropped hints as nicely as I could, but over time, her workplace grew funky. One by one, her clients, sensing the disconnect, went elsewhere. Eyes wide open, she let her lucrative business gradually fade away.

Like I said before, I never saw any self-employed sex worker age out of the business. But I saw plenty drift from making good money, to just getting by, to quiet desperation, to eventually dropping out. Along the way, they stopped doing the little things right. They didn't want to flat out quit the life; instead, they slowly fired themselves.

THAT ONE THING ...

There may be that one thing you just can't stand about the work. Maybe it's the texts and emails. Maybe it's the icky sticky stuff. Maybe it's stage fright. Maybe it's the grinding fear of violent clients. For me, not feeling pretty enough dragged down my days. What do you do when everything else about the job is manageable, but there's that one thing you're always going to hate about it? If there's something standing between you and loving your job, take some time to think about why. Treat it as though it's something a really good friend has to say, because it is—it's you. The single most important relationship you'll ever have with anyone in this lifetime is with yourself.

There most likely isn't an easy fix to that one-damned-thing-I-just-can't-stand issue, because if there were, you'd have done it already, but there's almost always some solution. If screening drives you out of your mind, maybe it's time to sign up with a service. If you can't stand wet work anymore, maybe it's time to switch to something less than full service. Hypnosis can work wonders for stage fright. Cultivating a consistent clientele limits risk. In my case, therapy helped me get to the root of my insecurities. Whatever it is, that one thing that makes you miserable, it's telling you it's time to make a change. Because if you don't, one day you will wake up, and you will be done. It will not be pleasant. It will not be convenient. At the very least, it will bring chaos and pain. One way to stave off that possibility is to make a lateral move.

LATERAL MOVES

Sometimes we just need to shake things up. It's good to try different things to see where our imaginations take off. However, sometimes we get in our own way, holding onto stubborn ideas that keep us stuck in place. If you're feeling burned out, don't limit your imagination, or engage in all-or-nothing thinking:

- ❈ *I'm getting too old for the Biz. I should just quit.*
- ❈ *If I can't charge what I used to, I don't want to do this anymore.*
- ❈ *I can't imagine doing what those [hippies/freaks/losers/perverts] do for cash.*
- ❈ *There's too much competition if I switch.*
- ❈ *I'll lose all my clients if I switch.*
- ❈ *The competition will think I'm a loser if I switch.*
- ❈ *My clients will think I'm a loser if I switch.*

You know what? It's fine to make a change for whatever reason. Don't stress about other people—they spend a whole lot less time thinking about you than you think they do. Don't get hung up on charging less or doing less. Job titles matter very little. What's important is loving your work, loving your life. Honor your sanity—something no one can give you, and no one can take from you.

Sometimes when we're in a funk, it's hard to imagine a different way of doing things, and we need a little nudge to imagine a different path for ourselves. It helps to know why you need to make a change, so give that some thought as well. In the appendix on page 284, I list books and websites for more information on many of these job titles, and here are a few suggestions for lateral moves:

❀ Phone sex if your body is out of commission for a while.

❀ Camming if you're tired of stripping for someone else or making porn.

❀ Verbal domination, fetish and body worship, cross-dressing, and hypnodomination (erotic hypnosis) if you're tired or injured.

❀ No-sex escorting (attending events and dining out) if full service is too much contact.

❀ Tantric or erotic massage or non-erotic hugging (professional cuddling) if full service is too much contact.

❀ Solo (masturbation) porn if full contact porn feels too intense.

❀ BDSM if prostitution or physical contact is getting you down.

❀ Subbing for a pro dom or sharing a dungeon if you need support and community for BDSM.

❀ Working for an escort service or massage parlor if screening is driving you crazy or you need support to feel safe.

❀ Independent escorting if working for a service is no longer right for you.

❀ Teaming up with a buddy as doubles specialists if you need support and community for escorting or erotic massage.

❀ Hiring an assistant and/or driver if screening is driving you crazy or you need support to feel safe.

❀ Finding a couple of Sugar Daddies/Mommies if you need a more structured, regular schedule.

> *Change is a part of life. It doesn't mean what came before was better; it doesn't mean what comes after will be a disaster. It's easy to hold tight to ideas about what makes us who we are, but rather than cling to a certain identity, our true commitment should be to our health, sanity, and authenticity.*

✳ KEEPING UP WITH NEW TECHNOLOGY (OR NOT ...)

Sex times technology equals the future.
—J.G. BALLARD

There's no escaping it—every time someone comes up with a new tech advance, someone will try to find a way to use for it for sex. Two seconds after that, someone else will try to turn a profit from it. Technological advances keep changing the Biz, but as we all know, change can be crazy-making.

I'm not here to offer advice on maximizing your tech prowess; this book is to help you find sanity in sex work and manage your time wisely. It's far more important to use basic technology well than be fluent with every new app. Always chasing the latest thing results in getting very little done. I know I'm howling into the hurricane when I advocate for less social media and more quality interactions in the "real" world as a strategy for staying grounded, but let me state my case just the same.

YOUR AD SAYS EVERYTHING ABOUT YOU

Let's start with the basics. Clear, consistent, and honest advertising creates reasonable expectations. When clients get their expectations met, or better yet, exceeded, they're happy. Happy clients make for a happy business.

All too often adult advertisers don't do the basics well, or try to do too much, or undermine their image. In the past, I've conducted online adult advertising surveys, asking clients what draws them in.

They told me useful ad copy and pretty pictures, and not in that order, so make sure you do those two things well. The very next thing they told me, however, are the professional flourishes that signal a high likelihood of a successful encounter: live links to interesting content, a banner that draws eyeballs, and engaging copy, proofread by someone who can spell. Do these things better than your competitors, if you can. If you can't, hire someone to do it for you.

What turns clients off? Misspellings, bad links, photos that have been obviously photoshopped or retouched to death. Buggy screening forms. Before your site goes live, ask a buddy to go through your site checking all your links and filling out your application to make sure everything operates as it should.

That's the technical stuff. On the creative side, be sure your site tells the story of your working persona. ***Advertising done well does half the work for you.***

SOCIAL MEDIA AS AN ADVERTISING TOOL

Once you've got the basics down, consider your next steps carefully. If everyone else is engaging with clients on social media, don't you have to, too? Not necessarily. In the next section, I discuss imagining your ideal client. If they are under the age of thirty-five, then social media is likely essential to your strategy. Clients in their fifties and sixties, however, at the height of their spending power, are much less likely to care about the latest platform. It helps to be clear on what age group you're targeting in order to advertise accordingly.

If you decide that tweeting, Snapchatting, or blogging should be part of your advertising plan, it should feel alive. A lot of content put out by sex workers isn't good marketing. As sex workers, we're already swimming upstream against stereotypes of flakiness and stupidity. Post only when you have smart, relevant things to say, and stick to a regular schedule. Nothing looks worse than weedy website content that hasn't been updated in months. Clients will assume you've dropped out and will move on to someone else.

Another turn-off is harsh messaging. So many times I've found myself dazzled by an escort's elegant website, only to be horrified by messy rants on their blog or Twitter feed. Tone is so important. All of your public messaging should be in alignment with your working persona. If you want to get political or unload your anger, do it under another name and keep it away from your working website.

Likewise, if your strategy to connect with regular clients is to share details from your personal life, do it from a private account the public can't access, so it feels special. Because it is special.

Above all, and I know this is hard because technology looms so large in the modern world, notice how online time makes you feel. Because all those hours spent in front of a screen, that's not fake life—*it's real life*. Online interactions contribute directly to our emotional state: outrage, fear, excitement, boredom, connection, and isolation. Given how crazy the adult industry can be, setting clear boundaries is critical. Block anyone who doesn't bring you joy, steer clear of content that drags you down, and set limits on the amount of time you spend online.

CLIENTS: AN INTRODUCTION

Hi, Sexy—

When I look back on the thousands of clients I encountered over the years, none was typical. Each brought their own charms and challenges. There were certain types, to be sure: married men, lonely bachelors, closeted kinks, and shy geeks. But one client—I'll call him D—does stand out as elemental.

At first, I liked D a lot. He was young and strong and smelled good. The sex was potent. He loved that I genuinely responded to him. He was a truck driver, distributing goods from the Oakland port throughout the Bay Area. Blue collar, not educated or interesting, but he always showed up on time. My fee stretched his budget so he couldn't see me often, but initially, he never made money an issue. However, after seeing me regularly for about a year, he called trying to negotiate a lower rate, which I refused. As it turns out, he'd lost his job and was having no luck finding a new one.

A few more months went by. Now he'd call wanting to see me for free. He'd want to tell me about his job search and his money problems. How he could no longer afford to buy Rogaine; he was losing his hair. I'd let the answering machine pick up when I saw his number.

My apartment at that time faced east towards downtown San Francisco. My building was set on a steep hill overlooking a gas station, which sat six stories below my window. I'd instruct clients to call me from the gas station pay phone—this was before cell phones were common—so I'd know when they had arrived. A couple of times D called from there, leaving long, rambling mes-

sages, begging me to see him "because things were so good between us." He might have known I was home, looking down on him. He probably guessed I would never pick up again when he called. I wondered just how weird he might possibly get. Not long after, I moved.

D's story illustrates several core client dynamics: the desire for pleasure, escape, and validation. Boundary encroachment. The pursuit of free sex on his terms. Behavior that guaranteed the exact opposite of his aims. Ironically, my sexual attraction to him complicated matters—if he sensed I was only going through the motions, things would have been simpler between us.

As sex workers, we navigate emotional landmines every day. Anyone making a living in the Biz needs to have some curiosity, some working theory about why clients come to see us, and a plan to attract and retain good ones. We need skills to counteract bullshit. I don't claim to have all the answers, but I'll share what worked for me and other successful sex workers I've known.

In this next section, I'll discuss what motivates clients, what they're looking for, what they need. I'll offer my thoughts on the competing pursuits of fantasy and reality. Then I'll talk about sending out the right signals to cultivate a clientele that enriches you. I'll suggest when to cut dead weight, and offer advice on managing coercion and intimidation because, unfortunately, some clients don't ask nicely. Speaking of not nice, I'll make a case for avoiding review sites, if at all possible, because the online world doesn't play by real life rules. And finally, I offer my best heartfelt advice on what to do when a client denigrates, humiliates, or frustrates you—demanding free sex, for example—or otherwise makes you feel like crap.

❀ WHAT DO CLIENTS WANT?

One way to … understand clients is as thirsty men who have found their way to a watering hole rumored by others to be poisoned. Their thirst wars with their fear: the decision to drink is often hard, but drink they do.

—CAROL QUEEN FROM "TOWARDS A TAXONOMY OF TRICKS: A WHORE CONSIDERS THE AGE-OLD QUESTION, 'WHAT DO CLIENTS WANT?'"

For every book or article written on clients, there must be a hundred about sex workers. Our critical gaze locks in on those getting paid. Why be curious about fans and patrons? We already know who they are—they just want to get off. It's easy to dismiss them as interchangeable.

However, anyone who's worked in the Biz for any length of time knows that there's a vast ocean of clients, fans, subs, and patrons out there, and their motives run the gamut. Carol Queen's essay, "Towards a Taxonomy of Tricks: A Whore Considers the Age-Old Question, 'What Do Clients Want?'" outlines many of the reasons clients see prostitutes: a desire for a variety of partners and activities. Convenience. Control. Similar impulses drive the clientele of pro doms, strippers, and porn actors.

Beyond the multiple motivations for seeing a sex worker, clients seek a range of emotional meanings. For some, it's a rare chance to be fully seen, cared for, and fed. Others crave the rituals of romance. I had clients tell me, "I love you," and want me to say it back. For others, avoiding love was the whole point, what I call "EMOTIONAL HYGIENE." Many clients chase their sexual fantasies; however, the opposite is also true. They hunt images, personas, and experiences that spark fantasy, searching for inspiration outside of themselves. Either way, they are driven by not having enough. This is important for understanding why clients behave as they do.

WHAT DO CLIENTS *REALLY* WANT?

Clients may be looking for fantasy, sure. They'll take fantasy, because that's what we offer, and they'll take what they can get. But deep down, many clients are on a hunt for the *real*, albeit in a fantasy, sometimes fantastical, setting. This is why a sex worker's ability to be present and authentic is so potent.

It helps to see things from the client's point of view. During paid sessions, they expose deep parts of themselves, what they crave, who they truly are. For some, this is as real as sex gets. So much of their bad behavior stems from unexamined, unexpressed shame at their helplessness. How terrible it must feel to believe we are unmoved by their desire, and that we only tolerate them because they pay. In the heart of every client, provided they are sane, are these questions: *Am I enough? When I touch you, when I tell you what I'm dreaming of, when I stand before you naked, am I acceptable?* Because they have to pay, they are terrified the answer can never truly be "yes." It is humbling to be in the presence of another person's aching fear. With practice, we can face that insecurity head on, letting them know with our words, our touch, our voice: *There is nothing wrong with you. I am happy to see you there.*

Now, many, many clients are knotted up in rage, it's true—their response to desire and need is fury. They like hating us, and they're not about to let it go. There's nothing to do about people like that except steer clear—you sure as hell don't need that in your life. But plenty of clients aren't. Once we look through the lens of compassion, alert to signs of insecurity and vulnerability, we can identify tenderness, an ache for authenticity and connection. That clientele is both sustainable and sustaining.

I was successful not because I was the most beautiful **PRO-VIDER**; I certainly wasn't exotic or gifted. But I could be kind, which attracted clients who could reciprocate. I offered the gift of gratitude, taking the sting out of my fee. They fed me and gave me the satisfaction of knowing I fed them too.

Here is the truth: As sex workers, if we throw up a bunch of shade, we are guaranteed to get shadow in return. If we promise deep erotic connection and yet deny access to our authentic selves, we can't be surprised when clients bang at our doors, raging to be let in. I'm not saying for a second pour honey on every head—not everyone is receptive to kindness, not everyone is worthy. Some clients make no more impression than a sneeze. But if you want to do this work for any length of time, connection is the path to financial and emotional sustainability. Put another way: if your business plan is to manage constant resentment and emptiness, both your clients' and your own, you will burn out, just as sure as you are reading these words. That is no way to make a life in the Biz.

EXERCISE: YOUR IDEAL CLIENT

In the last section, we identified work personas that complement our natural gifts and maximize our creative fire. Now it's time to complete the other half of the equation: Who is your ideal client? It's easy to think we have no control over our clientele, we just have to deal with whoever picks us, but that is not the case. Once we know what we want, we can focus on attracting it, and let everyone else go by.

Take a few minutes and sit in a quiet place. Find a blank piece of paper to write on. Close your eyes, take a few deep breaths, and imagine your perfect client, someone who leaves you feeling nourished rather than empty or depleted, or at the other extreme, sticky or drunk. Who leaves you with a smile on your face and your brain whirring with new ideas, energized and excited about your next call or shift. Who stimulates your mind, body, and bank account for years to come. You may already have someone in mind, a specific person you're fond of, but for the purposes of this exercise, let's set them aside. We want to focus on broad themes, not get hung up on individuals.

Try some free-form writing about this person: How does this ideal client reach out to you—what's the first thing they say to introduce themselves? What is remarkable about the sound of their voice or the quality of their emails? Do they feel familiar? Exciting and new? Are they professional or informal? Are they straightforward or a bit of a puzzle to be solved? Do they read your rules and follow instructions? How do they talk about your fee? What qualities do they possess that make you instinctively like or trust them? Do they seem confident, like they've done this many times before, or are they nervous, looking to you for guidance? How much do they talk, and what do they talk about? When you say "no" to a request, how do they react? Is this person curious about you and in what way? Do they like you already? Do they like themselves?

Now is a good time to list red flags, as well—those things an ideal client would never do: ask the wrong question, haggle, not keep their word, use profanity. Sometimes the littlest details can be a tell—every client I ever had who insisted on seeing me at an odd time, say, 4:10 P.M., always ended up being a jerk. Turns out, someone who needs to have things exactly their way isn't that much fun to be around. Trust your experience—when you spot a pattern, good or bad, write it down.

> *Once we envision our ideals, our deep intuition can get to work, attracting those who send the correct signals. We cut off those who don't come correct without guilt or second-guessing ourselves.*

❋ PRACTICAL ADVICE: CULTIVATING THE CLIENTS YOU WANT

When we look away from the importance of the erotic in the development and sustenance of our power, or when … we use each other as objects of satisfaction … to refuse to be conscious of what we are feeling at any time, however comfortable that might seem, is to deny a large part of the experience, and to allow ourselves to be reduced to the pornographic, the abused, and the absurd.

—AUDRE LORDE FROM *USES OF THE EROTIC: THE EROTIC AS POWER*

The sad reality is the vast majority of clients aren't ideal—they will test you on your time, your fee, and what you're willing to do. Many will try to bend your rules on all three. Sometimes their methods are subtle, sometimes crazy-in-your-face. Fortunately, problem clients often announce themselves right up front, asking for information clearly posted in your ad, demanding discounts, or requesting unsafe activities—I call them "**BOUNDARY CLOWNS**." This doesn't mean we can't achieve the clientele we want, but we do have to be clear in our communications, and be disciplined in cutting off yahoos.

If you want clients who respect your boundaries… enforce your boundaries. Post your rules prominently, apply them consistently. Reviews (if you allow them) will build your reputation for saying what you mean and meaning what you say. Good clients crave that kind of alignment. Clients who don't honor your rules are timewasters—don't engage them.

If you want clients who don't try to make you do things you don't want to do … be clear about what you offer and how much you enjoy it. Reward good behavior with your pleasure and good cheer. Clients who want to please will keep coming back. Fire those who need to be told again and again how to behave.

If you want clients who are happy to pay, rather than resentful ... demonstrate gratitude. Kiss that stack of bills with a big smile and a "thank you." Clients who want to "help" love a display of appreciation. Cut off clients who play games, like making you ask more than once for your money, or showing up with less than your full fee.

This is a process of cultivation. Jerks will always be a part of the Biz, there's no way to completely avoid them. But cutting off boundary clowns gets you clearer on what a good client looks like. You get better at sending out the right signals. Also, you're doing a service for other sex workers by notifying clients of their unacceptable behavior so hopefully they won't do it again.

Then there are those clients who have nothing else going for them except that one thing they do well. I'm thinking of this one guy I adored who also happened to be boring as hell. He'd tell the same three stories every time I saw him; I never learned a single new fact in his presence. But he never failed to let me know I was the best thing in his day. He'd walk through my door and give me the biggest, softest, most beautiful bear hug that would light up my body for hours. He'd hand over my fee with a smile—he loved taking care of me. Not a looker, not a big brain, not a tiger in bed. But he fed the hell out of me. Even writing about him now, all these years later, he leaves a glow. Gratitude: burnout's kryptonite.

It's helpful to reframe less-than-ideal clients as vitamins. Individually each one may not give you your recommended daily allowance of everything you need, but a killer back rub from one, a healthy political debate from another, a good laugh from a third, and taken together, you can achieve a happy balance.

What to do about the clients with no nutritional value other than showing up on time and paying your fee? Here's a suggestion—try getting curious about them. Use your imagination to find ways to shake up your time together. Ask if they'd be willing to explore something new. They might surprise you, and what do you have to lose? But if shaking things up doesn't help, let those clients go. Not all at once—I'm not suggesting jeopardizing your financial stability by cutting half your business loose. But systematically, say, one a month. Or, if that's too scary, fire your worst regular after establishing a new one you like better.

Make a list of all your regulars and rank them, best to worst. Circle the names of those who drain you, and promise yourself you will cross those names off your list in the next year. Imagine writing down the names of new clients you'll be excited to see again and again. If you backtrack—say that old problem client calls, and you see them out of financial need or boredom or some twisted sense of loyalty, that's okay—maybe they won't be as bad as you remember. Or, maybe they'll be just as soul-crushing as ever, and you can fire them for good.

Another thing you can do is raise your rates for those less-than-optimal clients. Most will move on, no great loss. But a few will pay more, and if nothing else, it's a boost to know they think you're worth it.

MYTH: CLIENTS HATE TO HEAR "NO"

Bad clients want you to say "yes" to everything, and if they can't have that, then for you to say "yes" after you say "no." You don't want clients like that—you don't want people like that anywhere near you. Good clients want to know you have rules, because they have rules. That you take care of yourself, because they take care of themselves. That you have limits, because people without limits are scary. They want to feel safe entering the magic circle of your enchantment, have their sexy fun, and leave knowing nothing will come back to haunt them later.

Here's how I managed this: I'd frame my boundaries not by what I wouldn't do, but what I liked to do. When screening a potential client, I'd say, "I don't do anything illegal or unsafe, and I always reserve the right to say 'no' if I'm not enjoying myself. However, the good news is, if I do something with you, you know it's because I want to be doing it. If the chemistry is right, we can go all kinds of places together."

My spiel attracted clients interested in my authentic presence and pleasure. They knew I'd assert myself, and I valued discretion. A wide range of activities was available if asked for correctly, but not for just anybody—that's what good clients like to hear. Notice there was no room for a conversation about specifics. Anyone wanting to know if I offered kissing or anal or a Porn Star Experience or whatever, would get frustrated and move on, making room for those clients looking to connect on more than one level.

We need to think for ourselves in this business. It's far too easy to get knocked out of our emotional orbits, falling prey to our insecurities. If you assert your boundaries and act professionally and display authenticity—I won't lie—you will lose clients, because each and every marketing choice you make will drive someone away. The important thing is you will also gain business. *These will be the clients worth having*.

TARGET NUMBER FOR REGULARS

Coming back to escorting in my thirties, fresh off a devastating breakup and $123,000 in debt, I had to make as much money as possible without burning out. My plan was to accumulate regulars who'd see me once a week, once a month, or even just a couple times a year. I figured with thirty regulars, my business would be stable. Along with an occasional new client every few weeks, I could meet my financial goals. A target number can be very helpful, even if it's arbitrary at first—yours could be twenty, thirty, or fifty. Over time, you'll get a sense of how many clients you need.

It took me about eighteen months to achieve, but a steady clientele did all kinds of good things for me. Although I always kept up at least one ad so my less-than-regular regulars would know I hadn't left the business altogether, I could cut back on advertising, saving money while limiting my exposure. I could be choosy about taking on new clients, and once I acquired a new, better regular, I could fire my least-favorite old one. Best of all, I could raise my rates with confidence, rather than pretending to be exclusive.

This strategy stood in sharp contrast to my nonexistent business plan from a decade before. In my twenties, I hardly ever fired a client because I was afraid I'd never get another one. As if there was some giant spigot in the sky that would shut off if I said "no." If they didn't stink, weren't rude, and showed up somewhere in the hour we were supposed to meet, that was good enough—I had no faith I could hold out for better. What I didn't know then was I'd only be able to keep working in the long run if I had a clientele I was excited about.

> *Trusting abundance makes it easier to let go of what doesn't work.*

❊ INTIMIDATION AND COERCION

Some clients use intimidation to get what they want, subtle forms of blackmail that fall short of physical violence. They hint they'll write a bad review, complain to management, refuse to pay, call the landlord or the cops. Then there's the threat behind the threat: They'll do something nasty behind your back you won't even know about until it's too late. It is ugly to be coerced into doing something sexual you do not want to do. In the moment, it can be difficult to think clearly, and sometimes it feels safer to comply.

Perhaps some clients don't realize how intimidating they sound. They're excited or are in unfamiliar surroundings, so they ask badly—that's called "**UNSKILLED BEHAVIOR**." It's easy to reject them as assholes, but this can be an opportunity for a teaching moment. Once they're told they'll catch more flies with honey, they straighten right out.

Then there are clients who are deliberately threatening, and they need to be managed. There's no way I can address every situation or offer foolproof advice, but let's game out a few ways to respond when a client makes us an offer they think we can't refuse.

If I'm not nice, what if they leave and don't come back? Short answer? Fuck them. You don't want clients who cross boundaries or make threats—period.

Here is an ironclad rule: If somebody scares you, that is reason enough to ***never, ever see them again***. Three strikes is baseball—this is real life. You have the right to cut someone off the very first time they misbehave. It doesn't make you weak, it doesn't make you overly fearful, it doesn't make you mean. It makes you *safe*. You deserve that. In the moment, you may have to go along, because it doesn't feel safe to say "no." But if you can, do. Hopefully they're decent and once they've realized they overstepped, they'll apologize, and you can continue on. If they don't like it and walk, well then, good riddance.

What if they'll write a bad review? My business will suffer. Predators rely on that kind of thinking. As scary as it might feel, asserting yourself lets them know you won't play their game. Say: "I don't offer [fill-in-the-blank], especially to reviewers. Because then you'll post that, and everyone will expect it. My answer is 'no.'"

Bad reviews are no fun—I get that. But allowing clients to set your boundaries for you is not acceptable. Anyone turned off reading what you won't do isn't a client you want anyway. A review reporting you enforce your rules, no matter how negative, reveals that you respect yourself, and lots of clients are looking for exactly that. And, don't forget, reviewers have their own reputations. Good clients can figure out which reviewers are boundary-pushing assholes—they make themselves very plain. Someone who respects sex workers will be repelled by those reviewers, not by you.

What if they say they'll sic the authorities on me? A client threatens to complain to management, call the cops, or tell your landlord—classic bullying behavior. Most talk big, but are too cowardly to follow through. Most likely, they wouldn't say anything if their true aim was to hurt you, rather than scare you.

There is never any guarantee, but in general, bullies back down when confronted. Call their bluff. Threaten to drag them into it. Let them know that you're not afraid. Tell them all you have to do is say the word, and they'll never be allowed in the club again. Say your landlord is your girlfriend and knows all about what you do, but she'll appreciate the note just the same. Tell them to go ahead, call the cops, and you'll direct them straight to the client's home address. As a general rule, anyone who can afford you has a lot to lose. Most clients don't want to be dragged out into the open any more than you do.

What if they destroy me, defame me, out me, DOX me, etc.? This can happen. I personally know an escort who had all of her personal information dumped online by a disgruntled ex-client after she cut him off. However, it's unlikely. Only someone who already has a screw loose is going to make it their life's work to ruin yours.

Again, never easy as it's unfolding, but you make yourself a less attractive target by being assertive. Bullies are looking for a reaction to their bad behavior. They want to see your fear, your shame, your compliance. My advice is to act bored. "You want to post my home address all over the Web? Go ahead, knock yourself out. Nobody cares. Now please leave." Don't give them the satisfaction of thinking that their threat is significant or exciting.

My final advice is use all available resources to protect yourself, both as deterrence before and then after the fact. That's what your screening protocol, support network, and management are for.

✿ REVIEW SITES

Online is the superhighway to the id.

—MONICA LEWINSKY

I am no fan of review sites. Yelp for sex workers—how can that possibly work in our favor? Online forums are hotbeds of cyberstalking and bullying, where scammers hide behind online anonymity to vent erotic rage, manipulate, and punish.

Review sites are founded on an ugly concept: Clients are entitled to explicitly describe, judge, and dominate sex workers. As if by offering ourselves sexually, we lose all claim to privacy. It is humiliating to have every aspect of our bodies catalogued down to how we groom our pubic hair. Our clients expect discretion, and yet the review boards strip that dignity from us. By detailing blow-by-blow accounts of our sessions, if we perform a certain act with one client, it's presumed that's available for anyone, undermining our authority to give consent.

Hobbyists justify the boards as necessary to keep from "getting robbed." If not fully satisfied, they'll ruin a sex worker's reputation. There's another term for this: sexual blackmail. *Do what I want, or I'll destroy you online.* Truthful negative reviews are scary enough, but the threat of fake bad reviews, impossible to defend against, strikes terror into the heart of any provider who relies on reviews to get business.

Even if reviews are mostly positive, unkind criticisms can get under our skin, eroding our self-esteem, causing us to doubt ourselves. I used to get calls from my working friends in tears over some casual devastating comment they had just read. One friend checked the review sites obsessively, dozens of times a day. She couldn't stop thinking about what other people were writing about her. When someone said anything remotely negative about her, it kept her up at night.

I understand that review sites provide many sex workers with a steady client base, but in my opinion, they carry a huge psychic cost. Research has shown that humiliation is felt more deeply than happiness or anger; online bullying feeds directly into suicidal thoughts; and forced subjugation and helplessness lead to anxiety and depression.

The trap we fall into is believing we have to engage. Consider this: many athletes and actors never read their critics. Nasty little voices inside their heads undermine their excellence, so they don't give them that power. Rather than reading your reviews yourself, I suggest having a trusted buddy read them for you every three to four months, no more often than that. Don't ask for gory details—all you need to know is they're mostly okay. Otherwise, ignore them, unless there is something truly out of line and actionable.

My best advice, however, is don't play the game. People who spend hours on the review boards aren't looking to become regulars. They're McDonalds clients—cheap, fast, and filling for a few hours, but as a steady diet, they make you sick. If you're currently using reviews boards to get business, I suggest you aim to get off as soon as possible. Ask your clients not to review you there, and provide reviews directly to your website instead. Build up your regular clientele from other advertising. Once I had my thirty regulars, I never saw another client who called citing my reviews—just mentioning them was disqualifying.

If you do work the boards, I recommend not feeding the trolls under any circumstances. Don't post looking for advice, because the responses will never be in your best interest. Don't get into flame wars, don't try to shout anyone down—trolls get turned on when you lose your cool. Exercise calm detachment, get what you need exerting the minimal effort required. Most importantly, the day you can be done with them, don't look back.

✴ HEARTFELT ADVICE: WHEN A CLIENT MAKES YOU FEEL LIKE CRAP

Sex work is customer service to the max, and some days it *sucks*. Getting stiffed or stood up. Getting ogled or groped or ignored. Enduring shitty comments, cluelessness, mind games, bad breath, funky toenails. As sex professionals, no matter what, we're expected to look good and smile, even while we're dying inside.

Given that our work is centered in our sexual selves, it often feels easier to just ignore bad feelings and hope they go away. But few of us truly have the ability to shake off negative encounters like they never happened. Instead, hurt and insult fester, poisoning our self-esteem, rattling our minds while shutting our bodies down. Dr. Robert M. Sapolsky, a neurologist who studies the neurobiology of stress, wrote in his essay, "Why Zebras Don't Get Ulcers," social stressors suppress our immune systems, leading to indigestion, insomnia, addiction, eating disorders, eczema, migraines, and so much more. Left unaddressed, these accumulated grievances and ailments lead directly to burnout. So when that crap day comes, recognize it for what it can be: a gift in disguise, a prime opportunity to be good to yourself. So let's get down to it.

First: Take care of your body. When we're humiliated, that hurt has to move through our bodies SOMATICALLY. Very few of us learn this as children. Instead, we're taught to rely on our intellect to process bad emotions. But our minds can't move what's stored in our muscles and joints and voice boxes and bones. So, as soon as you can:

❀ *Get right in the shower.* Wash the day away.

❀ *Eat moderately and mindfully, but only if you're hungry.* Don't starve yourself as punishment or stuff yourself in an attempt to dull the pain.

❀ *Unless the gym is your happiest place on earth, don't force yourself through your regular routine.* That's like piling on extra homework when you're already failing class. You'll either spend that time zoning out, or counting the seconds until your workout is over—neither is good. The best self-care is to be fully present, addressing your feelings directly.

❀ *Scream into a pillow, kick a punching bag, take a long walk or bike ride.* Play loud music, dance like you don't care, sing at the top of your lungs. Move hard and fast and long enough so that you're breathing hard. Wear yourself out with it

❀ *While moving, say what you're feeling out loud:* "Scared, scared, scared, scared." "Ouch, ouch, ouch, ouch." "Pissed, pissed, pissed, pissed." This lets you fully feel your emotions in your body, throat, and mind, allowing that energy to move through you.

❀ *Call a buddy, if you can—get yourself some sympathy, by all means.* For some perspective, it can help to ask the question: *Am I going to still be mad about this a year from now?*

This next step isn't easy, but it's part of the work we all need to do to make this world the place we want to live in. You know that moment of true inspiration—we hear someone righteous speak, or we read about an act of breathtaking kindness? That feeling that swells up in our chest, that poignant blend of awe and tenderness and gratitude, when we think, *Let there be peace on earth, and let it begin with me?* Here's your chance.

I know—it's not fair. Why do we have to be the ones to turn the other cheek when we're depleted and aggravated and insulted? But as the Buddha said, "You will not be punished for your anger, but by your anger." When we fight fire with fire, the whole world turns to ash. Instead, we fight fire with water.

That client who stood you up? Maybe they were in the middle of a shit day far worse than anything you can imagine. Maybe they just lost their job or their grandmother or their dog—send them a blast of unconditional love. That handsy fan with no manners? See them for what they are, someone lost in their neediness, stunted by desire for what feels just out of reach. That stupid, mouthy sub? Muster what compassion you can manage—people with happy lives don't act like fucktards. Picture your tormentor's face in front of you, and breathe into a simple prayer of forgiveness and acceptance.

This doesn't mean you have to be friends—take whatever steps you need to protect yourself in the future. But you are so much bigger and better than how they made you feel today.

While you're doing this, remember exactly who the hell you are—a gorgeous creature of delight, the breath of life. You bring sexual healing and inspiration and excitement into this world. Truly, it's too bad some people can't appreciate all your hard work and accept what you offer graciously. But **you know who you are**. Nobody can take that from you.

That's enough for one day—time for video games. Tomorrow will be a better day.

> Our job in life is to heal ourselves. As we do, we heal the world. We achieve this by first tending to our own needs, then turning our intention to others. It's never easy to extend unconditional compassion to those who have harmed us, but as Socrates said: "Those who are the hardest to love need it the most."

MONEY: AN INTRODUCTION

Hi, Sexy—

At the age of thirty-three, I moved back to San Francisco to return to escorting with one goal in mind: earn money fast. The prior five years had been rough. My partner and I had filed for personal bankruptcy. We had to put our farm up for sale because we couldn't afford the mortgage, but received no offers for more than eighteen months. To pay bills, we'd sold scrap metal and our plasma, and more than once scoured the sofa cushions looking for change to put gas in the car. These were lean, miserable years.

I came back to San Francisco half-convinced I was washed up. I scouted flophouses in the Tenderloin, because I wasn't sure I'd be able to afford a regular apartment. Fortunately, I had working friends to help me. The first three days back in town, I did four doubles. Having $950 in my pocket filled me with such deep relief, I could have wept.

That first week back, walking through North Beach, I spotted a gorgeous silver ring set with a blue pearl in a shop window. I entered and asked the price: sixty dollars. It'd been years since I had spent so much on myself. A little voice inside my head said I needed to be responsible—I couldn't possibly splurge on something so trivial, so I left the shop without it.

Lying awake in bed that night, that ring gnawed at me. The next morning, I went back and bought it. It was my Scarlett O'Hara moment: "I will never be hungry again!" I needed to prove to myself that I believed I could get my financial house back in order again, even after all those horrible years. Sex work requires us to take that leap of faith in our ability to earn over and over again.

In this next section, let's drill down on the emotions of money. How it makes us feel, what the common blind spots are. The sad fact is many top-earning sex workers end up with very little to show for their years in the Biz. That doesn't have to be you, but you cannot make the same mistakes. I'll explore specific money challenges, including earning enough, budgeting, and keeping money safe. I'll offer practical money management advice on how to get financial help, as well as setting goals and celebrating successes. I'll finish with the suggestion that one way to make peace with money is to consider how much we need to be happy, which might just be less than we think.

MONEY EXERCISES

Money is power. To say "yes;" to say "no." To live our lives how we want. Financial experts sell books on how to earn more or manage it better once we've made it. But what I see missing from most money conversations is curiosity about what it means, how it makes us feel, what we believe. It's astonishing that most of us aren't taught how money shapes our self-esteem. Especially for those of us selling our sexuality, it's worth taking the time to think about what we're working so hard for. Not until we turn and face money can we see it clearly.

Money profoundly impacts how we view ourselves. When we have enough, life feels full of opportunity. When barely eking out a living, we feel helpless and hopeless. It eats away at our energy, our self-worth, our ability to sleep through the night, and can be so difficult to talk about. When living hand-to-mouth, eating or paying rent are daily worries—hitting a target number in a budget can feel a million miles away. And plenty of rich people are miserable, proving that lots of money is not the automatic ticket to happiness.

A great book discussing the emotional meaning of money is *The Ask: How to Ask Anyone for Any Amount for Any Purpose* by Laura Fredricks, a successful nonprofit fundraiser. Her key observation is that it's easy to ask others to support worthy causes, but only after we get right with our own deep-seated beliefs about money. If we experience it from a place of fear, shame, a diminished sense of worth, confusion, or scarcity, we continually get in our own way. Fredricks points out that money has the power to determine:

- Where, when, and why we work
- Where we live

- ❀ What food we eat, what clothes we wear, whether we can afford a car and what kind
- ❀ How much we can borrow to buy a house or a car, start a business, or go to school, if we can borrow at all
- ❀ The quality of our health and our healthcare
- ❀ What we do in our free time
- ❀ How often and where we can go on vacation
- ❀ If and when we can retire
- ❀ How much we can save and invest
- ❀ Whether we feel we've made the right choices in life
- ❀ How we are viewed by our friends and coworkers
- ❀ Our status in our romantic relationships and families
- ❀ Whether or not we depend on loved ones, the state, or charity
- ❀ What we can give our loved ones now and in the future.

With all that baggage, is it any wonder that money is emotional? It can be the source of motivation, paralysis, fear, checked out and addictive behavior, guilt and shame, stress, joy, positive self-esteem, envy and greed, inadequacy, resentment, obligation, social awkwardness, dependency, generosity, feeling invincible or defeated, feeling competent or incompetent, and feeling like a grown up or a child. (So, funny thing. If you trade out the "money" for "sex," this list still makes sense. Coincidence? I think not ...)

WHAT DOES MONEY MEAN TO YOU?

Here's a simple exercise. Close your eyes, take a few deep breaths. Say the word "money" out loud.

- ❀ What words, phrases, or songs come to mind?
- ❀ How does it make you feel? Weak or powerful? Proud or shameful? Happy or sad? Afraid or in control? Safe or needy? Loved or all alone?

- ❀ Does money feel like love? Safety? Power? Health? Are these things you can ever have enough of?
- ❀ Is money something that rests inside your body or outside? Does it reside someplace far away where you can't see it, or is it nearby?
- ❀ Are you supposed to have enough money? Is everyone supposed to have enough money?
- ❀ Can you ever have too much money? Can other people have too much money?
- ❀ Do you want to take care of other people, or is your money only for you?
- ❀ Is it okay for you to receive money from other people when you need it, or is it your duty to provide for yourself?
- ❀ How does it feel to ask for money for your sexuality?
- ❀ How does it feel to receive money for your sexuality?
- ❀ How does it feel knowing no dollar amount can equal your sexual worth?
- ❀ What is your ideal relationship to money?

Pick three of the questions from this list that feel easy to answer. Write for five minutes answering them, putting down whatever comes into your mind. Now do the same for the three questions that are hardest to answer.

Take a few more deep breaths, and imagine you just got off work. Sitting right in front of you is a pile of cash you earned today. What does this money mean right now? Write for five minutes about what this money has to say.

- ❀ What do you need to survive? What do you need to be happy?
- ❀ What are you working towards? A target number, or something tangible, like rent, caring for your child, paying tuition, or saving up for surgery?

❀ How does working towards that goal feel? Does it feel impossible? Within reach? Exciting? Deadening? Endless? Not a big deal?

THE SHIT STACK

All of us have done things at work that we really, really, **really** did not want to do. We get home, and all we want is to forget what just happened. And there it sits staring at us, the SHIT STACK, the reason why we did what we did. Let's spend a little time with that dirty wad of bills.

Shit money contributes to a lot of bad behavior in the Biz. It's so easy to run out and blow it all on something to make us feel better. But then it's gone, and we still need money to live. Then we're faced with the prospect of maybe having to do something even worse. We're dirty for what we do to make cash, we're dumb for not managing it wisely. It's a vicious cycle.

Consider a cleansing ceremony for the shit stack—for all the money that we bring in, in fact. Create a ritual to discharge any negativity, and to let gratitude and abundance in. Designate a special place for it to sit for a time. Place it on an altar that you create to your goals, or in a sunny window, or in front of a picture of your child or your pet or your hero/ine. Stick it to the refrigerator with silly magnets. Let it air out, and absorb the love and clear intention you need to thrive. Let that money be restored to its rightful purpose: a resource that earns what you deserve in this world.

> *Money's importance is so huge that we often can't see it for what it is, a river of energy running through our lives. We can't help but manage money poorly when we turn a blind eye to what it really means to us.*

✳ PRACTICAL ADVICE: MONEY CHALLENGES

You must gain control over your money or the lack of it will always control you.
—DAVE RAMSEY

Sex + money = the sex industry. In sex work, there are endless emotional pitfalls around money, including reckless spending, **POVERTY CONSCIOUSNESS**, and poor decision-making.

It's all too common for sex workers to flame out after a couple of years with nothing to show for it—I don't want that to be your fate. **You don't have to make a ton of money to handle it wisely**. In fact, it makes doing the right thing even more important.

Trigger alert: I'm about to let all my middle-class biases hang right out here. I recognize not all sex workers will be able to follow my advice. Let me just say, however, even though I had a college education, money management took me a more than a decade to grow into. I needed a lot of handholding from an accountant who taught me how to save and invest—I never would have done it on my own.

As for you, I want you to be really good at money. This means having the practical skills and knowledge to manage it wisely, and the emotional wisdom to be in charge. Fortunately, there's no need to reinvent the wheel for day-to-day money management. Critical skills such as budgeting and managing credit scores, debt, and cash flow are the same as for other self-employed folks. For personal financial management advice, check out the resources in the appendix on page 273.

In this next section, I offer practical advice to address emotional money concerns: making enough and keeping it safe. Understanding how money makes us feel, and letting go of negative mental patterns. Taking charge, so our money works for us rather than the other way around. I'm a fan of investment, no surprise, and hope that not only your present is secure, but that you are saving for your future, whether that means a degree, house, business, retirement fund, surgery, or new life.

If you believe that's not possible, why not? Are you afraid you'll have to do everything yourself? You can get help. You'll have to keep secrets? You can find a financial advisor you can be honest with. You can't have nice things? Well, I call bullshit on that. Let's take some time to explore our sex-work-specific anxieties about managing finances, and put them to rest.

HOW DO I KEEP MY MONEY SAFE?

First things first: You must protect what you earn. Money is always safest sitting in a bank. Anyone in a cash business is vulnerable; sex workers doubly so. Not only is your hard-earned cash vulnerable to robbery, any bills found in a bust stuffed in your mattress or freezer will be confiscated. Whether or not you're convicted or even charged with a crime, you will never see that money again. Therefore, keep no more cash on your person, where you live, or where you work than you can afford to lose. Talk to your legal advisor about any legal recourse you might have if you get robbed.

ALWAYS HAVE MONEY SET ASIDE

I do not ever want you to accept a gig or a shoot or a shift that feels wrong. Before you do anything else with your cash, set aside a cushion to take care of your basic needs for at least three months. Savings mean you can afford to innovate and experiment. You can convey strength when screening clients. *Having the freedom to walk away at any time is the greatest wealth there is*.

For some of you, this may seem out-of-reach. You're working just to get by, with nothing left over. You've never been good at saving, all you ever do is spend. All I can say is, what is the plan if you get hurt or sick and can't work? Saving money is a habit; not saving money is a habit. I'll explain how I did it in this next section.

HOW DO I BUDGET AND CONTROL MY EXPENSES?

Has money always felt overwhelming and confusing, or like it belonged to other people but not to you? Many of us are attracted to sex work because those lump sums of cash make us feel rich for the first time in our lives.

Do you operate from a budget so you know your mandatory expenses? Because sex work income is almost always erratic, it's important to know how much you need to earn every month in order to break even. Also, as you probably already know, most sex workers experience seasonal slowdowns due to holidays, the school calendar, tax season, etc. I recommend either setting savings aside during your busy months so you have reserves during the lean times, or constructing your monthly budget based on projections of your slowest month.

Here's a simple monthly budget: tally up all of your regular expenses. Add 20% for incidentals, emergencies, and unexpected needs. Divide that by your average shift, session, or shoot—that's your target goal to break even for the month. My best advice is to hit that target by the end of the second week every month if you can, by the end of the third week if you must. That gives you a time cushion if business is slow.

The easiest way to save is to make it a habit, because we can always come up with excuses to spend. Here's how I managed my money when I worked as a call girl, putting ten percent into savings right up front. I kept seven envelopes labeled:

- ❀ Rent ($1,350)
- ❀ Food/Household Supplies ($600)
- ❀ Utilities/Health Insurance ($500)
- ❀ Reinvestment in my business ($300)

- ❀ Taxes (10%)
- ❀ Savings (10%)
- ❀ Discretionary

At the beginning of each month, I'd put forty dollars of each one hundred dollars earned (40%) towards rent, then ten dollars of each one hundred dollars earned (10%) into each of the other six envelopes. I'd use this breakdown until I earned rent for that month, and then set that envelope aside. After that, I'd put fifty dollars of every one hundred dollars earned (50%) from each call towards food and supplies, and ten dollars in each of the other five, until I hit that mark, then set it aside. Then the same for utilities and insurance, and reinvestment. Once I'd met all of my basic expenses, any money earned after that for the rest of the month would go to savings and discretionary spending, split fifty-fifty, after I set 10% aside for taxes. As Warren Buffett says, "Do not save what is left after spending, but spend what is left after saving."

At the beginning of each month, I might only be able to afford a movie or a burrito for fun, but by the end of the month, new boots. I knew I always had money set aside to tide me over the inevitable slow weeks and winter months, and core expenses were covered so I wouldn't have to scramble to cover my phone bill. No matter what, I'd always tithe ten percent to taxes and another ten percent to savings—I didn't even have to think about it. This system worked great for me—feel free to modify it so that it works for you.

WHAT IF I CAN'T MAKE ENOUGH MONEY?

I do not know your situation, where you live, your appearance, or your health. The last thing I'd ever want to do is make you feel ashamed or inadequate. But if you're barely scraping by in this work, that is not a good place to be.

Are you burned out? Have you fizzled out? Be honest with yourself about whether you're showing up all the way, managing your brand, making yourself available, and executing a well-thought-out marketing plan.

If those things seem solid, then perhaps it's time to enlist outside help. You can ask a buddy if they'd be willing to give you an honest assessment of your photos, website, and fee structure. Another way to get feedback is to hire a consultant. There are successful escorts, porn stars, and pro doms who offer their expertise for a fee to help you target your clientele. In the appendix on page 284, I list resources on most job titles, including professional domination, escorting, stripping, becoming a Sugar Baby, camming, etc. Sometimes a lateral move can raise your earning potential; there's also the possibility of relocating. What you offer might be better appreciated in a town with a different culture or clientele.

Finally, there is always the possibility that you aren't cut out for the work—there is absolutely no shame in that. It is far, far better to arrive at that conclusion yourself than to limp along until a crisis drives you from the Biz for good. If you're meant to do this, be the best damned sex worker you can be. If you suspect it's no longer a good fit, take some time with that idea, and follow where it leads.

WHAT IF I CAN'T MAKE AS MUCH MONEY AS [FILL-IN-THE-BLANK]?

The sex industry is a cutthroat climate, and it can be hard to feel secure. Very few of us have the total package. Most of us work knowing that in some way or another we fall short of the ideal. Since I was always insecure about my appearance, I'd tell myself I couldn't make as much money as the women I thought were so gorgeous. I couldn't shake that feeling even after attracting hundreds of clients, building up a loyal clientele, and earning six figures a year.

Looking back on all that wasted time and energy, my advice to you is: ***Don't compare yourself to others***. When we compare, we despair. You have no way of knowing what's going on inside another person. Look at how many movie stars and models crash and burn—they have money, beauty, fame, yet still they feel inadequate—it just seems to be the human condition.

Then there's that coworker who is always flashing their cash, boasting about some big score, or dropping their outrageous hourly rate into every conversation. That's all they have holding themselves together—without it, they'd be nothing. Just so you know, though, it's a dirty little secret—sex workers lie about what they earn. If not lie exactly, then inflate. Exaggerate. Extrapolate the rate they commanded on their most extravagant call to all of their business. Hey—we're all guilty of it at some time or another. It stems from insecurity, but it's understandable, considering we do the most intimate work imaginable.

You're three steps ahead of everyone else when you focus on what *you're* doing. Not wasting energy feeling inadequate is a gift to yourself. Take time every day to say out loud: "I am enough, I do enough, I have enough." Take into account your true wealth and worth, including your peace of mind.

I JUST MADE $$$$—I'M RICH, BABY!

In sex work, there's a flip side to feeling like we don't have enough, and that's the illusion that big lump sums solve everything. Not true. No matter the dollar amount, your fee alone does not secure genuine wealth.

In psychology, there's a principle called "INFLATION-DEFLATION," which describes the need to inflate one's ego in order to avoid feelings of insecurity and worthlessness. When we aren't grounded in healthy self-esteem and a realistic sense of ourselves, we swing wildly back and forth between two extremes: either we're on top of the world, or we're nothing. This leads to what I call "WHOO-HOO!" THINKING, or the irrational belief that sex work will provide endless easy money, and planning, saving, and budgeting will never be needed ever again.

It's that high we get when we make a ridonkulous sum for doing something sexy, and cash raining down on our heads feels like the

new normal. *I'm a genius! I'm the best! I've got this all figured out!*
Because that money happened so quickly, we tend not to treat it
carefully.

The downside to this juicy rush is what happens when the
phone stops ringing and the money stops pouring in. So we get mad
at the world: *I hate this town. I hate my clients. This job is fucked up.*
Or we're faced with the sickening prospect that we are to blame: *I'm
so stupid. I'm a piece of shit. I've totally ruined my life.*

The worst disaster in life can be achieving early success without
knowing why. For many sex workers, the job starts out as easy money,
and then gets harder. Or, to be more exact, something that resembles
reality. If you believe your job is robbing idiots blind, check yourself,
because that business plan requires an endless supply of rich idiots.
Knowing you offer value and believing those who seek your services
deserve value is a sustainable mindset.

SHOULD I DECLARE WHAT I EARN?

You and your money are safest when you handle it above board.
Deposit all cash and checks directly into a savings institution, like
a bank, credit union, or brokerage account. Declare every penny to
the IRS, and pay your taxes like every other law-abiding citizen. This
does two great things for you. First, you're operating under the law,
always a good thing. Also, you're paying into self-employment, Social Security, and Medicare. These benefits may seem far off in the
future while you're young and healthy today, but believe me, you'll
be glad to get them when you're older.

I know that temptation when you have a fat stack in hand. You
earned your money the hard way—why give any to the government?
However. Undeclared cash is nearly impossible to invest. Living expenses and consumer goods are things that only depreciate in value.
I've never known anyone who was able to retire on a closet full of
handbags and platform shoes.

I'm not a tax professional, but it's been explained to me that
the IRS doesn't care how you make your money. However, hiding

earnings is a crime, one they take seriously. Call yourself a consultant, performer, masseur/masseuse, event planner, video artist, excitement specialist, or any other damned thing you please, they just want their cut.

If you don't like the idea of paying taxes on your income, you'll like an audit even less. If the IRS suspects you operate an undeclared all-cash business, they will investigate. They have the right to assess your records and assets, including entering your home and place of business and itemizing your personal belongings. If you can't account for how you paid for things, they'll assume you bought them with undeclared funds and extrapolate your earnings from your hourly rate. You'll be on the hook for back taxes plus applied interest and penalties.

Here's the thing—that lump sum may make you feel rich in the moment, but how wealthy are you if you can't spend it how you want? If your goal in sex work is to build a future, buy a house, pay off student loan debt, or start your own business, then you have to declare your earnings. The good news is once that money is taxed and legal, it is yours for life.

WHAT IF I HAVEN'T FILED TAXES IN YEARS?

Interacting with the IRS can bring up all kinds of fear and shame. Fear we'll lose everything. Shame we let ourselves get into this mess in the first place. We didn't declare our earnings and file returns because we didn't pay taxes, but now we live with the threat of the IRS tearing our lives apart. It takes a lot of courage to come back into the light, and often it takes emotional repair work as well. We need to forgive our younger selves for putting us in this position. We need to thank them for taking us this far, for keeping us safe as best they knew how, but also let them know their way of doing business isn't working any more. There comes a time when an older, wiser version of ourselves needs to manage the finances.

It's never too late to file returns, pay back taxes, and get right with the IRS. However, you'll need a good tax professional and the determination to see a long process through to the end. Don't let your fears stand in the way of reestablishing yourself and reaping the benefits, such as repairing your credit, applying for jobs, buying a home, qualifying for Social Security and Medicare, and all the rest. We all make youthful mistakes. What's important is to not compound them by remaining stuck in the shadows.

FINDING TAX AND LEGAL ADVICE

To open a brokerage or checking account, there's no need to tell anyone what you do for a living. However, a tax preparer or investment advisor probably should know in order to give you the best advice. Ask your buddies who they use, but if you can't find someone that way, you'll have to find one yourself. Check out the Kink Aware Professionals Directory, and Mistress Lori A. St. Kitts's terrific book, *The Tax Domme's Guide for Sex Workers and All Other Business People* for references for financial professionals. If you can't find the help you need locally, you may have to work remotely.

When interviewing prospects, be honest about what you do. Don't roll your eyes, use air quotes, crack jokes, drop gory details, or otherwise undermine your authority, even if you're feeling uncomfortable. If you don't take your job seriously, you can't expect them to either. Remember: you're hiring them for their professional expertise, not to be your pal. Ask them point blank if they are okay with the fact that you work in the sex industry. Give them time to answer honestly; sometimes people need a moment to figure out how they really feel about something. If the situation doesn't feel right, honor your gut. Say politely but firmly, "This is not a good match moving forward, but thank you for your time," then leave. Don't pay a professional to make you feel terrible.

Escorting in my thirties, I worked with a sex-worker-friendly CPA; he also had a law degree, which came in handy. He insisted I declare my earnings and pay taxes. He helped me start a SEP and Roth IRA, along with a 401(k), and made sure I put in the maximum allowed by law every year. He took my future seriously, helping me feel safer about my money. More than that, he helped me imagine myself to be someone who would always be financially secure. This kind of care is possible for you, too—don't stop looking for the help you deserve until you find it.

BAD DEBT

Credit card debt is like excess weight—all it does is make life harder. Every month, it means throwing hard-earned cash away to pay interest. Even worse, the consumer goods we tend to buy with credit cards don't appreciate, but become junk over time.

For some, shopping and debt are sicknesses of the soul. If you find that your spending situation is out of control, consider joining Debtors Anonymous or Shopaholics Anonymous. It can be helpful to spend time with people with the same struggles. Also, these programs have helpful frameworks for understanding the underlying emotional logic of destructive shopping. If your spending habits don't rise to this level, but you need help, *How to Get Out of Debt, Stay Out of Debt, and Live Prosperously,* by Jerrold Mundis, is a useful book on the subject.

Unfortunately, student loans, which used to be universally seen as good debt, have become problematic. Mortgaging future earnings to earn a degree to increase future earning power used to be a no-brainer; now it's often a nightmare, saddling us with decades of useless loan payments that slow us from achieving anything else in life.

Bad debt sucks. And it's pretty easy to beat ourselves up if we find ourselves with a pile of it. As someone who returned to prostitution to retire $123,000 of bills after filing for personal bankruptcy, I can tell you, it left me with a mountain of emotional cleanup work. It took me years to feel like I was a grown-up again, someone who could be trusted to take care of herself. I needed to grieve that wasted time, and forgive my younger self for all the mistakes she made.

Escorting to pay off those debts had a complicated effect on my sense of self. Early on, there were days where I felt like a dumb loser who knew nothing about money, digging out of an endless hole. I felt like I'd ruined my life. But over time, as I paid my creditors off and my business grew, sex work began having the opposite effect, boosting my self-esteem. Soon enough, I was able to start saving. I could see that money in the bank growing into a nest egg that would care for me in my later years. My successes made me feel competent and accomplished.

If you are doing sex work because of bad decisions you made in the past, **don't beat yourself up**. The world isn't a better place when you wallow in self-loathing; you don't earn good karma by punishing yourself. Learn from your mistakes, and give yourself credit for taking responsibility for your actions. This situation is temporary, and in time, you'll move on to the next phase of your wonderful life.

TARGET GOALS

I'm a firm believer in setting target goals. In the introduction, I mentioned how target goals function as a sort of mental GPS. We program in where we want to go, and our brains chart the course on how to get there. *The Power of Habit: Why We Do What We Do in Life and Business* by Charles Duhigg is an excellent book on how we can train our minds to break bad habits and make good habits second nature. Duhigg points out that setting clear intentions is only half the job. The other half is acknowledging our achievements on the way to our goals. So often we ignore our progress, and then wonder why we can't stay focused. We may be human, but our base motivations are the same as any other mammal: when we're good we need a pat on the head and a treat.

If you're working towards a financial goal, visualize the progress you're making. You know those money thermometers nonprofits use to show how much they've raised? Make one for yourself and color it in as you put money away. If your aim is earning a college degree, post the list of requirements, and cross each one off every time you complete a paper or pass a class. Give yourself a gold star, while you're at it. Let yourself feel proud of what you've achieved. Whatever reason you got into sex work—to pay for surgery or rent, retire a debt, save for school, or care for your child—create a checklist with the steps to achieving your aim, and find ways to reward yourself along the way.

CELEBRATING MILESTONES

Whenever you reach a significant milestone—saving a big round number, scoring your thousandth client, retiring on your terms, whatever it might be—celebrate the hell out of it! Lord knows we drag our failures around like a sack of rocks.

We sex workers seem especially prone to ignoring our achievements, because to the straight world, our lives aren't worth memorializing. Aside from the AVN awards, most of us never earn a trophy for what we do. Of course, many of us were taught that it's wrong to draw attention to ourselves, or we don't deserve anything special just for doing our job. Well, screw all that. Attention must be paid.

Tara Burns, self-described ecowhore hobostripper, built an altar to honor the blowjobs she gave to pay off the land she owns in Alaska. One escort friend of mine performed a ritual celebrating the fact she made it to menopause without getting pregnant. Another escort friend threw herself a retirement party, inviting both her favorite clients and her fellow whores to celebrate her twenty years in the Biz.

When I finally dug myself out of debt and paid off my last creditor, I rewarded myself with a trip to Paris. I bought the cheapest ticket, slept on a friend's sofa, and ate bread and cheese for a week because I couldn't afford to eat out. I wasn't rich, but I was free. No better way to celebrate than a week in the City of Light.

> *Do not sell your efforts short—only you know what you had to do to get where you are. Sex work is hard work that requires bravery every day. Give the people who love you an opportunity to honor you, to be inspired. Write your accomplishments into the Book of Life through ceremony, spectacle, and celebration.*

�֍ VOLUNTARY SIMPLICITY

I talked about the emotional side of finances; they can have a spiritual dimension, too. One path to having a healthier relationship to money is to need less. The **VOLUNTARY SIMPLICITY** movement is a lifestyle that promotes self-reliance, ecological awareness, mindfulness, frugality, and disengaging from consumption. For those of us taught to measure success through earning more and buying more stuff, living simply can be a radical exercise. It can free up energy to make room for artistic pursuits, personal growth, and community.

Now, frugality isn't for everyone. For some, it will never feel like anything other than poverty. However, if you're someone who can never have enough, maybe you don't need more. You might consider rebalancing your relationship to external markers of success.

Plenty of books and blogs offer tips on how to downsize your living space, make do with less, or move away from fossil fuels—I won't advise you on all the broader points here. I bring up voluntary simplicity because it can be a powerful antidote to the toxicity of the sex industry's obsession with youth, image, and conspicuous consumption. We can feel endless pressure to present a glamorous look and bottomless appetite, at the very real cost of disconnection from our true selves. If you feel like superficiality is poisoning your life, you might consider a recalibration.

One way to disengage from the fantasy paradigm is by cultivating a **NORMCORE** look, wearing minimal makeup and ordinary street clothes instead of lingerie, designer clothes, and costumes. You might market yourself as someone who looks, talks, and sexually engages from a genuine place, willing to prepare a home-cooked meal rather than going out to a fancy restaurant. Your business might slow down, but not necessarily—there will always be a market for authenticity. For many clients, accessing the real is the dream.

Another possibility is to move away from mainstream genital and body-based sexuality. You might consider Tantra, erotic energy work, sensual massage, and other heart-based connections. For many, this can be a spiritual calling, trading "easy money" for integrity and clear intention.

> *Freedom from want is necessary for security;*
> *freedom from always wanting more is necessary*
> *for serenity. If we find ourselves running after*
> *something mindlessly, we must stop and face what*
> *chases us. It is valuable to know what we can truly*
> *live without, and the minimum we require to be*
> *comfortable.*

PART THREE:
SEX WORK AND SELF-CARE

In touch with the erotic, I become less willing to accept powerlessness, or those other supplied states of being which are not native to me, such as resignation, despair, self-effacement, depression, self-denial.

—AUDRE LORDE FROM *USES OF THE EROTIC: THE EROTIC AS POWER*

SEX WORK AND SELF-CARE: AN INTRODUCTION

Hi, Sexy–

We have come so far, conquering our demons and mastering the tools in our toolbox. Now it's time to pay some sweet attention to the mind-body connection, because self-care is the key to successful sex work.

I had to figure this out the hard way. When I worked in my twenties, what I thought I needed was for sex work to be fun. It had to thrill me, turn me on, take me places I'd never been. I pulled all kinds of crazy shit—having sex with clients on a bunk bed in a lesbian punk rocker's apartment where I was cat sitting. Travelling to sketchy parts of town without anyone knowing where I was going. Stepping into three-ways already in progress with total strangers. I met all kinds of people, had all kinds of adventures, and made fast cash along the way.

*But there was a serious downside—I had zero skills for when things turned **not** fun. I'd scream at club patrons and get them eighty-sixed for looking at me funny. I'd kick clients out of my apartment for tiny infractions, then get paranoid they'd retaliate and not answer my phone for days. One afternoon I walked out of a strip club mid-shift because I was bored.*

In my thirties, my outlook was completely different. Sex was a job now, a means to an end. I didn't expect it to entertain me; it was simply the fastest way I knew to make money. My number one goal was avoiding burnout.

A funny thing happened when sex work was no longer a sport, but a routine that required a healthy body and clear mind: the ex-

perience vastly improved. I screened rigorously, knowing a single asshole could rattle me for a week. I enforced my rules, because I knew I'd regret letting down my guard, even with clients I liked. I kept regular hours, rather than turning on my phone only when I felt like it, improving the quality of my clientele and making my earnings more predictable. I fired marginal clients to be available for better ones. In other words, I upped my game. Sex work became satisfying in a way it never had before.

So let's talk about self-care, what it takes to keep your mind fresh and open, your body sound and healthy. In this section, we'll discuss your support system, including buddies, coworkers, and a good therapist. I'll offer suggestions on how to manage trigger states, such as hunger, loneliness, and fatigue, to avoid the pitfalls of misusing food, drugs, and alcohol. I'll look ahead to the winter months, because that's an especially treacherous time of year for sex work. I'll address dissociation, because checking out can be an occupational hazard. And finally, I'll make the case to never forget pleasure. As Dr. Frank-N-Furter sings: "Don't dream it—be it."

✽ YOU NEED A BUDDY—BETTER YET, A BUNCH

Here's my dear friend, K, on how badly we all need working buddies: "Oh, my gosh, yes. Just try to keep your sanity sitting alone around your apartment all day and the only people you ever talk to are clients. And you're too afraid to go out to a bar or café or take a class because the very first question anyone asks is, 'So, what do you do for a living?' You've gotta have friends, girl, or you'll lose your mind!" Or as my close friend, C, likes to say: "It takes a village to raise a whore."

The shyness that runs through our industry is incredible, considering we're professional exhibitionists. For many of us, secrecy is the only way to feel safe, so we reflexively push people away in self-defense. Carol Queen tells the story of encountering a woman at a sex worker rights conference who had been in the Biz for years without ever meeting a fellow prostitute. Isolation can lead to depression, paranoia, and self-destructive behavior. I don't want that fate for you, Sexy Reader. Sex work can only be fulfilling when you have support.

I encourage you to act courageously when you meet someone in the Biz you think might be buddy material. Be direct, stating your intentions clearly: "Hey, you seem great. Any chance you'd like to meet and do something outside of work, just friends? No pressure." Light, breezy, no obligation. If they turn you down, no big deal. If someone suitable sends "Let's be friends" signals, be open to saying "yes." Accept social invitations even if you're not certain. Give new people a chance—don't make excuses and slink home to isolate. By being yourself and making yourself available, the right people will find you.

I have a few words of caution about the dynamics of friendship in the Biz, however. As important as community can be, sharing a common experience isn't always enough. This lesson didn't come to me easily: some people in the industry only want to be around you if you behave a certain way. If you don't, they withdraw or lash out. Be careful about giving your time to users just to avoid feeling lonely.

Sex work seems to attract certain personality types, like winners who only want to be around other winners. These are the people who never stop boasting about their latest most amazing achievements, who always have some new big "wow!" in their lives. Now, sure, an upbeat attitude is a good thing; but the inability to tolerate negativity is a defense mechanism to stave off feelings of inadequacy. These folks need to keep their flaming amazeballs in the air, because if one ever hits the ground, it will be a disaster. But here's the thing: sooner or later in sex work, balls fall. Don't be surprised if they don't have time for you when you're feeling sad or insecure.

On the other hand, be careful about those people who only love you when you're down. They have all the time in the world to listen to your problems or feed your outrage, but when you have good news to share, do they need to take you down a notch?

If someone is emotionally limited, that's okay. It doesn't mean you can't be friendly—just know they aren't about to change to meet your needs. Be honest with yourself about how they make you feel and maintain some distance. Sometimes we have to protect ourselves from people we want in our lives, but who are draining.

There can be other challenges to getting the support we need. Sometimes the most sex work-positive friends are the first ones to pressure us to get out when things get tough. Coworkers can feel threatened if we talk about wanting to leave the industry. It's not always easy to be genuine and not just talk in a way others want to hear.

My advice is to be direct and say out loud what support feels like for you. This requires both bravery and vulnerability, but there is no shame in teaching others how to love us better. One dear friend of mine is the best at this—whenever I'm in crisis, she doesn't try to be a mind reader. She simply asks, "What do you need from me right now?" A reality check? Reassurance? Advice? A shoulder to cry on? Active, loving listening? The best way to get the help you crave is to tell people what you need. Don't assume they know, don't make them guess.

My final piece of advice, and this is critical: **Make time for the people who count.** I know the job means crazy schedules and last-minute clients, but as the saying goes: Friends are like teeth—ignore them, and they go away. Be available to those precious folks who can accept all of our highs, lows, and mixed-up middles.

> *Making friends isn't just about getting our needs met. In building community, we give our lives meaning and richness by supporting others in return. We build emotional fortitude to be more gracious, more patient, more skillful in our work. Allied, fortified, and fully nourished, we can make the most of our gifts.*

❋ GET YOURSELF A GOOD THERAPIST—NO EXCUSES!

Compassion is not a relationship between the healer and the wounded. It's a relationship between equals. Only when we know our own darkness well can we be present with the darkness of others. Compassion becomes real when we recognize our shared humanity.

—PEMA CHÖDRÖN

It's a bitch, but negative emotions are a huge part of sex work—ignore that fact at your peril. Sex work carries tremendous stressors from all quarters. Even if you happen to be 100% okay with yourself, clients will show up on your doorstep bearing shitballs wrapped in shiny paper to set on fire right in front of you. Sooner or later, you'll find yourself managing other people's unconscious behavior soaked in self-loathing, resentment, and revulsion.

This work will let you know exactly where your wounds are and just how deep they go. If you wrestle with your weight; hate the way you look; have trouble asserting yourself or **CODE-SWITCHING** or maintaining clear boundaries or controlling your anger; have issues with authority, addiction, or keeping secrets; struggle with knowing what you want to be when you grow up or feeling connected to community or managing your money or making peace with your religious upbringing, sex work will gouge away at all that and more with a grapefruit spoon.

On the flip side, your baggage will be with you no matter what you do for money. Hopefully, sex work will give you the resources, time, and motivation to deal with it. If you commit yourself to being clear-eyed and truthful, dedicating yourself to self-care and lovingk-indness, you can get powerful work done, but you need someone you can talk to. Do not attempt sex work without a good listener in your life, someone trained to listen without judgment.

Therapy is a challenging, dynamic process that often isn't fun. Kind of like working out with a personal trainer, the individual sessions can be painful, and the long-term benefits aren't apparent for months or even years. So why do it? Because humans need to tell stories. We can do this on our own by journaling, making art, writing punk rock songs of murderous revenge, drafting letters we never send, ruminating for hours, and shouting ourselves hoarse as we hurtle down the freeway.

But an emotional alchemy occurs when another person who has earned our trust sits with us and allows us to say aloud whatever dark and dangerous thing we house in our core. It is an incredible gift to be fully seen and heard. The term, when done with kindness and wisdom, is "being held," such a lovely turn of phrase. Our stories, no matter how dreadful or unimaginable, become digestible. Our psyches are then able to break down meanings and incorporate them into our broader sense of ourselves.

What if you want to rely on your friends as your support network instead? Perhaps you're blessed with gifted amateurs in your life with loads of time to hear you out whenever you need it, but treating friends as therapists all the time makes you a lousy friend, just as treating partners as sex workers all the time makes you a lousy lover. I lost a longtime friend over exactly this. I'll never forget her pain, as she refused professional help. Whenever I'd suggest it, she'd bark, "What you're basically saying is I should pay someone to be my friend." She believed she should get what she needed from her social network. She wore a lot of people out, including me, I'm sad to say.

There are a lot of objections to therapy: It's expensive, and you shouldn't have to pay somebody to listen to your problems. How can you be expected to expose the rawest and most private parts of yourself to a total stranger? There's something so cold and artificial about relegating your emotional life to a fifty-minute session once a week. But, notice something about those objections? It's the exact same case against seeing a sex worker.

What a good sex worker and a good therapist share is the gift of their professional attention to something most of us do intuitively. If they're any good at what they do, they can set themselves aside to focus on you, the client. That's a true gift. (It also makes counseling a natural next career for sex workers, but that's a topic for a later chapter.)

My suspicion is that the fundamental objection to therapy stems from the belief that it reflects badly on us; it means we're selfish or defective or weak. We shouldn't let stuff get to us, and if it does, we should be able to work it out on our own. Well, I haven't lived forever, but up until now, I've noticed things don't work that way. Our wounds don't heal until we confront them; the only way out is through.

If you're worried about finding a therapist who won't judge you (no therapist should do that, but I understand the concern), a great place to look is the Kink Aware Professionals Directory. Take the time to find someone you feel deep compatibility with, because this is an investment in your ability to do sex work over time. For those of you on tight budgets, many therapists offer sliding scales. Another option is to looks for universities in your area that offer advanced degrees in psychology, social work, marriage and family therapy, or counseling—their graduated interns need hundreds of supervised counseling hours to meet their licensing requirements. Interns charge well below the market rate of fully licensed therapists, sometimes as low as ten or twenty dollars a session. The bad news is internships last only a year or two, which means you may have to say goodbye before you're ready to terminate the relationship. Check the appendix on page 281 for other low-cost mental healthcare resources.

> We arrive on this earth like kittens, filled with wonder and excitement and pure joy. Somewhere along the way, no matter how loving our upbringing, we get dropped and bent, sometimes broken. Therapists train to mend hearts and minds.
>
> You can learn to live with love or without it; the same is true for professional counseling. Like love, it has the potential to make our lives so much more worthwhile. And when facing the emotional issues that arise in sex work, it's no luxury.

❋ HAVE A HERO/INE

You need a hero/ine in this line of work—you really do. Sometimes we all need to channel an idol. I worked at my best when I stepped out of my comfort zone. Whether it was a complex situation, needing to think quickly on my feet, or to be more seductive than I'm comfortable with in real life, good things happened when I surprised myself just a little. As Erika Lyremark points out, even Beyoncé has an alter ego, Miss Sasha Fierce, to help overcome her stage fright—we're talking **Beyoncé**, people. Everyone can use someone to look up to.

Perhaps you have a short attention span, or it's hard for you to control your temper. Maybe you get insecure asking for money, or laugh inappropriately when nervous. Most likely those defense mechanisms were necessary when you were a child. However, if those traits have outlived their usefulness, let someone else step in from time to time to show how a hero/ine gets things done. Just to be clear—I'm not talking about behaving like a cartoon character, but channeling how our better, higher selves would act. As they say, "Fake it 'til you make it."

As an example, I was raised to be polite and avoid conflict at all costs, so I get all tied up in knots whenever I offend someone. All well and fine in normal social situations, but not ideal for sex work—sometimes you gotta be rude. Asserting myself in my personal life might be mortifying, but at work, I'd ask myself: *Would Catwoman give two shits about that asshole?* If the answer was no, I'd do whatever needed to be done and not beat myself up about it later. It doesn't matter if your hero/ine is real or fictional—over the years I've gotten enormous mileage from Susan Sarandon in *Thelma and Louise,* Pam Grier as Jackie Brown, and John Cameron Mitchell as Hedwig.

Here's a suggestion: devote a Pinterest or Tumblr page to your hero/ine. Link it to your website to attract clients who respond to the same archetypes you do. Build an altar or assemble a vision board. Keeping those images front-of-mind makes it easier to call on them when you need them.

> *Usually, we know in our gut the right thing to do, but somewhere along the way, we learned to doubt ourselves. Acting "as if" we were our own hero/ine empowers us to act in line with our core values, keeping our best interests in mind, without guilt or regret.*

✼ TRIGGER STATES

Managing basic human needs is a real concern in our line of work. When we're strung out, overwhelmed, or isolated, we tend to do things we know aren't good for us. We overeat or starve ourselves, act out or check out, overdo drugs and alcohol, or let down boundaries with clients. The irony is by trying to escape negativity in the moment, we set ourselves up for regret later on. Then it's easy to feel ashamed for making bad choices, setting a destructive cycle in motion.

The twelve-step community knows all about these vulnerable states that can trigger addictive or destructive behaviors. They use the acronym "HALT + B" to describe hunger, anger, loneliness, and tiredness, plus "B" for boredom. I've already discussed anger, so let's take a look at the others in turn, along with overusing drugs and alcohol.

HUNGER

I have low blood sugar, so hunger was always a huge issue for me—prostitution was especially depleting. Many times I worked lightheaded, desperate to get a client out the door so I could get something in my stomach. That starved state can be treacherous. After a difficult client or long shift, all we want to do is treat ourselves. Fried and sugary foods are fast, cheap, tasty, and tempting, but can leave us feeling disgusted with ourselves.

Then there's the problem of overdoing it. For many clients, an evening out means Binge Night: fancy dinners, expensive bottles of wine, endless desserts. Heading back to the hotel room for a "nightcap" after one of these food orgies can be as daunting as working half-starved. And don't get me started on the evils of flavored body oils, honey, whipped cream, and chocolate sauce—I don't know whose brilliant idea it was to mix goo food and sex, but all you end up with is a disgusting mess not suited to either eating or screwing. Not helping matters, of course, is the pressure to maintain an ideal weight, which for many of us means the endless diet. Our bodies become a constant battlefield of need, excess, and deprivation.

The solution is simple, if not always easy: keep your body in balance. Always have healthy food on hand, and don't keep sugary, salty snacks lying around. If you're going out to eat with a client, negotiate a lighter, healthier meal. Frame it as not wanting to be "too full for fun" later. When you treat yourself with food, make a conscious ritual to leave the house to get it, and only buy enough to enjoy that day. Take time to taste that wonderful thing—this is primal pleasure—you deserve it. Slow down to savor it.

LONELINESS AND BOREDOM

When I was working, I used to sit all day at home alone, becoming something of a vampire. Sometimes I'd go for days without leaving my apartment except to run errands. I'd start feeling sad and unlovable, living for my phone to ring. Even though most of my friends were sex workers, because we all worked weird hours, it made it hard to socialize. I'd turn down invitations because I was afraid they'd develop into obligations. I guarded my free time so well, I didn't want to do anything with it!

Long empty hours give us time to dwell on past slights. Ruminating feeds resentment and paranoia. Isolation compounds boredom, another trigger for bad decision-making. Plenty of times I went against my gut and saw a client I knew wasn't right because I'd been alone too long. And let's not forget how easily loneliness slides into depression. If you're stuck sitting around for work to make rent, that's sadder still. Burnout city.

Loneliness, isolation, and boredom are choices. We let them into our lives because we feel poor and undeserving, unable to afford connection, pleasure, and excitement. Of course, it's important to be careful with our schedules, but we also have to make time for beauty, connection, art, learning, nature, and all the other good things life has to offer.

We can take steps to defend against loneliness. One former rent boy friend of mine is prone to depression, so when he starts isolating and is at risk of becoming an "evil troll," in his words, he puts the call out on Facebook for some love. Ask your loved ones to call, text, or drop by—give them permission to pester you. It can be hard to re-member when we're feeling terrible that our sadness isn't a burden. Our friends *want* to be there for us. Maybe we learned at an early age that our bad feelings were too threatening for the adults around us. Now that we're grown, our work is to practice on a new set of grownups, ones who can be there for us when we're down.

Money is another excuse for isolating. Especially during the years when I was digging out of six-figure debt, I believed I couldn't afford to have fun. That's ridiculous thinking—there are so many free and low-cost ways to rejuvenate. Here are some suggestions for free things to do in your time off:

- ❀ Volunteer for a cause you love.
- ❀ Attend support meetings.
- ❀ Take long walks and hike in nature.
- ❀ Visit the beach or the park.
- ❀ Ride your bike.
- ❀ Babysit.
- ❀ Board your neighbor's pet while they're away.
- ❀ Housesit for a friend—turn it into a staycation.
- ❀ Make a date with your friends.
- ❀ Join a choir.
- ❀ Attend lectures and recitals. (If you live in a college town, these are often free or sliding scale.)
- ❀ Get politically active.

❀ Visit galleries and museums. (Most museums are free a few hours a week.)

❀ Search for clubs and social groups. Craigslist always has zany activities people want to do with total strangers. Meetup.com is another website with sliding scale and free events open to the public.

Here's a starter list of some fun low-cost activities:

❀ Enroll in junior college classes. (They offer everything from art classes to second-career training, and you'll get a student body card that gets you all kinds of discounts.)

❀ Try yoga, meditation, and tai chi classes.

❀ Check out cooking, sewing, and dance classes.

❀ Learn another language.

❀ Visit the zoo, the planetarium, the aquarium.

❀ Attend plays, concerts, and comedy clubs. (Search out half-price ticket venues in your town.)

❀ Go on a picnic.

❀ Camp out.

❀ Rent a car and drive someplace overnight or for the weekend.

❀ Learn new skills. There's always something new to learn in sex work, especially BDSM. If you spot someone whose talents you admire, reach out to them. Ask if they'll consult with you, or if you have a specialty, propose a skills trade. It keeps the job fresh, you meet potential buddies, and your clients will love you for it.

❀ Look for sexuality classes, a great place to meet like-minded folks. Or, if you've got a special skill to share, consider teaching a class yourself.

❀ Host a sex worker salon or support group. We have so much to learn from one another, and there's no better way to build community.

Notice what so many of these activities include? Getting outside, moving our bodies, nourishing our minds, or all three, and most take place in community. As humans, we're social creatures. Psychically, we need to rub on other people (even if our job is to *actually* rub on other people.) It's healthy to get outside of ourselves—sex work gets insular fast. It's too easy to forget there's a whole other world out there.

And to all you digital natives, I know you think your real life is online, but the digital world starves three of our five senses. Flashing screens can fill our minds, but our bodies need fresh air, human contact, and full-bodied sensory exploration. At the risk of sounding like your mom, step away from the me-machine, get outside, and play!

TIREDNESS

Fatigue seems to be the universal state of modern life, what some call "the exhaustion epidemic." We can't be at our best when we're tired all the time, so it's important to get our rest. This doesn't just mean getting enough sleep. We all need downtime, especially before bed. An hour before turning in, turn off all electronic devices and don't check your phone or email. Unless it's an emergency, the world can wait until morning.

Insomnia is a life-crusher, a thief of sanity. Researchers have discovered that not getting enough quality sleep is linked to all kinds of physical and mental health problems. If you find yourself awake and ruminating in the middle of the night, devote some daylight hours to addressing the problem. Don't save problem solving for nighttime. If you aren't able to sleep well for extended periods of time, talk to your doctor and/or therapist and get some relief.

Sometimes fatigue is a symptom of an underlying physical condition. If you're struggling to keep your energy up, get to the doctor. You could be suffering from allergies, anemia, hypothyroidism, adrenal failure, or complications from perimenopause, among other things. Give your body every chance to be as healthy as it can be.

Additionally, never underestimate the power of the mind-body connection. Physical weariness can stem from mental exhaustion, lack of exercise, depression, or anxiety. More and more Western practitioners are recommending meditation and mindful breathing to counter the stresses of modern life. Studies have shown meditation actually slows the rate of cellular aging.

Sitting with ourselves, clearing out our minds, with a focus on breath, is both calming and energizing, beneficial to our bodies and our sense of well-being. It costs nothing, and, best of all, we can practice anytime, anywhere. *Real World Mindfulness for Beginners: Navigate Daily Life One Practice at a Time*, edited by Brenda Salgado, can get you started with simple mindfulness practice. It's one of those wonderful books where you can open to any page and find something useful.

DRUGS AND ALCOHOL

Liquor is an occupational hazard of prostitution, and many strip clubs are soaked in it. If you are committed to sobriety, this can be a real challenge. Many clients can't loosen up without it—they crave the permission drinking gives their bodies and brains, and will get upset if you don't drink with them.

If you are clean and sober, advertise it loud and proud. It'll do two great things for you: attract sober clients and keep the partiers away.

If you do drink, don't work drunk, as tempting as it may be—it adds one more variable to an already complicated situation. You can lose track of time and awareness of your surroundings, and you're more likely to make bad decisions. Clients know it's easier to rip you off or push your boundaries. Promise yourself, "I will sip lightly." Watch your drink being poured. Better yet, pour it yourself, and keep your eye on it at all times, because alcoholic drinks are prime vehicles for date rape drugs.

Speaking of drugs, lots of clients like to party. Fine with me—adults should be able to do what they want with their bodies.

However, I rarely did drugs with my clients, preferring to work with a clear head. If drug use is a regular part of your work life, check out the *Ask Ms. Harm Reduction* column at titsandsass.com. She lays out best practices in plain English with no judgment. As her name implies, she's not trying to talk anyone out of anything. SWOP-NYC Harm Reduction Coalition is another good resource (harmreduction.org/connect-locally/new-york/swop-nyc/).

> *Too many of us engage in a kind of spiritual anorexia, as if starving ourselves of the fullness of life makes us better people. Or else we go overboard until we are drunk, stuffed, and disgusted with ourselves. You can strive to be the best you can be or you can let yourself down—the world will keep right on spinning either way. Why not make the most of this beautiful life?*

❀ SADNESS, DEPRESSION, AND SUICIDAL THOUGHTS

Sadness, feelings of stuckness, and wrestling with existential angst are a part of life, but they can make putting on the sexy a whole lot harder. Whether or not sex workers are more prone to emotional downswings than the general public, I can't say, but because of the stigma and danger we face, I believe many of us tend to associate any depression we do experience with our work.

Sex workers I've known tend to manage sadness one of two ways: they paper it over with addictive behaviors, or they resign themselves to it. Either way, the result is they live with depression like they deserve it. What I want for you, Sexy Reader, is something different. I want you to view depressive episodes as a part of the human condition, endurable and temporary, just like tax season, head colds, and Super Bowl Sunday.

Let me be clear: if you're feeling hopeless because you hate your job, then you need to take steps to get out of the Biz. But if you occasionally get down, same as everyone else alive, self-care is the key to loving your life again.

THE BLUES

Not wanting to bathe or go to the gym or feeling gross in our work clothes are signs our bodies are depressed—listen when that happens. Somatic depressive episodes are opportunities to treat ourselves with extra kindness. Consciously experiencing sadness as a sex worker can be scary—too often we ignore the warning signs out of fear that if we take a break from sex work, it'll stretch into a permanent vacation: *What happens if I'm depressed forever? I'll never work again.* But punishing ourselves and pushing through the resistance is a recipe for burnout.

How do you treat yourself when those sad, bad days roll around? Do you stop dead in your tracks, call in sick, and retreat? Do you force yourself through the day pretending nothing is wrong? Do you use it as an excellent opportunity to be sweet to yourself? Do you beat yourself up and call yourself horrible names? Do you reach out to those who love you most? Do you cruise Instagram for hours, stalking other people's seemingly perfect, happy lives?

I've learned over the years that the very best medicine for sadness is curiosity. Sorrow always comes with something it wants to say. Is your life changing in some way that you haven't acknowledged, or is some part of you going unfed? Do you miss someone or some part of yourself? Change is inevitable, and so is the sadness that comes with it. We need to take time to get to know and understand it. Once we do, wanting to look good, connect, dance, fuck, and all those other lively drives return.

Here's the thing. If you're afraid that deep down some part of you hates your job, you owe it to yourself to find out. Probably that's not the case at all. If most days you feel fine at work, I'm guessing you truly *are* fine—seriously, the vast majority of us are lousy at lying to ourselves. Now, maybe you need to take some time off or make a few changes. But don't ignore your melancholy because you're too afraid to learn what's at the root of it. You owe it to yourself to listen to what your sad spells are trying to say.

As for the issue of sex drive, there is no "right" amount of sexual desire. Certainly there's a perception that in order to do sex work, especially porn or prostitution, you either have to be hypersexed or altogether dead inside. Neither is true. It is absolutely fine not to want sex in your private life; it is absolutely fine to want sex outside of work. It's absolutely fine for your sex drive to wax and wane. What matters is you feel healthy, connected, and alive in your body.

Sometimes we don't feel actively sad, but it's like we've hit a wall. Who hasn't had those days feeling stuck, lazy, wanting to check out?

Then self-hatred comes rushing in because we should be doing laundry, going to the gym, and saving the world, when all we want to do is play Candy Crush.

The best attitude towards heavy, unmotivated stuckness is patience. Recognize that depression slows our bodies and minds down, and sometimes that's precisely what we need to be doing. Take a deep breath and say: *"I have no energy for saving the world today. All I'm good for is sitting here feeling like crap. Tomorrow, I'm going to wake up in the morning with plenty of energy, ready and rested."*

DEPRESSION

When sadness settles into stay, depression has come to visit, erasing any memory of anything good. Our bodies are the experiential seat of grief, hopelessness, and depletion; our minds make up stories to give those somatic symptoms meaning. It can be so hard to do the right things for ourselves when every muscle in our body aches, but we have to take action to get through it.

Body-based techniques have helped me through depression, including good diet and exercise, dancing and other forms of expressive movement, and the release of traumatic memories. I'm also a fan of lifting weights—studies show weight training can be as effective as anti-depressants. If you're looking for a book on the mind-body connection, I recommend *Unstuck: Your Seven Stage Journey Out of Depression* by Dr. James S. Gordon. *Unstuck* presents a seven-step body-based program for alleviating depression somatically. I offer additional practical advice to combat depression, SEASONAL AFFECT DISORDER, and the holiday blues in the appendix on page 263.

Of course, the mind needs attention, as well. I've gotten relief over the years with talk therapy, cognitive therapy, mindful meditation, journaling, and practicing positive mental feedback loops. Don't go without the support you deserve: I list resources to find low- and no-cost mental health care professionals in the appendix on page 280.

Finally, if you've been struggling for more than a few weeks, you might consider anti-depressants. Sometimes we need a pharmaceutical cushion against anxiety, despair, and intrusive negative thoughts; sometimes we need an assist to reset our brain chemistry. Talk to your doctor or a mental health professional about getting back to feeling good again.

SUICIDAL THOUGHTS

I wasn't sure if I should even tackle this subject—after all, I have no professional training. But the whole point of this book is to talk about difficult emotions as best I'm able, and, regrettably, suicidal thoughts are something many of us in this line of work struggle with. So, with full disclosure that I'm doing nothing more than offering amateur advice, I'm wading in. Feel free to skip this section if you're not ready for it right now.

If you're thinking about ending your life, stay with me—don't go anywhere. Be with me right here and now. Your life is so, so precious. I've never known anyone who hasn't at some time wanted the pain to go away. For each and every one of us, there are days when it's a struggle to just stay here. It can be especially easy as sex workers to fall into a black hole believing we are worthless, we mean nothing, nobody loves us, and Life Itself doesn't care if we live or die.

I can tell you right now, as powerful as that feeling may be, it is not true. I know this because everything had to go right for you to be alive. Thousands of people stretching back into the distant past had to meet, mate, and survive through winter, war, famine, and illness, all so you could be born and live to this day. If anything had gone differently, if some great-great-great-great-grandparent had tripped in front of a mad yak, you never would have happened. So Life does want you here, most definitely—it made sure of it.

The best book I've ever read on suicidal thoughts is Andrew Solomon's *The Noonday Demon*. It's a huge book, an encyclopedia of sadness, and I recommend it for anyone struggling with clinical depression. He studied what keeps people from ending their lives. We'd like to think that it's love, or family, or connection, all that stuff in the movies, but so often it's not. People who have come back from the brink report that what keeps them here are things like privacy—not wanting the neighbors to gossip about them after they're dead. Or pride—not wanting to give the lover who jilted them the satisfaction. Or the unwillingness to say goodbye to life's little pleasures, like a favorite meal. So often it's the littlest things.

I have my own story, which I'll share in the hope that someone finds it useful. When I was thirty-four years old, I was in graduate school and escorting, but became suicidal after a client broke my heart. I couldn't process the levels of shame and despair I felt having fallen for a married man. All I could obsess over was the fact that I was *that dumb whore*.

As I mentioned before, I kept a loaded gun in my apartment. I remember sitting on my bed and thinking, *I could just end it all here right now.* I came very close—I had everything I needed: motive, method, opportunity. Turns out I had a seminar that afternoon with a guest speaker I'd been looking forward to. I thought to myself, *Well, I'll go to class, and then if I still feel like it, I'll do it after I get home.* So I went to class. Honestly, I can't remember a thing about that lecture—it's not like I heard something earth-shattering. My situation hadn't changed, and my heart was still deeply broken. But I stepped outside into the sunshine, I rode the train, my classmates gave me hugs and asked how I was doing. It allowed me to forget my problems for a few hours. It wasn't much, but it was enough.

Intellectual curiosity kept me going that day. If you're feeling terrible right now, let's get you what you need to get through this awful moment to the other side, where you can remember all the reasons why you love your beautiful life. **Please reach out for help.** Talk to your friends, the ones who are there for you when things get really tough. Don't isolate, don't feel this way alone. Your despair is not a burden to others.

Call the nationwide 24-hour National Suicide Prevention Hotline (800-273-8255 | suicidepreventionlifeline.org). If you want to speak to someone fluent in trans* issues, call the Trans Lifeline

(877-565-8860 | translifeline.org). You'll be talking with someone who got out of bed this morning in order to help you, someone who wants to listen. Wherever you are, whatever the cause of your pain, your life has tremendous value, and you are not alone. You can find additional crisis hotlines and free and low cost mental health resources in the appendix on page 280.

Get outside, and breathe fresh air. Eat some tasty food, listen to soulful music. Sit in the park and wait for a friendly dog to come by—they're always so happy to see you. You ever notice that even when dogs have only two teeth and one eye and three legs, they never hate themselves? No matter what, they always believe they deserve a nice ear scratch, a treat, and a few kind words, and they are absolutely right. *You do too.*

As hopeless as I felt on that terrible day, I'm so glad I stuck around to find out how the rest of my life turned out. Who knows what marvelous things lie ahead for you, what love, what connection, what adventures? What will you do with your tremendous gifts? Promise me you'll find out.

> *Tasking our minds with pulling ourselves out of despair ignores the body's deep aquatic logic. When our bodies and hearts are tender, our intention must be gentle, gentle, like a mother soothing a heartbroken child. Sadness always comes with a message, and we must sit still enough to hear what it has to say.*
>
> *Depression is a natural part of life, a function of having a body and a mind, but it is not an inevitable state of constant being. There are times when each of us stares into the pit and wonders whether to jump. Remember there is always enough love for us, always some good we can do for others, always a reason for us to be here.*

❋ PRACTICAL ADVICE: WINTER

Sex work can get challenging during the winter holidays—it's a simple fact of life. If you're anything like me, dreary weather along with ubiquitous peppy messages to be merry, consume mindlessly, and spend time with loved ones is an annual assault on the spirit. If you're estranged from your family or in the closet, this can make the holidays especially difficult. Even if you adore winter—you were born at the North Pole and polar bear blood courses through your veins—it's still cold-and-flu season. Most clients have family and work obligations, so business invariably slows down. Seasonal realities of the sex industry can reinforce depression and isolation, resulting in a downward spiral. I've worked Christmas Day in a strip club; it takes a stiff spine to work that shift.

Year's end is also when people typically take stock of their lives, and it's no secret that people who pay for sexuality are usually working out (or, just as likely, denying) unhappiness in their lives. Clients, desperate to avoid drowning in disappointment and emptiness, act out or check out. Longtime regulars may resolve that this will be the year they quit seeing sex workers, so it can be a time of high attrition as well.

The first year I worked as a call girl, I made a huge mistake thinking the holiday slowdown was my fault—I just wasn't making myself available enough. So I set aside more and more hours to sit by the phone as it rang less and less. By the time Christmas rolled around, I was a hot mess. And then there was a terrible feeling of abandonment when that client who came to see me religiously every week didn't even text to say "hi" for the entire month of December. January rolled around, and he popped up again like nothing had happened. ***Bastard.***

While all that sucks, you are an adult, and it's your job to act accordingly. Holidays happen every year, you need to plan ahead. Set aside monthly allowances in the warmer months for the winter slowdown. Better still, budget to travel. Don't make my mistake of thinking that there will be some last-minute holiday rush.

Here's my best advice to you—one fine day during the sunny months, when you have a truly killer overnight call, or you find the most excellent groove slapping that hot sub around and they pony up for an extended session, or you perform an awesome lap dance and score a fat tip to match, take that cash and buy yourself a plane ticket someplace warm during Christmas week. And when winter rolls around, and you step off that plane into sunshine, take a moment and give a word of thanks for having such a truly freaking awesome job.

Perhaps this year that's not possible. Maybe the hotel down the road with a Jacuzzi and room service is what you can afford, and if so, do it. Make an end-of-year trip a stated goal for next year. You deserve it.

If you can't get out of town, plan ahead for how you're going to spend your time while work is slow. I provide an extended list of activities and tips for getting through the holiday blues in the appendix on page 263.

- ❀ If there's a creative project you've been ignoring, dust it off and dig in.
- ❀ Get out to movies, concerts, museums. Feed your artistic mind.
- ❀ Download a bunch of new music. Tickle your brain with new tunes.
- ❀ Line up your Netflix wish list and fall in love with some great new characters.
- ❀ Make sure you get to the gym every day, no matter what, unless you're dead on your back in bed with the flu. Depression flourishes in inertia.
- ❀ Take a dance or yoga class.

- ❀ Every single chance you can, get outside and walk. Fresh air and sunshine are depression's mortal enemies. Even if it's a cloudy day, look up. Take in what light there is in the sky.
- ❀ Don't discount purchasing a sun lamp or a membership to a tanning salon—I'm a big believer in the restorative powers of Vitamin D.
- ❀ Indulge in some retail therapy? Yeah, ok, if it feeds you. But just like drugs, food, and alcohol, the desperate spirit of the season cheers us on to mindlessly over-indulge. Hangover, self-loathing, and regret are the inevitable results. Practicing moderation, or abstinence if need be, is the true gift of self-care.
- ❀ Do not isolate—loneliness is depression's BFF. Accept invitations and offer them.
- ❀ Don't forget volunteering. It's amazing how the act of helping others gets us out of our shells.

Post fixed hours for responding to calls and emails, then stick to those hours. Get the hell out of the house or the dungeon when you're not available. Under no circumstances spend December thinking if you just check your phone every five minutes you'll land that last-minute call. If you find yourself obsessing, notice you're doing it, ask yourself to please stop, and redirect all that excellent energy into something positive.

If this is a spiritual time of year for you, feed that need. Denying your connection to the divine is dehumanizing. Please don't fall into the trap of seeing yourself as unworthy.

> *Surviving the holidays intact is a worthwhile goal. Strategize how to mitigate the pressures of the season ahead of time; don't wait until the last minute. It's an excellent time to practice the very best self-care and visualize your goals for the New Year.*

✳ DISSOCIATION

I'm just going to come right out and say it: Sometimes I would DIS-SOCIATE when having sex with clients. My mind is capable of sliding right off into outer space, leaving my body more or less to fend for itself. And while I can't go so far as to say that every sex worker I've ever known dissociates, the ones I'm closest to CHECK OUT from time to time as well.

What do I mean by saying I dissociated? At times, when doing things with clients I wasn't into, my mind would wander off for a while. One way to look at it was my brain was doing me a favor, keeping me at a distance, then bringing me back to reality when I needed to be fully present.

I know this is a loaded topic. Dissociation and other symptoms of PTSD, including depression, anxiety, and emotional numbness, are directly related to trauma, especially childhood abuse. This is a particularly sore spot for many sex workers because the straight world assumes we all must have been molested as children—why else would we do what we do?

Are all sex workers damaged goods? Was everyone mistreated in childhood destined to work a pole or walk the streets? Highly doubtful. But it is true there are all kinds of detached behaviors in the Biz, in sex workers and clients alike. To ignore that would be … well, denying reality.

I'm not here to romanticize trauma and its aftereffects. I don't believe dissociation offers powers of self-protection or the ability to read minds—nodding off like River Phoenix in *My Own Private Idaho* isn't noble or beautiful. However, sometimes we need to zone out. It's a defense mechanism, a bargain our minds made with our bodies years ago, and we need to honor it.

Here is what I believe: you can dissociate and still do sex work safely. This does not mean you are broken beyond repair, it doesn't mean you can't take care of yourself. If you can remember what happened after you've been gone in your mind for a time, if you're alert to dangers and know innately that you have the ability to act on them, then you can trust yourself to make good decisions.

However, if spacing out or obsessive negative thoughts are making it hard for you to do the work, consider mindfulness practice. These techniques help us to acknowledge and accept our thoughts, while detaching from their emotional charge. We can get better at not reacting, taking a step back, and watching ourselves with compassion. I already mentioned *Real World Mindfulness for Beginners: Navigate Daily Life One Practice at a Time,* a great place to start. A more advanced book on the subject is *Wherever You Go, There You Are: Mindfulness Meditation in Everyday Life* by Jon Kabat-Zinn.

Perhaps your symptoms are more severe, and your thoughts feel invasive, distressing, and persistent. I'm in no position to diagnose anyone, but I can recommend an excellent resource, *The PTSD Workbook: Simple, Effective Techniques for Overcoming Traumatic Stress Symptoms,* by Mary Beth Williams and Soili Poijula. This handbook does two things simply and gently: it explains why you might be feeling the way you're feeling, and offers exercises and checklists to help build emotional resilience.

Because of my propensity to dissociate, I used to worry that I was traumatizing myself when working. My fear was years later horrible memories would come roaring back to haunt me. Hollywood loves gory tales of repressed trauma destroying seemingly put-together people, but honestly, how many times have you encountered that scenario in real life? Most of us aren't delusional. When we're miserable, we know it, and we want desperately to make it better. I can report I've waited more than twenty-five years for a delayed reaction that never came. Other sex workers in my social circle report the same. So if you feel like you're handling the work, even if you need to separate for a spell, then you probably are. ***Trust yourself.***

The flip side is if you feel like you're not handling it, if your little mental side trips leave you feeling anxious and undefended, you need to honor that. Whether or not you used to be okay with the work, or you think you should be able to manage it, all that's beside the point. At the end of the day, the only person you are accountable to is you. If your brain is trying to tell you something feels bad, then it's time to make a change.

✵ PLEASURE

Within the celebration of the erotic in all our endeavors, my work becomes a conscious decision, a longed-for bed which I enter gratefully and from which I rise up empowered.

—AUDRE LORDE FROM *USES OF THE EROTIC: THE EROTIC AS POWER*

People say all the time, "Follow your passion." Sounds like excellent advice. So … why not a job where we get to play with passion all day long? Our job is to shimmy and to strip and to suck and to squirt and to flirt and to spank and to tease and to screw and to come. And it's a whole bunch of other things, too, but can we just stay right here for a moment? Done right, our job is downright juicy and delicious. We get to be sensual. We get to be gorgeous. We get to give and receive pleasure. ***Never fucking forget this***.

Sure, a lot of the time, there's nothing fun about it—it's boring, it's repetitive, it's exasperating—you might say it's like telling a CPA they should enjoy filing taxes. But shuffling paperwork isn't the same as putting on clothes that make us look good, moving in ways that make people's eyes dance.

Many people believe that commodified sex must always be zero-sum, extractive, and sad. If someone is paying for sexuality, then it is automatically empty; if we're getting paid to do it, then we're just going through the motions. But we know it doesn't have to be that way. I'm not suggesting for a second that you connect authentically with every client—god knows, deep connection is rare. But always remember pleasure. Look for it, seek it out—it's your inheritance. Nobody gains when we just go through the motions. The world isn't a better place when we feel dead inside.

Annie Sprinkle, former prostitute, fountain of kindness and acceptance, is my heroine. In her list, "Forty Reasons Why Whores Are My Heroes," Annie reminds us, for all the discrimination and dangers we face, sex workers **sparkle**. We make the world a more luscious place. We get paid to play in the sandbox of the erotic imagination, with some of the biggest toys there are: bodies, emotions, imaginations, and desires. Never lose sight of that fact. **Enjoy yourself as much as you let others enjoy you.**

PART FOUR:
SEX WORK AND RELATIONSHIPS

Out beyond ideas of wrongdoing and rightdoing there is a field. I'll meet you there.

—RUMI

SEX WORK AND RELATIONSHIPS: AN INTRODUCTION

Hi, Sexy—

I followed this one kickass call girl blogger for years—she was a pistol. Sharp, political, funny, and she loved her job. But one vulnerability came up again and again in her writings—the fear that she could never make a long-term romance work. Her relationships tended to be short-lived, which she blamed on escorting. She'd often write about her belief that once she retired, the truth about her past meant she would face a terrible bind: Lie and live with the fear of her secret coming out, or spend the rest of her life alone.

*All my years in the sex industry, both as a participant and an observer, this is one of the most common anxieties I've seen: The fear that true love is off limits to the likes of us. I am here to say **that is just not the case.** I've known plenty of sex workers in successful long-term relationships, and I've been fortunate enough to find love both while I was working and after.*

Now, it's fair to say that there are challenges. The worship of monogamy in our society is foundational, so deep most of us don't question its force in our lives. The belief that A) there is only one person who should meet all of our romantic and sexual needs, and B) we should mesh with them mind, body, soul, and bank account, and C) we shouldn't be romantically or sexually involved with anyone else ever is the basis of practically every love song ever written.

As sex workers, we queer that paradigm—it's a key factor in the stigma we face. As unattached sexual agents, we aren't afforded the privileges the monogamous enjoy. But it doesn't mean we are disqualified from romance and commitment.

Fearing rejection because you do sex for a living holds you back from living life to its fullest. Take some time to unpack where that fear comes from. It's easy to fall into the trap of feeling unworthy because you don't save your sexuality for a special someone.

But here's a welcome piece of news: plenty of people aren't constitutionally suited to monogamy—they don't need it or crave it. They believe sexuality is an infinitely renewable resource that can't be used up or contaminated. Loving someone doesn't mean owning or controlling them. They're no more threatened by the notion of their partner going off to a shift at the club or the massage parlor or the dungeon than a shoe factory. We can find the love we crave while working in the sex industry.

In this section, I'm going to share some of the wisdom of our fellow sexual adventurers, the polyamorists and other ethical sluts—they have a lot to teach us. I'll discuss what a healthy partnership looks like while doing sex work and provide a list of relationship red flags. I'll explore jealousy and honesty, and finish up by discussing how to work with a broken heart, even when it's a client who broke it.

❋ SEX WORK AND RELATIONSHIPS

Many sex workers live with the fear of never finding love, but as it turns out, the world is very wide. Many folks don't view sex work negatively at all—they find it a turn-on, aren't prone to jealousy, or see the work for what it is—a job. In the past twenty-five years, I've encountered sex workers in every conceivable romantic arrangement: both partners working, separately or as a team; one working to support the other; open relationships; working within certain rules (no kissing, no penetration, no doubles with a member of the same sex, etc.); one person working on the down low, the other oblivious; partners living together, emotionally but not sexually committed; and partners living apart, but romantically and sexually committed. There's no one right way to do it, and there's no reason there isn't someone out there for you!

I realize, however, that we can't just expect all of the societal expectations we're raised with to just disappear. Sex work has real implications for our personal lives. How do we uncouple love and romance from sexual exclusivity? I think it's helpful to start by challenging the chokehold that monogamy has on our culture's imagination.

POLYAMORISTS, ETHICAL SLUTS, AND OTHER SEXUAL ADVENTURERS

POLYAMORISTS, those intrepid emotional explorers who pursue the state of being in love or romantically involved with more than one person at a time, challenge the status quo by asking: What's so great about bonded-pair relationships in the first place?

Polyamorists question our culture's blind assertion that we should get all our needs met from a single special person. They propose that each of us should be responsible for our own self-esteem and fulfillment. Against the monolith of monogamy, imagine the power of a simple set of ideas: each and every one of us, whether we have a partner, a hundred lovers, or are celibate, is whole and complete just as we are. Love and sex are not zero-sum—romance or sex with one person takes nothing away from anyone else. Each of us is free to explore our infinite capacities for love, pleasure, experimentation, and excitement with as many people as we please.

Freed from the belief that there is only a single person fated to love us, polyamorists view sex, romance, and deep connection from a place of adventurism, excitement, courage, self-reliance, bounty, and empowerment, and isn't that a world we'd all rather live in? It's not an easy path, but monogamy is no walk in the park, either. Polyamorists have a huge amount to teach the rest of us about living consciously, honestly, abundantly, and fearlessly in the moment.

Now, maybe an open relationship will never be right for you. But even if finding a One True Forever Love is your heart's desire, shouldn't monogamy be a conscious decision, made with a full awareness of all relationship possibilities, rather than an unexamined default position because that's all we ever see in the movies?

To learn more, I recommend two books: Dossie Easton and Janet Hardy's classic *The Ethical Slut: A Practical Guide to Polyamory, Open Relationships and Other Adventures* is filled with firsthand accounts. *More Than Two: A Practical Guide to Ethical Polyamory* by Franklin Veaux and Eve Rickert has easy-to-understand discussions of the emotional work that goes first into loving ourselves, and then making ourselves available to be loved by many, many others.

By all means, don't let society's hang-ups about sex hold you back from pursuing a relationship, if that's what you want—don't starve yourself for love, don't sell yourself short. We just need to be aware that there may be certain challenges, as there are in any relationship. Let's begin by laying out what we want.

HEALTHY RELATIONSHIP CHECKLIST

What does it feel like to be in a loving, adult partnership with someone who really gets what sex work is about?

- ❀ You can be authentic, with no pressure to look a certain way or keep up a façade.
- ❀ You have sex only when you want to and the way you want to. You can say "no" to sex, and that's okay.
- ❀ Finances feel equitable, and you can discuss money freely.
- ❀ Your money is fully appreciated, not resented.
- ❀ There's recognition that your money may carry a special emotional charge because of how you earn it.
- ❀ Your workspace and schedule are honored, not undermined.
- ❀ Privacy is respected between the two of you and with outside people.
- ❀ It's okay to talk or not talk about your work, as you both decide.
- ❀ It's okay to share your work-related fears without concern it will contaminate your relationship or cause your partner to unduly worry about you.
- ❀ It's not threatening to have a really good day.
- ❀ If you have a really bad day, you don't feel pressured to quit.
- ❀ If jealousy arises, it is articulated respectfully, addressed fully, and resolved.
- ❀ Trustworthy behavior, intimacy, and connection aren't taken for granted. Instead, they're consciously acknowledged and built upon.
- ❀ Agreements can be openly discussed and, if need be, renegotiated.

- ❀ Slip-ups can be acknowledged; apologies and amends can be made. Mistakes and misunderstandings don't have to be fatal.
- ❀ It's okay to ask how your partner is feeling and thinking; it's okay to ask for reassurance and affirmation.
- ❀ And every day, in every way, everyone keeps checking in!

Now, I recognize—that is a big, hairy list. None of us are perfect, and no relationship is going to be ideal all of the time. Just remember: navigating big issues like jealousy, sexual compatibility, finances, and expressing negative emotions responsibly isn't unique to sex work—it's called being an adult. But because our society is fundamentally warped around sex and money, it's important not to sugarcoat the heightened potential for conflict when sex work is a part of the relationship mix.

SEX WORK AND RELATIONSHIP PITFALLS

Ambivalence and resentment can manifest in all sorts of ways. Be mindful of patterns that make you uncomfortable, with emphasis on the key word "patterns." All of us have those no-good-very-bad days when we regress and act out. That's when we have to apologize and make amends—one or two bad episodes don't have to mean a relationship is over. However, if you find yourself in the same bad rut again and again, and honest communication doesn't improve things, it may be time for that relationship to end. You do not deserve, nor should you tolerate:

- ❀ Emotional acting out—outbursts or moody silences
- ❀ Fights that go in circles or skirt something unspoken
- ❀ Passive-aggressive behavior, such as over-sharing with other people
- ❀ Feeling disrespected, shamed, or belittled
- ❀ Not feeling emotionally safe or supported
- ❀ Punishment for honesty or vulnerability

❀ Blame for your partner's depression or low self-esteem

❀ Pressure to meet unrealistic expectations of sexual availability or performance

❀ Sex that feels like work

❀ Being made to feel guilty for your work schedule

❀ Having your earnings taken for granted, or resented, or both

As I've mentioned before, the money we make from sex work is emotional—you owe it to yourself to be especially mindful how you share funds and expenses with your partner. While I've known a few couples who made it work, supporting a partner for an extended period of time doing sex work can be a recipe for disaster—resentment and low self-esteem can be the result for both parties.

JEALOUSY

Jealousy is one of those hidden, shameful emotions that can be so difficult to acknowledge. As sex workers, we need to be sensitive to its hidden dynamics. No matter how vulnerable, how stigmatized, how abandonable we might feel because of our work, to our partners, we are desirable. We are powerful. We can always walk or be stolen away. Even while we routinely encounter rejection on the job, to our partners, we get told every day how hot we are by people with money. (One trans* man I know called his wife's escort clientele her "Boyfriend Club.")

Grinding insecurity causes people to act badly. When it comes up, you need to address this dynamic directly, taking conscious steps to let your partner know they are safe. The more your partner knows about the realities of your work, the less power fear has.

Another side effect of jealousy can be indifference to *our* insecurities. When we don't get the approval we crave, it's easy to assume it's because our partners don't need us, and can cast us aside at any moment. How quickly our minds rush to the conclusion that when we don't get the love we want, it's because we are unlovable. Withholding can be devastating, but with compassion, we can see why: love can paralyze. For many people, acknowledging how much power their beloved has over them is terrifying, so they shut down and hold back.

If on some level your partner feels threatened by your sexual magnetism, earning power, freedom, or some other perk of your job, they may find it hard to praise you or soothe your insecurities. It's not admirable, but it's human. It's okay to ask for what you need, and to tell them what it feels like when you don't get it: "When I ask you to [fill-in-the-blank], and you don't do it, it feels like you don't love me anymore."

IS HONESTY ALWAYS THE BEST POLICY?

Honesty is an important feature of trust—true partnership can't be built on lies and secrets. However, our work requires discretion. We do private things for pay, and whether we should aim to be transparent in everything we do or not is an important question.

In my opinion, full disclosure is an ideal to strive towards, but not to achieve at all costs. You don't need to tell your partner absolutely everything you've ever said, done, or dreamed about to have a close, respectful relationship. What matters is that your rules are clear, mutually agreed upon, and honored. Each and every one of us has private moments, intimate thoughts, parts of ourselves that belong to us and us alone. That takes nothing away from the people we love.

> *Rumi writes: "Your task is not to seek love, but merely to seek and find all the barriers within yourself that you have built against it." We know that right now and always there will be enough love in the world for us, partnered or not, because we never abandon ourselves.*

❊ HEARTFELT ADVICE: HOW TO WORK WITH A BROKEN HEART

Ah, my sweet, sad Sexy one—if I knew how to eliminate heartbreak, I'd be a gazillionaire. The pain of loss can be so sharp while doing sex work. Dolling up for a stranger feels cruel when we've been rejected. Checking out with food or drugs can be so tempting when our hearts are blasted open.

Loss is a part of life. You need to take care of yourself, and time to work through it. Much of this advice is basic self-care, because when we're feeling sad it can be hard to remember to do the right things.

- ❀ *Don't overeat or starve yourself.* Eat healthy food and take care of your body. As hard as it can be when every muscle aches with grief, get your exercise.
- ❀ *Don't overdo drugs and alcohol.* If you're in recovery, now is the time to go to meetings and call your sponsor.
- ❀ *Unplug from social media.* Don't hunker down in the dark, scrolling endlessly through other people's vacation photos and happy selfies.
- ❀ *Get outside.* Spend time with your friends, make some new memories.
- ❀ *Lean on the people that love you.* Rely on your therapeutic providers.
- ❀ *Do something nice for someone less fortunate than yourself.* Simple acts of kindness give perspective.
- ❀ *Remind yourself that love in our lives is a gift.* As difficult as it can be, try to say a few words of gratitude every day.

Feeling thankful for what you've lost, even while grieving it, lets you know you've turned a corner in the process.

❀ *If you have a mindful practice, practice.* If you find peace in prayer, pray. If you find a connection to the divine in nature, get outside. Remember that you are part of something much bigger than yourself, and that your life story is not defined by this moment in time.

No matter the circumstances of your loss or breakup, no matter what was done or said, nothing changes the fact that you are a wonderful, worthy human being, and you deserve happiness. Nothing changes the fact that there is enough love in the world for you. Any grandmother will tell you when you're feeling devastated: "This too shall pass, my beloved darling." Turns out the Nanas are always right about that.

SEX WORK DURING HEARTACHE

Grief lives in our bodies, so here's some advice for the heartsick sex warriors out there:

❀ *Steer clear of anyone who triggers you or makes you feel inadequate.* You don't need that in your life right now.

❀ *Give yourself permission to sidestep difficult clients when you're emotionally overwhelmed.* Having a rainy day fund means this won't hurt your finances.

❀ *Only work with people who make you feel good about yourself.* Don't be shy about asking to do doubles or sex shows with a buddy. Touch feels good when you're hurting, even if it's just for show. If you've ever wondered how much physical affection we need to be happy, just ask a pet owner how many times a day their dog or cat demands to be petted.

❀ *Try to enjoy your favorite clients.* The ones that nourish you, make you laugh, make you feel gorgeous, make you come.

❁ *Don't use your broken heart as an excuse to relax your boundaries.* I lost way too many good clients doing things I normally wouldn't because I was sad—letting my guard down backfired every single time. Either they'd expect those same privileges later, which, if I tried to claw back, never ended well. Or they'd sense my emotional desperation, which is a huge turnoff. Drowning your sorrows in the arms of your favorite client can feel good in the moment, but is bad, bad, bad for business.

❁ *Don't let your negativity bleed into your sessions.* You'll damage your business, so you need to stop. No need to beat yourself up—we've all let our emotions get the best of us at one time or another. Notice you're doing it, and apologize if appropriate. Tell someone you trust—a friend, a therapist, a buddy—and ask them to hold you accountable for better behavior in the future.

❁ *However … pro doms have the luxury of working stuff out on the asses of their subs.* If it's consensual, by all means, whack away!

The body is the seat of sex and love, of heartache and sadness. At the same time, it's our vehicle for making our living. There's nothing easy about performing erotic labor through emotional pain. When we are processing loss, we need to take extra care of ourselves. As always, we seek to arrive at a place of gratitude for the love we have in our lives, even while we say goodbye to it.

WHEN A CLIENT BREAKS YOUR HEART

I can hear some of you snort at this—the idea of falling in love with a client is inconceivable. Feel free to skip ahead if this is advice you know you'll never need. For the rest of us, however, falling for a client is an occupational hazard. The intersection of sex and love is fertile ground for poets down through the ages. I felt a wide mix of attraction and affection for my clients ranging from tolerant amusement to the great love of my life. Working after a client punched a hole in my heart was one of the hardest things I've ever had to do.

If you fall in love with a client and it ends badly, you may feel waves of shame, humiliation, and inadequacy roaring up. Try to remember that we swim in the deep end of the ocean when it comes to sex, fantasy, projection, and emotions. Sometimes we get swept away—we're only human. Your initial temptation may be to stop working. However, my firm advice is to wait. Make that decision consciously with your head *and* your heart. Take your phone off the hook or your name off the schedule and wait a few days. If retirement is right, it'll still be right a week from now.

> *Our job is to perform the rituals of seduction and sex play that can lead to love in real life. Just because we're professionals doesn't make us immune to their power.* **The heart wants what it wants.** *Sometimes it wants a client. If heartache causes you to question your job, take time to make a measured decision about your future.*

PART FIVE: LIFE AFTER THE LIFE

Everything that occurs teaches and prepares you for the next phase of life. Nothing is lost.

—ZIG ZIGLAR

LIFE AFTER THE LIFE: AN INTRODUCTION

Hi, Sexy—

Let me tell you the story of how a good friend of mine got out of the Biz. It illustrates how many of us move through major transitions in life, often without even realizing it.

For years, M and I used to meet regularly for lunch every couple of months. We'd talk about all kinds of things, but mostly he'd want to talk about burnout. M was in his mid-fifties with a robust BDSM clientele, but he was getting tired—he knew he needed to make a change. And yet the prospect of not working anymore was daunting. He loved that his job title for the last twenty years had been "Leather Daddy." How could he support himself otherwise? Could he ever find meaningful work? Would he ever get laid again?

After a year or so of inertia, M started taking baby steps in other directions. He went back to school and took a few accounting courses. He started dating a man from North Carolina. They travelled through the South together, a part of the country he had never seen before. He fell into a gig as a lobby ambassador for an upscale apartment building for a few shifts a week.

These developments weren't enough for him to quit pro domming, but I noticed his shift from fear of the future to excitement about other opportunities. Sex work, which before had seemed like his only option, now seemed too small to contain him. Interestingly, whether this was because of choices he was making or a coincidence, his business started to drop off. After another six months or so, he'd talk about BDSM with frustration—he was clearly over it.

At the same time, his relationship grew more serious, and he put in for a promotion at the lobby job. A year later, he was living in Charlotte with his boyfriend, working as an assistant at a real estate office, studying to get his real estate license.

Getting out, which initially seemed so far off and unlikely, just kind of happened. His transition took more than two years, but it was **gentle**. At the outset, the boyfriend, North Carolina, and real estate weren't part of the plan—they weren't even on his radar. But over time, he made small changes that led to bigger changes, and he seized opportunities as they came up. While an important chapter had ended, his life was fuller and richer than before.

Our lunchtime sessions were a part of his process. He needed to bitch and fret and be encouraged. When planning for that next step, we all need support, to hear our thoughts out loud. Don't struggle with the question of what comes next on your own—let your friends be there for you.

Another lesson from this story: M was a prime example of fizzling out. That's a problem if the goal is to keep making a living in the Biz. But if it's time to do something else, then winding down—not hustling for new clients, turning down work, and all the rest—that's how we make room in our lives for new things. There's no need to beat ourselves up about this perfectly natural tapering off process.

I encourage you to think about how you've made changes in the past. Are you a planner or a procrastinator? A dreamer or a doer? Do you wait for things to fall into your lap or do you shake things up, even if it means leaping into the unknown? Does the future feel full of promise or dread? Do you feel skillful at making your life into what you want, or has that process always seemed mysterious and cruel? Understanding yourself, trusting that you know how to get from one stage of life to the next, is important.

This next section examines transitioning out of the Biz. First, I'll talk about the emotional side, both leaving on your own terms and getting bounced out involuntarily. I'll discuss sex work in the rearview mirror, because one thing none of us can know now for certain is how we'll feel about this job in the years to come. I'll offer my thoughts on the "Pretty Woman" fantasy, or marrying out of the Biz, because as it turns out, real life ain't always like the movies. Then I'll tackle the practical side, listing sex work skill sets that naturally translate to other careers. Finally, I'll make some suggestions of side jobs that can bring in some extra money or serve as a cover career.

❋ HEARTFELT ADVICE: WHAT TO EXPECT GETTING OUT

Something's, like, crossed over in me, and I can't go back.

—THELMA FROM *THELMA AND LOUISE*

Love or hate the Biz, stepping back into regular life can be a process. I'll discuss the challenges and the opportunities of straight work in a minute, but first I want to talk about the emotional realities of giving up sex work for good.

LEAVING THE LIFE VOLUNTARILY

Exiting the Biz on your terms is a worthwhile goal, I've said many times, but even when voluntary, it's not always easy. My advice for this transition period is be gentle with yourself—listen to your body, do what it tells you. You're stepping out of one phase of life into another. Take the time you need to adjust.

It might be helpful to hear what I experienced. Both times I left the Biz, it was my choice. However, both times I went through a contractive period when my mind and body turned inward. Doing sex work I had to be on, using all parts of myself. It was a huge high; I was *alert*. But it also took its toll, and in the weeks and months after I stopped, the adrenaline receded. I found myself recovering from an unexpected emotional and physical deadening. Real life seemed drained of color. I put on weight, felt irritable, and wasn't interested in sex. My body was both shut down and oversensitive to stimulation. My brain felt numb—it wasn't depression exactly, more like the wired-tired feeling after a rock concert.

I didn't miss the Biz or regret leaving—I was glad to be done. However, both times I worried that I'd permanently fried my nerve endings and would end up spending the rest of my life feeling both jangled and dull. It took several months, but real life did eventually get its snap and color back, and my overworked senses and sex drive returned to normal.

LEAVING THE LIFE INVOLUNTARILY

Some of us will get unlucky and be forced out of sex work against our will. We'll get sick, we'll burn out, we'll get busted beyond repair. If this happens, it's natural to go through a period of mourning. Take the time to feel your sadness all the way, to grieve what is irrevocably lost. Recognize that the depths of your feelings reflect how meaningfully this job impacted your body and mind. Really let yourself say goodbye.

The normal grieving cycle can get distorted and amplified if it's mixed with panic—fear plus sorrow can be a devastating mix. Take some time to separate the two. Hopefully, you've set aside resources to give yourself some breathing room. Your emotional state may be complicated by waves of self-loathing: *I fucked up so badly, I'm such a loser, I've wasted my life. Nothing I try ever works. I hate myself.* Those are powerful feelings, but that is all they are. Just about every single one of us on earth has felt them many times, including me.

Here's when you need to be your own best friend. Those emotions are no more real or permanent than clouds passing over the sun. Take a step back and say, *"I'm feeling this for one minute, but once those sixty seconds are up, I'm moving onto something else. I am not stuck here. This is nothing more than a moment in time, and there's a big, wide, beautiful life waiting for me on the other side."*

WRITE YOURSELF A LETTER

On your last working day (and may it be the day of your choosing), write yourself a letter. Tell all those future yous the story of what brought you here. Explain why you got in in the first place, what made you stay, what you learned along the way. What you gained, what you lost, your triumphs and regrets. What you'll miss the most, and what you're *so* glad you'll never have to do again.

There may come a time when you grow distant from this moment, making it harder to make sense of things. You may grow to regret becoming a sex worker; you may regret quitting. This chapter of your life may seem like a dream that happened to somebody else. All your older selves will have to reckon with this decision, so make sure to tell them your story.

SEX WORK IN THE REARVIEW MIRROR

How you deal with the fact you were once a sex worker is up to you. Some of us turn the page like it never happened; some of us maintain our friends from the Biz for life. But for many of us as the years go by, we gradually drift away.

Don't feel bad for not identifying with the industry as you did when younger. Don't beat yourself up for evolving, for becoming the person you are growing into. It doesn't mean you're ashamed of your younger self. Feeling less connected to our earlier lives is natural—as toddlers we wore diapers; we don't anymore. We all know stunted people unable to let go and move on. It is so much better to grow and to change.

You may feel guilty disconnecting from old coworkers. It can be especially hard when folks you were once close to make bad choices. However, we are allowed to let go of people we no longer connect with authentically. Recognize that each of us is on their own journey. Just because you shared important experiences with someone years ago doesn't make you responsible to them for the rest of your life.

Moving on doesn't mean we regret the past—it means we've filled up with new things. The Biz will always be a part of our history, but we have every right to write new chapters in the books of our lives.

> *If you own your story, you get to write the end of it.*
> —BRENÉ BROWN

DON'T FEAR THE FUTURE

The problem with worrying about the future is the rest of your life is a really long time. Who can say whether your checkered past will ever come back to haunt you? That fear, because it extends to the entirety of your time on earth and your reputation once you're gone, can feel enormous. Getting outed does happen. So does getting doxxed, harassed, evicted, fired, and all the rest.

What if you find yourself someday facing the full Monica Lewinsky scrum, your name a national punch line for something you did years ago? In her TED talk on shame and empathy, Monica talks about her parents' fear that shame would drive her to take her own life. It's not just her. A friend of mine, a former porn star and escort, took rational professional risks. He was cautious in his advertising and a low-key member of his local sex worker community. However, when he became involved with a famous client and the press found out about it, his life exploded. His name, image, and reputation were scandal fodder for years.

What I've learned from the people I've known directly and indirectly who've had sex work thrown in their faces is this: ***It is survivable.*** It's not pleasant, and it can take time. Worst case, you may have to move, find a new job, or change your name. But even Monica, our most widely shamed slut in a generation, came through it. There's no way to know for sure whether you'll suffer later in life for doing sex work. However, I do think it's helpful to break that fear down into its component parts. Not all disaster scenarios are equally likely or dreadful.

Let's start with the nightmare, the full-court Eliot Spitzer/Ashley Dupré national media horror show. As long as you steer clear of celebrities—which, by the way, I recommend in no uncertain terms for precisely this reason—the odds are miniscule. Unless you're involved with someone famous, the media won't give a damn about you. Even if you're a celebrity yourself, it's worth remembering that however big you are today, the Biz moves on. New blood feeds the beast. Big names today will mostly likely be forgotten a few years from now. Think about the millions of former sex workers alive right now—how many can you name that were stars back in 2010?

Now, if you run for the Senate, a shady past might damage you, sure, but usually these fears are overblown. Unless you have a criminal record, there's no real way to be found out. Investigative journalists don't dig up dirt on ordinary people. That treatment is saved for celebrities because there's money in it. If you don't use your real name, if you use discretion in your advertising, how is anyone going to make the connection?

I can hear you saying, *What about my reviews? All those gory details* ... Review sites don't keep old profiles up. Who wants to read about a sex worker nobody can see anymore? If you don't believe me, in researching this book, I went back and tried to find my old working persona online. (I left the Biz in 2005.) I could find none. Same for my friends who aren't out as writers and activists—no trace anywhere. Then, doing due diligence, I researched all the links in Magdalene Meretrix's *Turning Pro: A Guide to Sex Work for the Ambitious and the Intrigued.* I wondered how many of her online resources from 2001 were still valid. Of more than forty websites listed, only two were still active, even using an archive search engine—that's five percent. That's not to say that *your* information, *your* profile, *your* story won't live forever online, but the saying that the internet is written in pen, not pencil, may prove not to be so true as it ages. It is far more likely that a few years after you retire, it'll be as though you never worked at all.

Perhaps your fear is that some future employer or professor or loan officer will recognize you, and your new life will be destroyed. Let's take some time to think that fear through. First, start with the fact that off-duty sex workers tend to look a whole lot like normal people. Much of our allure stems from context. Leave open the possibility that outside of the club or the dungeon or the porn set, you don't make the same impression in your street clothes.

Now, it's true if you live in a small town, or if you had an especially large presence online, people might recognize you. You might feel safer moving or changing your look. But I can report I've run into several old clients around town in the years since I stopped working; they didn't even notice me. No more than a flash of recognition on my part, and I went on with my day. Odds are, I've been spotted as well, but if so, it happened without my knowing. So, in reality that prospect might not be anywhere near as grisly as we build up in our minds.

Also, anyone who recognizes you was once a client or coworker themselves. While it's not impossible they'll call you out, tear you down, blackmail you, or otherwise make your life an unholy hell, it's unlikely. It's the kind of scenario screenwriters love that has very little to do with real life, like aliens blowing up the White House. Remember: everyone has their own lives to protect. Most likely they'll be more afraid of the damage you could do to their reputation than you are of them. Really, it boils down to this: most people aren't evil. Chances are old clients will be delighted to see you, displaying some combination of embarrassment and curiosity, while rooting for your success in your new life.

There are professional fears. Then there are personal fears. How will it be to make new friends and have a love life with sex work in your past? At the core of that worry is the belief that sex work has stained us, making us unworthy and unlovable. That we have only two possibilities for the future: keep secrets, or face rejection if we tell the truth. I'm here to tell you that the fear of the loss of all future love is a sad, scared myth. There are plenty of people in this world ready to adore us just as we are.

Still, it's a big fear. Here's my response: Just as I'm pretty sure I'm never going to fall in love with someone who thinks waterboarding is sound policy or global warming is a hoax, I can't imagine ever feeling a soul connection with anyone who thinks sex work is despicable. Someone with that worldview has a very tiny chance of ever making it off the front porch of my heart to be welcomed into the parlor.

Take a moment to ask yourself: Do you think you're going to be attracted to narrow-minded people in the future? Probably not. It's a whole lot more likely you're going to continue to live your life with integrity, and you'll never grow into someone you don't recognize.

There's another way to look at all these anxieties, because another terror beats at the heart of them all. What many of us really fear is that *we'll* be the ones that make our lives miserable in the future. *We'll* be the ones who can't live with what we did. You hear about sad cases, like Linda Lovelace from *Deep Throat* fame, going from porn poster child to born-again Christian, denouncing everything she ever did in the Biz. It's safe to say that anyone who bounces between extremes like that would struggle with self-acceptance no matter what they do in life, but, of course, tragedy happens every day.

The response to that fear is trusting we won't grow into someone we despise. Or, for that matter, into someone who would despise our former selves. We know and love ourselves well enough that we will never reject our history. No matter who we become in the future, we will honor the choices we made when we were younger.

> *We are the children of our past, just as we are the parents of our future. We give ourselves all the love, acceptance, and forgiveness we need to embrace ourselves in our entirety, confident and resilient to face whatever life brings next.*

✻ WHEN FALLING IN LOVE MEANS GETTING OUT OF THE BIZ: MARRIAGE AND RETIREMENT

The *Pretty Woman* fantasy of meeting that dreamy client and falling in love is powerful stuff—marriage as a ticket out of the Biz can seem like the perfect happy ending. In real life, however, that scenario gets complicated in a hurry. I married a client and have close friends who did too, and I'm here to say, it can be challenging, whether or not you keep working.

To start with, fellow sex workers can be cruel to clients who cross the line to become lovers, making it difficult to socialize as a couple. Many of us might like clients well enough as people, but on some level, they're still the enemy. I've seen client-lovers treated as chumps, losers, and ATMs—after all, they're getting for free what they used to pay for. Also, we know there's no way we'd be treated well in their world, so why should they get access to ours? That resentment can blow back on you. You may find yourself being treated rudely because you "won the game." One time, ostensibly congratulating me on my engagement, a fellow pro called me a gold-digger to my face.

Now, some of that spite is envy. Who in the Biz hasn't longed to hear the words, *"Let me take you away from all this"* at one time or another? The fantasy of being rescued can be extraordinarily potent, especially with our unique working relationship to desirability, money, and power. On the other hand, in fairness, some of that bitterness can be preemptive, stemming from the fear of betrayal. That's because so many sex workers marry out of the Biz like entering the witness protection program: they change their names, move to another town, and never look back. It's easy to see how feelings can get hurt all around.

I'm not saying it's inevitable, but it's best to be prepared for insensitivity and disrespect. Even after years of marriage, I've had people call my bond with my husband nothing more than a business transaction, as if there couldn't possibly be a happily-ever-after for us because of the way we met. Which is ignorance, but hurtful just the same. Speaking of disrespect, heaven help you if you break up an existing relationship. Whether you leave your lover for a client or your client leaves someone to be with you, expect to be the bad guys. Whoever gets left behind will most likely garner all the sympathy.

Holding onto friends who know all the gory details of how you got together isn't always easy; maintaining a public face for the straight world isn't either. The question "How did you two meet?" can be stressful in casual social situations. Secrets can forge a sweet, sexy bond, but they can also be a wedge, a source of anxiety, shame, and resentment. At worst, they can be used as emotional blackmail.

Don't discount how hard it can be to leave the Biz for someone else. Landing back in the straight world can be a strain under the best of circumstances. If you find yourself financially or socially dependent, you may feel pressure to conform, to make the relationship work no matter what.

The challenges of coming together as client and sex worker can result in other ripple effects—once we're out of the industry, it might not always be easy to be truthful about our past. We may find ourselves hiding our genuine feelings about our history, even from our partners. Sexual authenticity can be a source of anxiety as well. The arc of most sexual relationships passes through a passion phase before settling into companionship, but getting real takes on a whole new meaning when we first come together in fantasy. Monogamy and trust issues can hang over the relationship—when hitting a rough patch, either partner may feel threatened the other will revert to their old ways.

I don't write any of this to discourage you from following your heart. If you and your client fall for one another, may you find every happiness—I certainly did. Just be aware that when crossing such a large social divide, you'll face challenges and changes. You may find yourselves grappling with sex, money, trust, power, status, fidelity, and identity, and you might lose people along the way. Working in the Biz we face these struggles every day, but when it's our private lives, the stakes can feel higher.

One final thought—if you ever find your life soaked in tears because you've run off with a client, consider this: even the greatest scandals have one potent antidote, and that is time. Prince Charles and Camilla Parker Bowles are Exhibit A. When their affair became public, especially after Princess Diana's death, Charles and Camilla were considered hateful, contemptible, selfish, unforgivable. After twenty-five years, however, the world has come to accept them as a couple and a great love story. Hopefully in your life nothing as monumental as the succession to the throne of Great Britain hangs in the balance—just something to keep in mind.

❈ HEARTFELT ADVICE: WORK AFTER SEX WORK

Whether we love sex work or hate it, it can be hard to walk away. After the high of the punk rock life, returning to respectability can seem like a long way down. Regular jobs can seem boring as hell and hardly worth the peanuts they pay us. Even if we're crispy fried and desperate to make a change, the prospect of a regular job can be scary.

Perhaps you've been thinking about leaving the Biz, but holding you back is the epic list of "I can'ts":

- ❀ *I can't get hired for a straight job.*
- ❀ *I can't explain the gaps in my resume.*
- ❀ *I can't launch a career this late in life.*
- ❀ *I can't work a forty-hour-a-week job.*
- ❀ *I can't do the same damned thing day after day.*
- ❀ *I can't play office politics.*
- ❀ *I can't sit behind a desk.*
- ❀ *I can't work for someone else.*
- ❀ *I can't risk anyone finding out what I did in my previous life.*
- ❀ *I can't make enough money to support myself.*
- ❀ *I can't make the kind of money I'm making now ever again.*
- ❀ *I'm burned out, I know I have to do something different, but …*
- ❀ *… I'm too old, I'm not smart enough, someone's going to find out about me.*
- ❀ *I just can't.*

Okay. So, all that might be true, but you know what? I highly doubt it. These specific, self-hating "I can'ts" are the shapes that our fundamental, existential fear takes: *I am not safe. I am not good enough. Nothing is certain.* Fresh White says, "Whatever life you are living right now is the one you dreamt for yourself at one time." Where you are today is no accident. Your next step, whatever it may be, takes some dreaming. Then it takes some doing.

DON'T SELL YOURSELF SHORT

Whatever your dream job may be, a way of life that feeds you in every way, there's a path to it. It may require going back to school, launching your own business, or starting at rock bottom and working your way up. It all boils down to whether you're willing to do what it takes to achieve it. Know that your voice, your skills, your insights are what this world needs, and that there is more than enough money in the world to support you.

Don't let the fear of resume gaps keep you from looking for employment. Unless you're looking to make partner in a law firm, what you've done previously shouldn't matter much to prospective bosses. However, if you do need a cover story, you can mention that you started a small business, took time off to tend to an ailing family member, or inherited some money and decided to travel or study abroad. Don't be afraid to tap your coworkers as references—your clients, too, if they can be trusted. Just make sure you've filled them in on your cover story beforehand.

One other thought—I've struggled with not knowing what to do my whole life, envious of anyone born knowing their true calling. When we know we need to make a change but don't know what we want to do next, it can be excruciating, fueling those voices in our head that tell us we're not good enough.

Rather than beating ourselves up, how much kinder is it simply to acknowledge that we're scared. Try to be patient with yourself during those uncomfortable, empty, in-between periods. Think of them as fallow seasons, necessary downtimes before tackling some-thing new. It's okay to say: "I have no idea in hell what I'm doing right now, but inspiration will strike. When it does, I'll be rested and ready, filled with all the energy I need to take the next step."

> *The most difficult times for many of us are the ones we give ourselves.*
>
> —PEMA CHÖDRÖN

❋ PRACTICAL ADVICE: WORK AFTER SEX WORK

Sex work takes a mad set of skills! Don't talk to me about easy money—it requires the get-up-and-go of an entrepreneur, the wardrobe skills of a quick-change artist, and the patience of a saint. Spend any amount of time in the Biz, and you'll learn a ton about yourself and other people. Translating those talents into other careers takes some imagination, but the possibilities are endless. If you've had any degree of success in the sex industry, then you're probably also a natural born:

- ❀ Entrepreneur
- ❀ Creative type
- ❀ Problem solver
- ❀ Risk taker
- ❀ Self-inventor
- ❀ Self-starter
- ❀ Self-promoter
- ❀ Iconoclast

All of these are excellent qualities when working for yourself. Additionally, if you have had any degree of success in the sex industry, then you probably also:

- ❀ Have excellent people skills
- ❀ Have good communication skills
- ❀ Conduct yourself professionally
- ❀ Recognize the importance of discretion

❀ Practice good time management

❀ Execute good money management

❀ Navigate shifting circumstances gracefully

❀ Take care of yourself emotionally

❀ Know how to handle high-pressure situations

❀ See many sides to a story

❀ Tell a good story

❀ Are a good listener

❀ Read between the lines

❀ Provide a quality experience

❀ Meet and exceed expectations

❀ Are an excellent competitor

❀ Clearly state your boundaries and needs

❀ Know the value of your time

❀ Have an excellent sense of humor

❀ Aren't afraid to take a deep breath and dive in.

Just look at that skill set—you're a bit of a badass! You might well make a fantastic employee, but with those skills, shouldn't you be the boss? Your *own* boss. Let's link job titles to our sex work-related talents. I'm guessing you probably also:

❀ Are comfortable interacting with high net worth individuals:
- Realtor
- Personal assistant
- Luxury sales
- High end hospitality
- Broker

❀ Are great at asking other people for money:
- Nonprofit fundraising
- Sales

❈ Love beauty/fashion/glamor:
- Interior decorator
- Personal shopper
- Style consultant
- Color consultant
- Beautician/Hairdresser/Barber
- Wedding consultant

❈ Are good at reading people:
- Therapist
- Social Worker
- Life Coach

❈ Know something about marketing:
- Marketing consultant

❈ Know something about videography and photography:
- Professional photographer/Videographer
- Video editor

❈ Have a loving touch:
- Massage therapist
- Tantric healer
- Acupuncturist
- Physical therapist

❈ Have a background in dance, fitness, or other forms of movement:
- Dance instructor
- Fitness trainer
- Pilates instructor
- Yoga teacher

❀ Have an interest in health:
- Nutritionist
- Homeopath
- Safer sex counselor

❀ Have a few things to say (about sex and other good stuff):
- Author
- Comedian/Performance artist
- Actor
- Political activist

❀ Have a few things to teach (about sex and other good stuff):
- Motivational speaker
- Workshop facilitator
- Teacher
- Consultant

What do most of these titles have in common? First off, there aren't a whole lot of nine-to-five desk jobs on this list. These are service and creative careers, which means either starting out on our own, or working for someone else for a few years. Once we're established, we become indispensable. Most don't require a rock solid resume or a degree from a fancy school. Many command top dollar once we've made a name for ourselves. Most are open-ended with potential for lifelong learning and development. However, most require some training, schooling, and/or licensing. And most won't pay much starting out, taking time to build. In order to be credible, we have to act credibly, so if you see your future on this list, the time to start working towards it is today.

If your dream job seems out of reach, try making contact with someone who does it for a living. Ask to schedule an informational interview and offer to pay their hourly rate—after all, your time isn't free. Not everyone will say "yes," but someone will. Ask how they got started, what education and experience paths they recommend, and what mistakes to avoid starting out. What do they love about their job and what do they dislike? What qualities are necessary to succeed? What's the outlook in their field in the next five, ten, twenty years—is their field growing or contracting? Do they recommend becoming a specialist or a generalist? If you're so inspired, ask if they might consider hiring you one day, and what qualifications you would need to make that happen.

Hopefully, this person will be straightforward and honest about your prospects to help you to decide whether it's the right path. Although it can be disappointing to learn that what you thought was going to be your dream job turns out to be a dead end, you'll save yourself all kinds of headaches determining that today and not years from now.

SIDE WORK AND THE PORTFOLIO CAREER

Full-time sex work isn't for everyone. Many of us get into it looking to supplement a straight job, picking up a shift or a shoot or doing a double here and there. Likewise, a lot of us transition out in stages while picking up other work on the side. My friend calls his balancing of straight and erotic massage, professional housesitting, and catering jobs his "portfolio career," a great term. Not being married to a single endeavor is a perfectly valid choice. Many of us prize flexibility and free time, and can only thrive when different sides of ourselves are engaged.

Of course, a portfolio career does require discipline and initiative. However, most side jobs don't require much start-up training or investment, just a willingness to put ourselves out there and a business card. If you find yourself needing to pull back from sex work or take a break altogether, consider these side gigs:

- ❀ Driver for rideshare service
- ❀ Personal assistant
- ❀ Personal chef
- ❀ Personal shopper
- ❀ Gardening services
- ❀ Yard work
- ❀ Virtual assistant
- ❀ Babysitter
- ❀ House sitter
- ❀ Professional organizer (cleaning people's closets, pantries, garages, storage spaces)
- ❀ Dog walker/Pet sitter
- ❀ Car detailer
- ❀ Graffiti removal (inspecting a property and painting over graffiti for a monthly fee)
- ❀ Interior house painter
- ❀ Blogger (monetizing your site)
- ❀ Resume writer
- ❀ Tutor
- ❀ Altering clothes
- ❀ Making clothes, arts and crafts, etc., and selling them online
- ❀ Masseuse
- ❀ Photographer
- ❀ Web or Graphic Designer
- ❀ Social media consultant

If you live in an apartment building, you can advertise to do routine maintenance tasks such as changing out HVAC filters, prepping air conditioners for the winter, or disposing of used Christmas trees for a fee. Of course, anything you can do well, you can teach others: play guitar, cook Chinese food, pole dance.

We focus so much on money, but for many of us, freedom is what we truly crave. Don't get caught up on job titles or meeting other people's expectations. Give yourself permission to find a work mix that works for you.

> *It doesn't matter if inspiration for our life's work comes right away or takes years while getting by doing other things—it's always worth striving for. Believing in something bigger than ourselves, loving something more than ourselves, doing work that makes the world a better place—this is the path to fulfillment, a full-bodied sense of belonging to life that transcends simply earning a paycheck.*

CONCLUSION

The most successful people in life recognize that they create their own love, they manufacture their own meaning, they generate their own motivation.

—NEIL DEGRASSE TYSON

[The erotic] flows through and colors my life with a kind of energy that heightens and sensitizes and strengthens all my experience.

—AUDRE LORDE FROM *USES OF THE EROTIC: THE EROTIC AS POWER*

We are each other's harvest; we are each other's business; we are each other's magnitude and bond.

—GWENDOLYN BROOKS

CONCLUSION

My Sweet Darling Sexy—

We've traveled a long way together, and we're almost to the end. After all we've discussed, let's go back to the beginning, and re-visit my list for thriving in sex work.

1. You are truly thriving in sex work when: You love yourself; you love your life.

You experience little hits of joy and satisfaction and peace throughout your day. You're not continually stuffing down negative feelings. Gratitude rules your heart. I'm not talking about loving every moment of life—everyone has rough days and blue periods. But when these inevitable downturns occur, you're gentle with yourself and don't work in a funk for months on end.

2. You are truly thriving in sex work when: You take care of your health and have interest in physical pleasure.

You are clean and well groomed. You feel sane about food, drugs, alcohol, and your weight. Most days and in most ways, your body craves somatic pleasure of some kind: hiking in nature, salsa dancing, picnicking in the park, cuddling with your cat on the sofa, or laughing your ass off watching stupid movies.

3. You are truly thriving in sex work when: You have time and energy for outside interests.

You have creative spark in your life; you don't just live to make money. You volunteer, are creative, go to school, have hobbies that turn you on.

4. You are truly thriving in sex work when: You have love in your life, including friends, family, coworkers, pets, and/or romantic partners, and a sense of community.

You make warm-bodied creatures outside of work your priority.

5. You are truly thriving in sex work when: You have a personal support network that gets you and your decision to be a sex worker.

And, if the time comes, your decision to get out. You can discuss your fears and irritations, your joys and successes honestly, without feeling pressured to act or speak a certain way.

6. You are truly thriving in sex work when: You have a professional support network.

This includes tax preparers, lawyers, social media and website consultants, financial planners, credit counselors, and of course, health care providers. You get advice from experts who respect and understand your work and support you as a person.

7. You are truly thriving in sex work when: Your clients provide you with the money and gratification you deserve.

Your clients value your unique gifts and make you feel energized and rewarded.

8. You are truly thriving in sex work when: You understand, have weighed, and made conscious decisions about the risks you take.

You've taken all necessary steps to protect yourself physically, legally, emotionally, and financially. There's no way to mitigate every danger, and disasters do happen. However, you've looked squarely at the hazards of your profession and made clear-headed, reality-based choices.

9. You are truly thriving in sex work when: You have a financial plan.

You manage your money according to your goals while mitigating your fears. You take concrete steps towards getting an education, starting a business, saving towards retirement, buying real estate, having surgery, or paying off debt.

10. You are truly thriving in sex work when: You choose to do sex work.

If something doesn't feel right, you walk away. If you want to stop altogether, you can. You have a fallback plan if, for any reason, you are no longer able to do it.

I'm adding an eleventh element, and this one might be the most important one of all:

11. You are truly thriving in sex work when: sex work exceeds your expectations, and your life is better than when you started.

Most days, in most ways, erotic adventure, great clients, good money and a general sense of well-being characterize your life.

Borrowing from Margaret Cho, former pro dom and phone sex operator: **Loving yourself and living fully as a sex worker is a gorgeous act of radical rebellion.**

BACK TO THE FUTURE

I wrote in the introduction that I wanted to help fellow sex workers navigate the negativity associated with erotic labor. My vision for you, Sweet Sexy, is far larger than that: I want to see a future sex work world worth working in.

Some day soon, I hope making porn becomes no more than a rite of passage for everyone but the Amish, sort of like starting a band in your parents' garage. Having some old sex video floating around on the Interwebs will be no more embarrassing than dorky prom pictures. (I feel like that day is practically already here.)

Strippers will be viewed as exactly who they are: performers, dancers, acrobats. Twinkly people with hot bods and great personalities who make the world a more gorgeous place, honored for their beauty and good cheer with fat bills stacked at their feet. Pro doms will be viewed as combination life coach/personal trainers who know more about your own body than you do. Folks who get inside your head to get you off—your friends will feel kinda sorry for you if you don't have a good one.

Full service sex workers will be acknowledged for the heavy emotional lifting they do providing loving, healing, erotic touch. Somatic therapists who don't just listen and nod, but who instead take risks and act with their whole beings. Providers for humanity's enormous, endless need for beauty, variety, arousal, connection, and release, pleasures we all crave.

How about clients? I envision a world where the widespread desire for novel sexual experiences is honored for everyone. No matter what someone looks like; no matter their age; single people and those in committed partnerships; the able-bodied and the disabled;

women, men, and everyone in between, each person is allowed to fully explore their bodies and fantasies. Where those who use our services are treated with compassion and respect. Where we recognize not everyone will attract a compatible sexual partner in this lifetime, and all of us at times find ourselves alone. Where skill and compassion keep sexual shame and stigma from being offloaded onto others.

And I look forward to a time where there are thousands of books and blogs, written by all different kinds of sex workers across the globe, relaying their wisdom, fostering an extended conversation on weathering the emotional realities of the Biz so this industry is humane and worthwhile across the entire spectrum of sex worker experiences.

How far off is the day that sex work is seen as an important, life-affirming service that can be safe, sane, and freely chosen? For that to happen, people's minds must change. As autonomous, healthful, conscious sex workers, we can begin with ourselves. I leave you with these words from the St. James Infirmary, a San Francisco-based health collective for sex workers: "Never be afraid of who you are. Never be afraid to ask for what you want and need. You are not a waste of resources; you *are* one."

APPENDIX

SPECIAL THANKS & ACKNOWLEDGEMENTS

It took a village to write this book. I couldn't have done it without the professional help and loving care of Sarah Moser, Allison Moon, Fresh White, Carolyn Higgins, Kristy Lin Billuni, Claire Nobles, Pat Mazzera, Freddie Hovey, Carol Queen, Clair Farley, Matthew Miller, Mel Honowitz, Jasmine Valandani, Butch Young, Albert Ochosa, and Rob Siders.

And especially Felicia Gotthelf,
who scoured every line a whole bunch of times.

To Christina & Karin—
may our conversations be forever ongoing.

And to Barry & Max
who make everything possible.

ABOUT ME

My name is Lola Davina, born in 1968 to a middle-class nuclear family of European descent. Although I haven't done any kind of sex work for more than a decade now, I consider myself to be a sex worker. Those experiences inform my sexuality and my career path. The most succinct description of my identity is bi/queer/transphile/cis-blurry female-identified sex worker, although that that really doesn't explain the half of it.

As a kid, I was always fascinated by the adult industry. I can recall knowing about three kinds of sex work: stripping, pornography, and prostitution, and later on learning there was this other thing called "phone sex." At the age of ten, I wrote in my journal, "I want to grow up to become a prostitute." Don't ask me why...

Ever goal-oriented, when I graduated from college in 1989 and moved to San Francisco, I made a to-do list: volunteer in the raging AIDS crisis, work as a cocktail waitress, and spend two hundred hours stripping. In my budding researcher's mind, these constituted a "real world" internship. So, I signed up to deliver Open Hand meals to people living with HIV/AIDS. I got myself hired at a Cuban salsa joint, slinging booze. And one dark, rainy day in January 1990, I auditioned my way on to the stage of the Lusty Lady, a live peep show theater.

The Lusty was not your typical strip joint. Back then, it was an epicenter of Riot Grrrl punk, ACT-UP fueled activism, and sex-positivity. Those two years taught me sex workers are kickass rule-breakers, making the world a better place, all the while looking fabulous. I met some of the fiercest, most fun, ferociously brilliant people, several I'm lucky enough to call my closest friends today.

Someone once said stripping is a gateway drug. Fellow Lustys paved my way to professional domination and prostitution. I didn't have what it took for contact stripping, but I made porn videos, ran sex parties, wrote erotica, and worked briefly for a madam, whiling away a couple of stupendously boring afternoons in a brothel.

So, I consider myself someone who has directly experienced much of the sex industry, albeit in a specific place and time. Additionally, I've read a broad cross-section of academic sex work research, as well as followed the popular dialogue on sex work online up to the present day. I've also been on the client side of the exchange, visiting strip clubs and purchasing the services of pro doms and escorts.

My time working for other people is limited, since I mostly worked with and for women I considered my peers, not laboring under a typical employee/management dynamic. Without exception, I worked inside: apartments, porn sets, dungeons, a brothel, or sex parties, almost exclusively in the Bay Area. When I traveled for work, it was always to upscale hotels—I could have been anywhere in the money-bubble world.

While working, I earned an M.A. in Human Sexuality Studies, and later, an M.S. in Nonprofit Fundraising. It's always been about sex and money for me—go figure. My human sexuality master's thesis was on sex work and Social Contact Theory. My research found that people who personally know a stripper, porn actor, pro dom, or prostitute are more likely to have a favorable impression of both the sex industry and sex workers than people who don't know anyone in the Biz—just something to keep in mind next time you're wondering whether to come out.

As for my personal life while working, there were stretches when I was single. I dated several butch lesbians who weren't threatened by my job, living for a time with one woman while I worked out of our apartment. I dated several couples and a few clients, mostly disastrously, until one stuck, so I married him.

Finally, in my post-sex work career, I'm a writer, educator, fundraiser, and playwright.

DEFINITIONS

BBW: "Big Beautiful Woman/Women." Women of size.

BDSM PROFESSIONAL: A person of any gender who provides professional bondage, domination, sadomasochistic, and/or role-playing services as a dominant, a submissive, or both. *Includes:* Professional Dominant, Professional Submissive, Pro Dom, Pro Domme, Domina, Dominatrix

BOUNDARIES: Limits one sets on one's behavior and others in order to maintain one's dignity and sense of self. Boundaries can be consciously stated rules such as, "No sex without a condom," or, "No appointments after midnight." Or a boundary can be an unstated, internal limit that is only known once it's been breached.

BOUNDARY CLOWN: A potential client who opens negotiations with an unreasonable, illegal, or rude request.

BRAZEN HUSSY: A person of any gender out as a sex worker or other sexual minority in order to engage in political activism.

BUDDY: A fellow sex worker or colleague who is part of your support system.

BURNOUT: The syndrome of being no longer able to do sex work due to emotional or physical exhaustion. *See also:* Hitting the Wall

CAMMER: From "webcamming." Live online sex performers, combining video chatting with stripping/sex shows. *Includes:* Webcammer, Cam Boy/Girl/Queer, Webcam Model

CHECKING OUT: The propensity to disengage from reality for periods of time. A psychological phenomenon ranging on a spectrum from daydreaming to fugue states. *See also:* Dissociation

CISGENDER: Relating to a person whose biological gender corresponds to their gender identity. *In contrast to:* Transgender, Trans*

CLIENT: A person of any gender who pays for sexual services or products from a sex worker. *Includes:* Patrons, Subs, Fans

CODE-SWITCHING: The practice of alternating between two languages or cultural modalities in order to fit in. For sex workers, this can mean modifying one's behavior between the straight world and the adult industry.

CONTACT SEX WORK: Jobs that require sex workers to physically interact with clients, such as stripping and prostitution, as opposed to camming and phone sex.

CONVENIENCE CLIENT: A client seeking a drop-in appointment, rather than scheduling a day or more in advance.

DEMON: An emotional state that causes pain or distress.

DISSOCIATION: The propensity to disengage from reality for periods of time. A psychological phenomenon ranging on a spectrum from daydreaming to fugue states. *See also:* Checking Out

DOXXING: Releasing personal and/or confidential information, including real name, bank accounts, home address, etc., online, especially with the intent to blackmail or punish.

EMOTIONAL HYGIENE: An interaction characterized by the understanding that there will be no emotional entanglements or obligations for either partner.

EMOTIONAL LABOR: The effort workers put into checking their emotional reactions within a professionally acceptable range. In sex work, emotional labor is expanded to account for a sex worker's responsibility for the positive emotional state of their clients.

FAN: Admirer of a particular porn star who purchases their products and attends their public appearances.

FIZZLING OUT: The syndrome of letting one's business decline due to neglect.

FOUND FAMILY: Friends who are as close as family.

FULL SERVICE SEX WORK (FSSW): Synonymous with escorting or prostitution.

HALT + B: A Twelve-Step acronym for hunger, anger, loneliness, and tiredness, plus "B" for boredom. Negative states that can trigger addictive or destructive behaviors.

HITTING THE WALL: The syndrome of being no longer able to do sex work due to emotional or physical exhaustion. *See also:* Burnout

HOBBYIST: Review site jargon for a client who visits many different sex workers.

IMPOSTER SYNDROME: Chronic feelings of self-doubt and inadequacy, even when facts indicate the opposite is true. In sex work, this means not feeling attractive or classy or intelligent enough, even when making good money.

INFLATION-DEFLATION: The psychological need to inflate one's ego in order to avoid feeling insecure and worthless.

LAST FUCKABLE DAY: Comedienne Amy Schumer's skit about Hollywood actresses in their forties and fifties celebrating the last day they are considered attractive enough to star as romantic leads. After that, they face a future of mom roles in turtleneck sweaters.

LOOKISM: Socially constructed standards of attractiveness, and the judgment people face from how well or poorly they meet that standard.

LOW SELF-ESTEEM: Feeling incapable, incompetent, or not good enough.

NORMCORE: Fashion trend of unpretentious clothing and appearance.

OUTSOURCING SHAME: Consciously or unconsciously making another person feel bad in order to dispel one's own feelings of shame or inadequacy.

PATRON: Client at a strip club.

POLYAMORY: The philosophy or state of being in love or romantically involved with more than one person at a time. *Related to:* Polyamorist

PORN ACTOR/PORN STAR: A person of any gender who performs sexual acts to be recorded or transmitted to be sold for sexual stimulation.

POVERTY CONSCIOUSNESS: Beliefs, feelings, and values that presume a lack of material and financial resources, usually involving fear.

PROSTITUTE: A person of any gender who has sex in exchange for money or other remuneration. *Includes:* Escort, Call Girl, Rent Boy, Whore, Hooker, Streetwalker, Provider, Courtesan, Full-Service Sex Worker (FSSW)

PROVIDER: A full service sex worker.

PTSD: Post Traumatic Stress Disorder. A mental health condition triggered by trauma, either from witnessing it or experiencing it directly. Symptoms may include flashbacks, nightmares, or a generalized feeling of dread, as well as uncontrollable, racing thoughts.

SEASONAL AFFECT DISORDER (SAD): Winter-related depression.

SAPIOSEXUAL: Someone who finds intelligence sexy.

SEX INDUSTRY: Businesses providing sex-related services and products. *Synonymous with:* Sex Trade, Adult Industry, Erotic Labor

SEX WORKER: A person of any gender performing sexual services or providing sexual products in exchange for money or other things of value. A blanket term that includes strippers, BDSM professionals, porn actors and cammers, Sugar Babies, and prostitutes. *Synonymous with:* Adult Performer, Erotic Laborer, Sexy Professional

SHAME: A deep-seated belief of being bad, dirty, or wrong.

SHIT STACK: Money earned doing something we did not want to do.

SOMATIC: Relating to the body, especially as distinct from the mind.

SSCA: Sex that is safe, sane, consensual, and between adults.

STIGMA: The anxiety or pressure to hide because of other people's judgment; a mark of disgrace.

STRIPPER: A person of any gender who professionally performs a striptease; one who dances naked or removes clothing in a sexually suggestive way. *Includes:* Exotic Dancer, Bachelor/ette Party Dancer, Striptease Artist, Peepshow Performer

SUB: Client at a dungeon; does not necessarily mean submissive.

SUGAR BABY: A person of any gender available for an ongoing relationship with a Sugar Daddy/Momma, where companionship and sex are exchanged for money and gifts, usually involving a regular stipend.

SURVIVAL SEX: Sex driven by extreme need in exchange for basic requirements such as food, shelter, protection, or drugs.

THE BIZ: Shorthand for the sex industry. More specifically, the mindset of living as a sex worker from direct participatory experience, rather than as an abstract concept or observed from a distance. *See also:* The Life

THE LIFE: Shorthand for the sex industry. More specifically, the mindset of living as a sex worker from direct participatory experience, rather than as an abstract concept or observed from a distance. *See also:* The Biz

THE NORMAL WORLD: Life outside the sex industry. *See also:* The Straight World

THE STRAIGHT WORLD: Life outside the sex industry. *See also:* The Normal World

TRANS*: Relating to a person whose biological gender does not correspond to their gender identity, encompassing individuals across the full transgender, gender-different, and gender-nonconforming spectrum. *Includes:* Transgender, Transman, Transwoman, Trans-Identified

UNSKILLED BEHAVIOR: Acting in a way that guarantees a different result than what one hopes for.

VOLUNTARY SIMPLICITY: A lifestyle that values a simpler and more meaningful life, rather than money and material things.

WHOO-HOO THINKING: The irrational belief that sex work will provide endless easy money, and no planning, savings, or budgeting will ever be necessary again.

WINTER AND DEPRESSION SURVIVAL CHECKLIST

Combatting depression and the winter blues takes effort. When I get down, I forget to take care of myself, so I need constant reminding. Take a moment to take a deep breath, exhale, and say: *I am doing the very best job I can to get through today.* That's all anyone can do. And remember, sad days don't last forever.

EVERY DAY

- Exercise at least 20 minutes every day. An hour is better.
- Enjoy maintaining a healthy weight.
- Be judicious with sweets and booze.
- Take St. John's Wort or something stronger, if you have to.
- Vitamins. (Do it!)
- Before you go out, primp! Take time to look your best.
- Dress warmly.
- Wear gloves!
- Look up at the sky.
- Breathe!
- Smile at strangers.
- Ask for and receive reassurance and compliments.
- Write about your feelings.
- List your accomplishments.
- Turn off the television.
- Don't dwell. If you do, notice you're doing it and redirect.
- Cultivate color.

EVERY WEEK

- ❀ Call one long-distance friend.
- ❀ Go out with friends to dinner or a movie.
- ❀ Do something really nice for someone else.
- ❀ Go to a movie, concert, play, opera, etc.
- ❀ Get a mani-pedi or a massage.
- ❀ Cook for yourself.
- ❀ Buy flowers.
- ❀ Start an interesting book.

QUICK PICK-ME UPS

- ❀ Yoga
- ❀ Crochet
- ❀ Massage
- ❀ Facial
- ❀ Perfume
- ❀ Exercise
- ❀ Hot Tub
- ❀ Bath
- ❀ Call a friend

REMEMBER...

- ❀ Winter doesn't last forever. But it's long enough to require strategies to survive it.
- ❀ The question isn't whether anyone else finds you loveable. The question is: Do you treat yourself as if you are?
- ❀ The depth of the pain that you feel is an indication of how much you need loving care.
- ❀ Say "yes" to social invitations, and offer them, too.
- ❀ Celebrate the good days and hours.
- ❀ How much love you have in your life.

❀ If you need it, ask for a check-in list from your friends—they are there for you.

❀ Having a lover is not the magical answer to every problem.

❀ Being in a relationship doesn't prevent the holiday blues.

❀ There is another side to every story.

❀ When you compare, you despair.

❀ Don't skimp! Summer is the time to save.

❀ PMS is real, it's a bitch, but it does pass.

❀ Always keep cold meds on hand.

❀ Most days aren't holidays!

❀ Focus on the moment—don't dwell on the past or future-trip.

❀ Dream and set goals.

❀ Things change, and it's okay for goals to change.

❀ Cultivate satisfying, life-affirming rituals.

❀ Celebrate victories, milestones, and for no reason whatsoever.

❀ Some people feel nothing around the holidays, good or bad.

❀ The holidays can be hard on a lot of people. ***But they don't have to be hard on you.***

BIBLIOGRAPHY

These are the books I read leading up to and during the writing of *Thriving in Sex Work*, intended for the general reader who is interested in sex work, self-care, and personal finances. For specific recommendations made in the text, please see the next section.

ACADEMIC STUDIES

Chapkis, Wendy. *Live Sex Acts: Women Performing Erotic Labor.* New York: Routledge, 1997.

Ditmore, Melissa Hope (ed). *Encyclopedia of Prostitution and Sex Work.* Westport, Conn.: Greenwood Press, 2006.

Ditmore, Melissa Hope, Antonia Levy and Alys Willman (eds.) *Sex Work Matters: Exploring Money, Power, and Intimacy In the Sex Industry.* New York: Zed Books, 2010.

Grant, Melissa Gira. *Playing the Whore: The Work of Sex Work.* New York: Verso Books, 2014.

Laing, Mary, Katy Pilcher and Nicola Smith (eds). *Queer Sex Work.* New York: Routledge, 2015.

Weitzer, Ronald (ed.) *Sex for Sale: Prostitution, Pornography, and the Sex Industry.* 2nd ed. New York: Routledge, 2010.

❀ ESSAYS & AUTOBIOGRAPHIES

FIRST PERSON ACCOUNTS + THEORY

Nagle, Jill (ed.) *Whores and Other Feminists.* New York: Routledge, 1997.

Q, Siouxsie. *Truth, Justice, and the American Whore.* Berkeley: ThreeL Media, 2016.

Queen, Carol. *Real Live Nude Girl: Chronicles of Sex-Positive Culture.* Pittsburgh, Penn.: Cleis Press, 1997

Tiefer, Leonore. *Sex is Not a Natural Act & Other Essays.* Boulder, Col.: Westview Press, 2004.

FIRST-PERSON SEX WORKER STORIES & AUTOBIOGRAPHIES

Burana, Lily. *Strip City: A Stripper's Farewell Journey Across America.* New York: Hyperion, 2001.

Burns, Tara. *The Collected Whore Diaries.* Audible: 2014.

Delacoste, Frédérique and Priscilla Alexander. *Sex Work: Writings by Women in the Sex Industry.* Pittsburgh, Penn.: Cleis Press, 1987.

Keefe, Tim. *Some of My Best Friends Are Naked: Interviews with Seven Erotic Dancers.* San Francisco: Barbary Coast Press, 1993.

Lee, Jiz (ed.) *Coming Out Like a Porn Star: Essays on Pornography, Protection, and Privacy.* Berkeley, ThreeL Media, 2015.

Leigh, Carol. *Unrepentant Whore: The Collected Work of Scarlot Harlot.* San Francisco: Last Gasp, 2004.

Oakley, Annie (ed.) *Working Sex: Sex Workers Write About a Changing Industry.* Emeryville, Cal.: Seal Press, 2007.

Sterry, David Henry. *Chicken: Self-Portrait of a Young Man for Rent.* Berkeley: Soft Skull, 2013.

Sterry, David Henry and R.J. Martin Jr. (eds.) *Hos, Hookers, Call Girls and Rent Boys: Professionals Writing on Life, Love, Money, and Sex.* Berkeley: Soft Skull, 2009.

Sterry, David Henry and R.J. Martin Jr. (eds.) *Johns, Marks, Tricks, and Chickenhawks: Professionals and Their Clients Writing About Each Other.* Berkeley: Soft Skull, 2013.

Sycamore, Matt Bernstein (ed.) *Tricks and Treats: Sex Workers Write About Their Clients.* New York: Harrington Park Press, 1999.

❋ SELF-HELP & SPIRITUAL GUIDANCE

Bornstein, Kate. *Hello Cruel World: 101 Alternatives to Suicide for Teens, Freaks, and Other Outlaws.* New York: Seven Stories Press, 2006.

Chödrön, Pema. *Comfortable with Uncertainty: 108 Teachings on Cultivating Fearlessness and Compassion.* Boston: Shambhala, 2008.

———. *The Places That Scare You: A Guide to Fearlessness in Difficult Times.* Boston: Shambhala, 2005.

———. *Start Where You Are: A Guide To Compassionate Living.* Boston: Shambhala, 2004.

———. *When Things Fall Apart: Heart Advice for Difficult Times.* Boston: Shambhala, 2002.

de Becker, Gavin. *The Gift of Fear and Other Survival Signals that Protect Us from Violence.* New York: Dell, 1999.

Duhigg, Charles. *The Power of Habit: Why We Do What We Do in Life and Business.* New York: Random House, 2012.

Easton, Dossie and Janet Hardy. *The Ethical Slut: A Practical Guide to Polyamory, Open Relationships and Other Adventures.* Berkeley: Celestial Arts, 2009.

Hạnh, Thích Nhất. *Fear: Essential Wisdom for Getting Through the Storm.* New York: HarperOne, 2012.

Gordon, James S. *Unstuck: Your Guide to the Seven-Stage Journey Out of Depression.* New York: Penguin, 2008.

Kabat-Zinn, Jon. *Full Catastrophe Living: Using the Wisdom of Your Body and Mind to Face Stress, Pain, and Illness.* New York: Bantam Books, 2013.

———. *Wherever You Go, There You Are: Mindfulness Meditation in Everyday Life.* New York: Hyperion, 2005.

Lamott, Anne. *Small Victories: Spotting Improbable Moments of Grace.* New York: Riverhead Books, 2014.

Mitchell, Stephen A. *Can Love Last? The Fate of Romance Over Time.* New York: Norton, 2002.

Richo, David. *How To Be An Adult: A Handbook on Psychological and Spiritual Integration.* New York: Paulist Press, 1991.

———. *The Five Things We Cannot Change: And the Happiness We Find in Embracing Them.* Boston: Shambhala, 2005.

Salgado, Brenda (ed.) *Real World Mindfulness for Beginners: Navigate Daily Life One Practice at a Time.* Sonoma Press, 2013.

Stendhal, Renate. *True Secrets of Lesbian Desire: Keeping Sex Alive in Long-Term Relationships.* Berkeley: North Atlantic Books, 2003.

Veaux, Franklin and Eve Rickert. *More Than Two: A Practical Guide to Ethical Polyamory.* Portland, Ore.: Thorntree Press, 2014.

Weiss, Joseph. *How Psychotherapy Works: Process and Technique.* New York: Guilford Press, 1993.

Whitfield, Charles L. *Healing the Child Within: Discovery and Recovery for Adult Children of Dysfunctional Families.* Pompano Beach, Fla.: Health Communications, 1987.

Williams, Mary Beth and Soili Poijula. *The PTSD Workbook: Simple, Effective Techniques for Overcoming Traumatic Stress Symptoms.* 3rd ed. Oakland, CA: New Harbinger, 2013.

✳ SEX WORKER SEXPERT BOOKS

FOR THE GENERAL PUBLIC

Christina, Greta (ed.) *Paying For It: A Guide by Sex Workers for Their Clients.* Emeryville, Cal.: Greenery Press, 2004.

Lyremark, Erika. *Think Like a Stripper: Business Lessons to Up Your Confidence, Attract More Clients & Rule Your Market.* Minneapolis, Minn.: Bascom Hill, 2013.

Monet, Veronica. *Veronica Monet's Sex Secrets of Escorts: Tips From A Pro.* Indianapolis, Ind.: Alpha, 2005.

Queen, Carol. *Exhibitionism for the Shy: Show Off, Dress Up and Talk Hot!* San Francisco: Down There Press, 2009.

FOR OTHER SEX WORKERS

Brooks, Amanda. *The Internet Escort's Handbook Book 1: The Foundation.* Golden Girl Press, 2006.

———. *The Internet Escort's Handbook Book 2: Advertising & Marketing.* Golden Girl Press, 2009.

Green, Lady. *The Sexually Dominant Woman: A Workbook for Nervous Beginners.* Emeryville, Cal.: Greenery Press, 1998.

Jones, Taylor B. *The Sugar Daddy Formula: A Sugar Baby's Ultimate Guide to Finding a Wealthy Sugar Daddy.* R&D Publishing, 2014.

Meretrix, Magdalene. *Turning Pro: A Guide to Sex Work for the Ambitious and the Intrigued.* Emeryville, Cal.: Greenery Press, 2001.

❋ THEORY

Bartky, Sandra Lee. *Femininity and Domination: Studies in the Phenomenology of Oppression.* New York: Routledge, 1990.

Bell, Shannon. *Reading, Writing and Rewriting the Prostitute Body.* Bloomington, Ind.: University Press, 2004.

Freire, Paolo. *Pedagogy of the Oppressed.* New York: Continuum, 2000.

Goffman, Erving. *Stigma: Notes on the Management of Spoiled Identity.* New York: Simon & Schuster, 1986.

hooks, bell. *Feminist Theory: From Margin to Center.* Boston: South End Press, 1984.

Lorde, Audre. *Uses of the Erotic: The Erotic as Power.* Brooklyn: Out & Out Books, 1978.

Rubin, Gayle. "Thinking Sex: Notes for a Radical Theory of the Politics of Sexuality." From *Pleasure and Danger: Exploring Female Sexuality*, Carol Vance (ed.) Boston: Routledge & K. Paul, 1984.

✻ EXTENDED READING

Baldwin, James. *The Fire Next Time.* New York: Vintage. 1992.

Barry, Lynda. *One! Hundred! Demons!* Seattle: Sasquatch Books, 2005.

Berkowitz, Eric. *The Boundaries of Desire: A Century of Good Sex, Bad Laws, and Changing Identities.* Counterpoint, 2015.

Brown, Chester. *Paying For It: A Comic Strip Memoir About Being A John.* New York: Farrar, Strauss and Giroux, 2011.

Burgo, Joseph. "The Difference Between Guilt and Shame," *Psychology Today,* 2013. Accessed March 2017 at https://www.psychologytoday.com/blog/shame/201305/the-difference-between-guilt-and-shame

Erickson-Schroth, Laura (ed.) *Trans Bodies, Trans Selves: A Resource for the Transgender Community.* New York: Oxford University Press, 2014.

Estés, Clarissa Pinkola. *Women Who Run With The Wolves.* New York: Ballantine Books, 1992.

Ronson, Jon. *So You've Been Publicly Shamed.* New York: Riverhead, 2015.

Sapolsky, Robert M. *MonkeyLuv and Other Essays on Our Lives as Animals.* New York: Scribner, 2005.

Sprinkle, Annie. *Providing Educational Opportunities to Sex Workers.* [Ph.D. Dissertation]. 2002. Accessed March 2017 at http://anniesprinkle.org/media/dissertation.pdf

———. "Forty Reasons Why Whores Are My Heroes." Accessed March 2017 at http://anniesprinkle.org/forty-reasons-why-whores-are-my-heroes/

Sycamore, Mattilda Bernstein (ed.) *That's Revolting! Queer Strategies for Resisting Assimilation.* Brooklyn: Soft Skull Press, 2008.

Tanenbaum, Leora. *I Am Not a Slut: Slut-Shaming in the Age of the Internet.* New York: Harper Perennial, 2015.

✼ TED TALKS

Brown, Brené. *The Power of Vulnerability*. [video file]. June 2010. Retrieved from TEDx Houston, https://www.ted.com/talks/brene_brown_on_vulnerability

———. *Listening to Shame*. [video file]. March 2012. Retrieved from TED2012, https://www.ted.com/talks/brene_brown_listening_to_shame

Lewinsky, Monica. *The Price of Shame*. [video file]. March 2015. Retrieved from TED2015, https://www.ted.com/talks/monica_lewinsky_the_price_of_shame

Mac, Juno. *The Laws that Sex Workers Really Want*. [video file]. June 2016. Retrieved from TEDX East End, https://www.ted.com/talks/juno_mac_the_laws_that_sex_workers_really_want

Satyarthi, Kailash. *How to Make Peace? Get Angry*. [video file]. March 2015. Retrieved from TED2015, https://www.ted.com/talks/kailash_satyarthi_how_to_make_peace_get_angry

RESOURCES REFERRED TO IN TEXT

Expanded resources promised in the text. Focused mainly in the U.S., current as of this writing, and will not be updated. I keep living lists of sex worker resources on my website, loladavina.com.

❋ FINANCE AND BUDGETING

EMOTIONAL SIDE OF MONEY

Benson, April Lane. *To Buy or Not To Buy: Why We Overshop and How To Stop*. Boston: Trumpeter, 2008.

Fredricks, Laura. *The Ask: How to Ask Anyone for Any Amount for Any Purpose*. San Francisco: Jossey-Bass, 2006.

Robin, Vicki and Joseph Dominguez. *Your Money or Your Life*. New York: Penguin Books, 2008.

Stanley, Thomas J. and William D. Danko. *The Millionaire Next Door: The Surprising Secrets of America's Wealthy*. Lanham, Md.: Taylor Trade Pub., 2010.

Tessler, Bari. *The Art of Money: A Life-Changing Guide to Financial Happiness*. Berkeley: Parallax Press, 2016.

A New Age pain in the ass, overflowing with Tessler's stories about rewarding herself with chocolate every time she sits down to balance her checkbook. However, it's the single best book about the emotional life of money I've ever read. She talks about the "Money Story" that we as small children learn about what money "means." Highly recommended.

PRACTICAL MONEY ADVICE

Edwards, Paul and Sarah Edwards. *Finding Your Perfect Work: The New Career Guide to Making a Living, Creating a Life.* New York: J.P. Tarcher, 2003.

Edwards, Paul. *Home-Based Business for Dummies.* 3rd Ed. Hoboken: Wiley Pub., 2010.

Luhrs, Janet. *The Simple Living Guide: A Sourcebook for Less Stressful, More Joyful Living.* New York: Broadway Books, 1997.

Kobliner, Beth. *Get a Financial Life: Personal Finance in Your Twenties and Thirties.* 3rd Ed. New York: Simon & Schuster, 2009.

Mundis, Jerrold J. *How to Get Out of Debt, Stay Out of Debt, and Live Prosperously.* New York: Bantam Books, 2012.

Orman, Suze. *The Money Book for the Young, Fabulous & Broke.* New York: Riverhead Books, 2005.

———. *Women & Money: Owning the Power to Control Your Destiny.* New York: Spiegel & Grau, 2007.

Ramsey, David. *The Total Money Makeover: A Proven Plan for Financial Fitness.* Nashville: Nelson Books, 2013.

St. Kitts, Lori A. *The Tax Domme's Guide for Sex Workers and All Other Business People.* CreateSpace Independent Pub, 2013.

❊ LEGAL RESOURCES

FREE AND LOW COST LEGAL ADVICE

Even if you're unable to afford to hire a lawyer, with persistence, you can find legal professionals to answer your sex work-related questions for little or no cost. Remember—it's not a crime to ask questions.

AVVO

avvo.com

> Free legal advice website for straightforward questions. Sex worker friendly. Easy-to-use form to submit your question anonymously, and licensed attorneys will respond. This is a site for lawyers to generate business, so you can look here to hire a lawyer as well.

CALIFORNIA PRO BONO

californiaprobono.org

> When seeking free or low cost legal advice, you will most likely be talking to lawyers at the beginning or the end of their careers. California Pro Bono can connect you with law students and retired attorneys in state; they provide national resource links as well.

LAW HELP

lawhelp.org

> Clearinghouse website for free nonprofit legal aid services in the U.S.

NATIONAL LAWYERS GUILD SF CHAPTER (NLGSF)

nlgsf.org

> Excellent online legal resource for sex workers: a list of sex worker criminal law resources (CA and national), and the *Sex Worker Know Your Rights Manual*.

PRO BONO NET

probono.net

> National clearinghouse website for pro bono attorneys helping the poor and disadvantaged, serving 22 U.S. states and internationally.

PROS NETWORK CHICAGO (PROVIDERS AND RESOURCES OFFERING SERVICES TO SEX WORKERS)

prosnetworkchicago.org

> A directory of direct service providers and legal, medical and mental health professionals who are capable of providing non-judgmental, client-centric and harm reduction-oriented services to individuals in the sex industry.

QUORA

quora.com

> "Ask the Experts" website, sex work friendly. New attorneys answer questions here to attract business, along with fellow sex workers and the broader hive mind. It may take some time, but crowdsourcing your legal issues can get good responses. Be specific about where you live, precise about the details of your situation, and check the credentials of the responders.

REDDIT

reddit.com/r/legaladvice/

> Upside of the Legal Advice subreddit is it's anonymous and free. Downside is you have no idea if the respondent who claims they've practiced law for thirty years is in junior high. But an excellent place to get background information. If your access to an attorney is limited, honing your knowledge first on reddit means you can use your paid time wisely.

SAN FRANCISCO TRANSGENDER LAW CENTER

transgenderlawcenter.org

> San Francisco-based legal advocacy group for trans* community.

STATE BAR OF CALIFORNIA

calbar.ca.gov/Public/Pamphlets/HiringaLawyer.aspx

> "How To Find the Right Lawyer" page with helpful guidelines on everything to ask when hiring an attorney. They have a helpful pro bono page as well.

SWOP CHICAGO CALA CLINIC

SWOP-Chicago.org

> Free, full-service legal clinic for individuals currently or previously involved in adult industries/sex work or impacted by the stigma and criminalization of sex work. Providing a wide-range of criminal and civil law services from advice and community legal education to representation. All legal services, including full representation, are free of charge to clients.

SYLVIA RIVERA LAW PROJECT

srlp.org

> NYC-based legal assistance and advocacy for the trans* community, especially low-income folks, people of color, and the incarcerated.

TRANSFORMATIVE JUSTICE LAW PROJECT OF ILLINOIS

tjlp.org

> Provides free, zealous, life-affirming, and gender-affirming holistic criminal legal services to low-income and street based transgender and gender non-conforming people targeted by the criminal legal system.

❇ INTERACTING WITH LAW ENFORCEMENT BEFORE, DURING, AND AFTER ARREST

NATIONAL LAWYERS GUILD

nlg.org/know-your-rights/

> Free online booklet available in English, Spanish, Arabic, Urdu, and Bengali: *You Have the Right To Remain Silent.*

NATIONAL LAWYERS GUILD SF CHAPTER (NLGSF)

nlgsf.org

> Legal guide for interacting with police officers. Protocol for what to do if you have been the victim of police misconduct.

RED LIGHT LEGAL CHECKLIST

redlightlegal.org/police-misconduct-checklist/

> Checklist for reporting police misconduct.

SWOP CHICAGO

redlightchicago.wordpress.com/in-case-of-arrest-what-not-to-do/

> Written by an attorney, ten simple steps when under arrest: *In Case of Arrest: What NOT to Do!*

❇ TRANS* SEX WORKER RESOURCES

As of this writing, these organizations are committed to trans* rights and expressly advocate for sex workers.

EL/LA PARA TRANSLATINAS

ellaparatranslatinas.yolasite.com

> Building a world where TransLatinas feel they deserve to protect, love and develop themselves. Support in protection against violence, abuse, and illness. San Francisco.

NATIONAL CENTER FOR TRANSGENDER EQUALITY

transequality.org

> National social justice advocacy organization winning life-saving change for transgender people. Washington D.C.

RED UMBRELLA PROJECT (REDUP)

redumbrellaproject.org

> A peer-led organization based in Brooklyn. Community organizing and advocacy to make policy and systemic change to support the rights of sex workers.

SAN FRANCISCO TRANSGENDER LAW CENTER

transgenderlawcenter.org

> Legal advocacy group for trans* community.

SEX WORKERS PROJECT

sexworkersproject.org

> Providing client-centered legal and social services to individuals who engage in sex work, regardless of whether they do so by choice, circumstance, or coercion. New York.

SWOP BAY

swopbay.org

> Dedicated to the fundamental human rights of sex workers and their communities, focusing on ending violence and stigma through education and advocacy. Bay Area.

SYLVIA RIVERA LAW PROJECT

srlp.org

> NYC-based legal advocacy group for trans* community, especially low-income folks, people of color, and the incarcerated.

TGI JUSTICE PROJECT

tgijp.org

> Working to end the human rights abuses committed against trans* people in California prisons, jails, detention centers, and beyond.

TRANSFORMATIVE JUSTICE LAW PROJECT OF ILLINOIS

tjlp.org

> Provides free, life-affirming, and gender-affirming holistic criminal legal services to low-income and street based transgender and gender non-conforming people targeted by the criminal legal system.

�֎ MENTAL HEALTH RESOURCES

CRISIS HOTLINES

NATIONAL DOMESTIC VIOLENCE HOTLINE

(800) 799-SAFE (7233) | thehotline.org

> Free 24-hour national hotline for services and trained support for victims of violence. Anonymous, confidential, and available to all genders.

NATIONAL SEXUAL ASSAULT HOTLINE

(800) 656-4673 | rainn.org

> Free, anonymous, confidential, and available 24 hours a day to all genders.

NATIONAL SUICIDE PREVENTION HOTLINE

(800) 723-8255 | suicidepreventionlifeline.org

> Free 24-hour, national suicide hotline that will connect you to a trained counselor in your area. It is anonymous, confidential, and available to all genders.

THE TRANS LIFELINE

U.S.: (877) 565-8860 Canada: (877) 330-6366 | translifeline.org

A crisis hotline by and for trans* people.

THE TREVOR PROJECT

(866) 488-7386 | thetrevorproject.org

LGBTQ youth suicide hotline. Free, anonymous, 24-hour.

✳ FREE/LOW-COST MENTAL HEALTH AND EMOTIONAL SUPPORT

Note: These are not suicide prevention resources. If you're in crisis, please see resources listed above.

AMERICAN GROUP PSYCHOTHERAPY ASSOCIATION

agpa.org/home/membership/affiliate-societies

Group therapy can be a lower cost option than private sessions, and some of us do our best work interacting with others. Affiliated certified group psychotherapists in most states offer group therapy sessions.

ANXIETY AND DEPRESSION ASSOCIATION OF AMERICA

adaa.org/finding-help/mobile-apps

Website listing apps for managing anxiety, depression, OCD, PTSD, and related disorders. Most range in price from free to $4.99.

COMMUNITY HEALTH CENTERS (CHC)

Locator map: findahealthcenter.hrsa.gov

Federally funded non-profits providing health care to the underserved, with or without insurance. Sliding scale.

MENTAL HEALTH AMERICA

mentalhealthamerica.net/find-support-groups

> Support groups are one way to find safe community; they are often free or very low-cost. National list of every kind of support group imaginable on website.

NATIONAL ALLIANCE OF MENTAL ILLNESS (NAMI)

(800) 950-NAMI (6264) | nami.org

> A helpline with trained staff who can answer questions on your mental health symptoms, treatment options, and resolving legal issues. They don't provide direct counseling, but can help you find an affordable mental healthcare facility that fits your needs.

PROS NETWORK CHICAGO (PROVIDERS AND RESOURCES OFFERING SERVICES TO SEX WORKERS)

prosnetworkchicago.org

> A directory of direct service providers and legal, medical and mental health professionals who are capable of providing non-judgmental, client-centric and harm reduction-oriented services to individuals in the sex industry.

QUEER MENTAL HEALTH

queermentalhealth.org

> Online mental health community for LGBTQ, Two-Spirited, and Genderqueer people.

TALKSPACE.COM AND 7CUPS.COM

Online counseling services offering internet therapy with licensed therapists at a fraction of the cost of in-person counseling.

UNIVERSITIES

Universities that offer advanced degrees in psychotherapy, social work, counseling, and therapy produce graduates every year, who need thousands of supervised counseling hours to meet licensing requirements. Interns often charge well below the market rate of fully licensed therapists. Look for university-affiliated mental health clinics near you.

✾ SEXUAL HEALTH

ADULT PERFORMER ADVOCACY COMMITTEE (APAC)

apac-usa.com/porn-101-video

> Check out their "Porn 101" video featuring big name porn stars. It covers basic STD transmission information, along with advice for maintaining safety and sanity on the porn set. It's worth watching even if porn isn't your career; for folks who make fantasy for a living, they sure know how to get real!

CENTER FOR DISEASE CONTROL (CDC)

cdc.gov/std/

> If you don't know about sexually transmitted diseases, or want to refresh, a "just the facts" website. Transmission, symptoms, prevention, and treatment for all STDs, along with useful statistics.

ST. JAMES INFIRMARY

stjamesinfirmary.org

> Peer-based occupational health and safety clinic for sex workers and their families in San Francisco.

SAN FRANCISCO SEX INFORMATION (SFSI)

(415) 989-SFSI (7374) | sfsi.org

> The sex ed hotline to end all sex ed hotlines. That crazy out-there sex question that you don't know who to ask…? SFSI has seen, heard, and done it all.

SCARLETEEN

scarleteen.com

> Ostensibly for teens and young adults, simply the best sex-ed website around. If you have basic questions about sex or sexual health, Scarleteen will break it all down in a thorough, matter-of-fact, and often funny way that'll leave you feeling better about the human race.

SWOP HOTLINE FOR ADULT WORKERS

(312) 252-3880 | swop-chicago.org

> A community support "warm-line" (not staffed all the time), for current and former sex workers, activists, organizers, and allies.

✳ RESOURCES FOR SPECIFIC SEX WORK JOB TITLES

BLOGS, BOARDS, AND WEBSITES

AMBER CUTIE

ambercutie.com

> Open forum for cammers and their fans.

APAC

apac-usa.com/blog-1

> Blog for porn performers.

CAM GIRL SURVIVAL GUIDE

camgirlsurvivalguide.tumblr.com

> Blog for cam performers.

THE EROTIC REVIEW

theeroticreview.com/discussion-boards/index.asp

> Closed, moderated escort discussion boards.

I LOVE STRIPPING

ilovestripping.wordpress.com

>   Stripper blog.

MAX FISCH DOMINA GUIDE HOSTS: THE HANG

maxfisch.com

>   A closed, moderated discussion board for pro doms.

O CAMGIRL

ocamgirl.com

>   Camming advice website.

PREFERRED411

preferred411.com

>   Closed escort discussion board.

REDDIT SEX WORKER AND STRIPPER FORUMS.

reddit.com/r/SexWorkers and reddit.com/r/stripper/

>   Anonymous and heavily moderated; asshats are swiftly
>   dispatched.

SEX WORKER HELPFULS

sexworkerhelpfuls.tumblr.com

>   Tumblr page with helpful info provided by fellow sex workers.
>   Definitions, FAQs, tips, and lots more.

STRIPPER WEB

stripperweb.com/forum/forum.php

>   Stripper forum.

SUGAR DADDY FORMULA

thesugardaddyformula.com

>   Taylor B. Jones, Sugar Queen.

SURVIVE THE CLUB

survivetheclub.wordpress.com

> Self-help blog for strippers.

TITS & SASS

titsandsass.com

> Blog written by and for (mostly) female escorts.

YNOT AND YNOTCAM

YNOT.com and YNOTcam.com

> Resource websites for cammers.

BOOKS

Brooks, Amanda. *The Internet Escort's Handbook Book 1: The Foundation.* Golden Girl Press, 2006.

———. *The Internet Escort's Handbook Book 2: Advertising & Marketing.* Golden Girl Press, 2009.

Jones, Taylor B. *The Sugar Daddy Formula: A Sugar Baby's Ultimate Guide to Finding a Wealthy Sugar Daddy.* R&D Publishing, 2014.

Meretrix, Magdalene. *Turning Pro: A Guide to Sex Work for the Ambitious and the Intrigued.* Emeryville, Cal.: Greenery Press, 2001.

ADDITIONAL RESOURCES

✻ ADVOCACY FOR SEX WORKER RIGHTS

ADULT PERFORMER ADVOCACY COMMITTEE (APAC)

apac-usa.com

> Advocating to maintain and improve safety and working conditions in the adult film industry by giving adult performers organized representation in matters that affect health, safety, and community. Providing terrific online resources, including their Performer Bill of Rights and Performer Code of Conduct.

BAY AREA SEX WORKERS EDUCATION NETWORK

bayswan.org

> Academic, political and occupational safety/health information for use in sex work policy.

BEST PRACTICES POLICY (BPP)

bestpracticespolicy.org

> DC-based pro sex work advocacy, dedicated to supporting organizations and advocates working with sex workers, people in the sex trade and related communities in the U.S.

DESIREE ALLIANCE

desireealliance.org/wordpress/

> A diverse, sex worker-led network of organizations, communities and individuals across the U.S. working in harm reduction, direct services, political advocacy and health services for sex workers.

EROTIC SERVICE PROVIDERS LEGAL EDUCATION AND RESEARCH PROJECT (ESPLERP)

esplerp.org

> Community-based erotic service provider-led group that seeks to empower the erotic community and advance sexual privacy rights through legal advocacy, education, and research.

LAMBDA LEGAL ADVOCACY FOR FULL CITIZENSHIP RIGHTS FOR LGBTQ

lambdalegal.org

> Sex work positive.

RED UMBRELLA PROJECT

(347) 927-3867 | redumbrellaproject.org

> Peer-led organization based in Brooklyn, New York. Community organizing and advocacy to make policy and systemic change to support the rights of sex workers.

SEX WORKERS OUTREACH PROJECT-USA (SWOP)

(877) 776-2004 | swopusa.org

> National and international social justice network dedicated to the fundamental human rights of sex workers and their communities, focusing on ending violence and stigma through education and advocacy. Search for "SWOP" and your town on Twitter to find a chapter near you.

COMMUNITY

SEX WORKER OPEN UNIVERSITY

sexworkeropenuniversity.com

> Community building, public education and advocacy for sex worker's rights.

DESIREE ALLIANCE

desireealliance.org/wordpress/

> Sex worker-led network of organizations, communities and individuals across the U.S. working in harm reduction, direct services, political advocacy and health services for sex workers.

HOOK ONLINE

hook-online.com

> Online community site for men working in the sex industry.

SWOP BEHIND BARS

swopbehindbars.org

> SWOP's new project to support women, including transwomen, in prison.

WHORECAST

thewhorecast.com/podcast/

> A podcast sharing stories, art and voices of American sex workers with Siouxsie Q.

DRUG USE HARM REDUCTION

ASK MS. HARM REDUCTION

titsandsass.com/?s=harm+reduction

THE HARM REDUCTION COALITION OF SWOP-NYC

harmreduction.org/connect-locally/new-york/swop-nyc/

PRIVACY

Blue, Violet. *The Smart Girl's Guide to Privacy: Practical Tips for Staying Safe Online*. San Francisco: No Starch Press, 2015. Certainly not just for smart girls.

Luna, J.J. *How to be Invisible*. 3rd ed. New York: St. Martin's Press, 2012. E-book on protecting your online identity.

HACK*BLOSSOM

Hackblossom.org

> DIY feminist cybersecurity website with information on how to protect yourself online, including encryption.

ELECTRONIC FRONTIER FOUNDATION

eff.org/deeplinks/2014/07/
protecting-your-anonymity-how-sex-workers

> Free online guide: *Protecting Your Anonymity and Privacy: A How-To for Sex Workers.*

SAFETY

ST. JAMES INFIRMARY'S OCCUPATIONAL HEALTH AND SAFETY HANDBOOK

stjamesinfirmary.org/wordpress/wp-content/uploads/2010/10/sji-rg-v3-2010.pdf

> St. James Infirmary literally wrote the book on safety and sex work, available for free online.

STAYING SAFE IN THE SEX INDUSTRY

redlightchicago.wordpress.com/resources-for-sex-workers/
staying-safe-in-the-sex-industry/

> SWOP Chicago's useful safety articles across job titles.

UK NETWORK OF SEX WORK PROJECT (UK NSWP)
uknswp.org/wp-content/uploads/RSW2.pdf

> Paid for by British lottery funds. (!) Sex worker safety brochure offering basic safety information for all genders across job titles, including indoor and outdoor prostitution.

There are additional ways to keep yourself safe as a sex worker, but these methods rely on discretion, so I am not listing them here. Preferred411.com and theeroticreview.com are closed sex worker forums; the sex worker forum at reddit.com/r/SexWorkers/ is open, but heavily moderated. I encourage you to ask questions and learn more there.

CPSIA information can be obtained
at www.ICGtesting.com
Printed in the USA
BVHW07s1729240918
528346BV00001B/161/P

9 780998 892030